NICE JUMPER

Tom Cox

BLACK SWAN

NICE JUMPER
A BLACK SWAN BOOK : 978 0 552 77935 7

Originally published in Great Britain by Bantam Press,
a division of Transworld Publishers

PRINTING HISTORY
Bantam Press edition published 2002
Black Swan edition published 2003

3 5 7 9 10 8 6 4 2

Set in 11½/14pt New Baskerville by
Falcon Oast Graphic Art Ltd.

Black Swan Books are published by Transworld Publishers,
61–63 Uxbridge Road, London W5 5SA,
a division of The Random House Group Ltd,
in Australia by Random House Australia (Pty) Ltd,
20 Alfred Street, Milsons Point, Sydney, NSW 2061, Australia,
in New Zealand by Random House New Zealand Ltd,
18 Poland Road, Glenfield, Auckland 10, New Zealand
and in South Africa by Random House (Pty) Ltd,
Endulini, 5a Jubilee Road, Parktown 2193, South Africa.

The Random House Group Limited supports The Forest Stewardship
Council (FSC®), the leading international forest certification organisation.
Our books carrying the FSC label are printed on FSC® certified paper.
FSC is the only forest certification scheme endorsed by the leading
environmental organisations, including Greenpeace. Our
paper procurement policy can be found at
www.randomhouse.co.uk/environment

MIX
Paper from
responsible sources
FSC® C016897

Printed and bound in Great Britain by Clays Ltd, St Ives PLC

2i

Cox's writing has appeared in the *Daily Telegraph*, *Sunday Times*, *Observer*, *Mail on Sunday*, *Jack* magazine, *The Times* and the *Guardian*, for which paper he was Pop Critic between 1999 and 2000. He is the author of two books: *Nice Jumper*, which was shortlisted for the 2002 National Sporting Club Best Newcomer Award, and *Educating Peter*. He was born in 1975 and lives with his wife in Norfolk.

Acclaim for *Nice Jumper:*

'The *Fever Pitt* of golf, an engaging tale of sporting obsession and adolescent fumbling for identity . . . consistently entertaining and often extremely funny . . . "Is golf sort of like, really boring, Tom?" asks a girlfriend. "Well, yeah and no," he replies. In Cox's hands, very much the latter'
Martin Fletcher, *Independent*

'*Nice Jumper* captures both the intoxicating sense of being "the one" and the icy douche of adulthood that soon follows. Thank the Lord for those crazy dreams, and the writers, such as Cox, who can make us laugh at them . . . an enormously fun read'
The Times

'Extremely funny – often laugh-out-loud funny, occasionally a threat to the intercostal muscles . . . a large fizzy can of Diet Bobby'
. . . Webb, *The Times*

'. . . probably do more here to interest the non-putting community in the sport than Tiger Woods and P G Wodehouse put together'
Guardian

'At last a book about growing up populated by characters who aren't entirely hateful. In fact *Nice Jumper* is knitted with real warmth and passion, my two favourite things apart from wanking and Bowie. And the golf stuff isn't a problem'
Adam Buxton, of Adam and Joe

'Hilarious true story about East Midlands teenager ignoring the traditional lure of cider, ecstasy and music for the world of golf and the Cripsley Edge golf club. Lashings of insight, sarcasm and slapstick. Fore!'
Jack

'*Nice Jumper* is certain to strike a chord with most golfers – it's funny and it's well written'
Sunday Times

'Hugely enjoyable début ... *Nice Jumper* treads similar ground to *The Commitments* and *Fever Pitch*, but with a depth and humour very much of its own. Recommended'
The Leeds Guide

'A charming and funny coming of age story . . . this book, as Julie Burchill pithily observes on the cover, can be described as "*The Catcher in the Rye* meets *Caddyshack*"'
The Times Literary Supplement

'An enjoyable look at childhood obsessions told with an amusing self-deprecation that makes you turn the pages all the quicker'
Sunday Express

'This is a wry fable of sporting par-adise lost'
Time Out

For Jo, Mick, Edie and AB

On the golf course as nowhere else, the tyranny of causality is suspended, and life is like a dream.

John Updike, 1973

Oi! Stop throwing tee pegs at my head!

Tom Cox, 1989

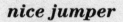

nice jumper

A Confession

As far back as I can remember, I never wanted to be a golfer.

I was born in Nottingham in May 1975, several miles from the nearest golf course, to parents who never thought to dress me in a miniature tartan cap and plus fours. My first word wasn't 'Carnoustie', 'fore!' or 'Nicklaus', and as a toddler I didn't pick up random gardening tools and swing them in the direction of makeshift flagsticks constructed from mop handles and discarded pants. The first record I bought was ABC's *Lexicon Of Love*, an album which features an absolute lack of songs about pitching wedges, hanging lies or steep-faced bunkers. When the European Ryder Cup team made history by beating their American counterparts for the first time, in 1985, I was probably watching *Cheggers Plays Pop* on the other channel, having my life unchanged. I never met a distant uncle called Rex, who took me out to the local pitch and putt, loaned me his spare set of clubs and taught me words like 'shank' and 'mulligan'. I didn't have a distant uncle called Rex.

If you had met my pre-pubescent self and asked me what I wanted to be when I grew up, I might have listed a fickle variety of occupations, ranging from Rock Star past Han Solo all the way to Willie Wonka. What I almost certainly would not have said was, 'Seve Ballesteros.' Amid the clutter of my parents' well-thumbed paperbacks and hippie vinyl, you wouldn't have found one errant ball marker, tee peg, or pitch-mark repairer. Similarly, among the friends they knew from their teaching jobs and CND connections, you wouldn't have found one set of Gore-Tex waterproofs or novelty St Andrews towels.

In fact, it is probable that at no point during the first thirteen years of my life was there even the most tenu-ous hint that I would one day stand upon a strip of immaculate, spongy grass in a pair of bad trousers, waggle a shoddy nine-iron and holler, 'Yes! This is it! This is the answer!'

For golf and me, it really was this simple: one day we woke up and found ourselves utterly, inexplicably in love.

Between the summer of 1988 and the summer of 1993 – a period that encompasses the peak years of my adolescence – I played golf virtually every day, usually all day. Without warning, the game seemed to meta-morphose from some stupid old man's pastime that occasionally mucked up the scheduling of Saturday morning kids' telly, to the core of my very being. I didn't stop to question this at the time. It simply happened, as if it was another part of the inexorable, disorientating onset of puberty. The only difference between golf and nocturnal emissions was that nobody sat me down for a quiet chat and warned me about golf.

I didn't just play golf; I dreamed, walked and talked it. When I was forced to accompany my parents on a family hiking expedition, I didn't amuse myself by play-ing air guitar; I did it by playing air five-iron. When I was cajoled into visiting relatives, I made use of the time by examining their garden for contours, texture and speed, while my somewhat embarrassed mum explained to a befuddled aunt or grandparent that I was 'reading' their lawn.

Every life lesson had a golfing metaphor, the key to a balanced teenage existence no more important than the key to a dependable swing plane. I evaluated com-plete strangers, friends and family members in terms of their potential backswing, not their personality. Anyone who didn't play my favourite sport seemed to me a slightly lost, inferior being. I shut out art, culture, music, literature and school work. I faked migraines in order to miss second-period Geography and catch the early stages of the Dunhill British Masters. I recorded every moment of every terrestrially televised golf tournament. I made wallcharts, on which I recorded every round I played, every fairway I split, every green I hit in regulation, adhering exactingly to the blue-for-under-par, red-for-over-par code employed by the BBC. I was in a zone of my own, and nobody who knew me outside the context of golf knew quite what to do with me.

For more than four years, I devoted every fibre of my being to becoming East Midlands' answer to Lee Trevino. At night, when the golf course was closed and my classmates were at the school disco, I was in my back garden, uprooting clods of earth and psychotically checking the shoulder turn of my reflection in the kitchen window, or in my bedroom memorizing every winner of golf's four major championships since what, for me, was the dawn of history (what was the point of acknowledging life before golf?). On my bedroom wall, where there had once been pop posters cut meticulously from *Smash Hits* magazine, there hung a collage of photographs featuring Tom Watson and Greg Norman in midswing, made up from the pages of *Golf Monthly*, *Today's Golfer* and *Golf World*.

On my final-year report card for GCSE Biology, it says this: 'Tom has no interest in this subject because he "wants to be a professional golfer".' I didn't take this as sarcasm; I took it as a stone fact. I daydreamed away my school life doodling dogleg par fours in the margins of my exercise books, in the precise place where decades of classroom tradition held that I should be doodling hideously deformed genitals. If I saw a girl I fancied, I didn't wonder if she'd let me take her behind the bike sheds; I wondered if she'd let me take her up to the driving range. I wasn't popular or swotty or nerdy; I was just 'that kid who plays golf'. Yet golf probably did more damage to my exam results than drugs, drink, crime and sex could have done with one gargantuan combined effort.

It's painful enough to have acne, girls, hormones and bad taste to deal with. I had all this, and golf. Within the rigid boundaries of a private golf club, with all its scientifically questionable dress codes and arcane customs, I was expected not only to deal with the conflicting hopes and desires of a teenage psyche, but also to form some kind of sociably pliable character, fit to see me through the trials of adulthood. This is the place where I grew my hair, shoplifted, violated a wheelie bin, wore the wrong-coloured socks, smashed windows, set fire to a close friend and got admonished for hiding in a bush. This, in short, is where I spent the most pivotal period of my life.

And I've spent the last eight years pretending it wasn't.

This book is firstly a confession and secondly a personal investigation. There are people with whom

I've built close relationships who will read it and feel shocked and compelled to re-evaluate my worth as a friend and human being. Even my wife, who knows me best, and my parents, who saw the whole sorry episode close up, will recoil, stunned and double-crossed, from much of the information within. But nobody, perhaps, will be as surprised as me.

Over the years, I've been consistently amazed at the ease with which I've been able to edit my own past. When I stopped playing golf, in July 1993, my life resumed its course more or less as originally ordained. I fronted a diabolical, unsuccessful punk rock band for a short time and dressed in shapeless clothes, as you might have expected a kid with left-wing, arty parents to do. I eventually and inescapably adopted the musical taste of the people I grew up with, as you might expect of someone who'd been weaned to the sound of Neil Young's *After The Goldrush*. And, although I failed miserably in my mission to become a leather-trousered intergalactic chocolate-factory-owning pin-up, I started to make a living by writing about rock music, which turned out to be a satisfying enough second best to actually making the stuff.

The fact is, if you take the first thirteen years of my life and sew them to the last eight, it makes a pretty seamless whole. Unlike my clandestine stash of golf photos where, leaning rakishly on my putter in pleated slacks, I look an entirely different *species*, the pictures of pre-teen me depict a smaller, unsideburned version of 26-year-old me. Hence these are what I carry around in my mind as the Truth; these are what I display to the world, if it happens to be paying attention at the time. Most of the friends who witnessed my golfing aberration have drifted away or been conveniently compartmentalized, so I haven't got anyone to snitch on me. Obviously I've been required to brush up on my knowledge of the watershed moments of late eighties and early nineties popular culture (not something that required any significant amount of time or intellectual strain), but, on the whole, deleting almost five years from my life has involved remarkably little groundwork. I don't even feel like I'm covering anything up any more. It's got to the stage where I've got myself convinced almost as thoroughly as everyone else that I had a normal adolescence.

So why dredge up the awful truth?

There are four main reasons, I think, why I have to write about my experience as a teenage golf nut. The first is exactly what I've just said: that I can feel it slipping away from me. I half wonder if it happened to me at all. Will it disappear into the dustbin of personal history if I don't write it down for posterity?

The second is the Dream. I've been having the Dream ever since I terminated my mission to be the world's best golfer, and for every year I put between myself and my golf life, it intensifies. In recent months, it's become unbearable.

The Dream begins with a squall of feedback. It's always the same: I think I'm at a rock concert, only to turn round and realize the noise is coming from a microphone set up on the first tee of a golf course. A throat clears and a voice pipes up, the flavour of fake leather upholstery and pipe smoke.

'On the tee, representing Cripsley Edge Golf Club: Tom Cox!'

Polite applause pitter-patters around me and I slide my driver out of my bag. The place is almost familiar – an amalgam of three or four great courses I competed on as a teenager. Suddenly, as I sink my wooden tee peg into the ground and position a brand new balata-covered golf ball on top of it, I'm struck by the sensation that this is the most important tournament of my life. All around me, spectators – thirty or forty of them at least, none of whom ever have faces – hold their breath, and I begin my backswing, coiling my shoulder muscles for a powerful shot.

The ball falls off the tee peg.

I repeat this series of actions numerous times – anywhere between fifty and a hundred on a bad night – but the ball never stays on its perch long enough for me to complete my stroke. I hear mumbling from behind the tee where my playing partners, who have both bisected the fairway, are loitering. Palms clamming up, I bend down to examine the tee peg, to find that the bottom of the peg is round, while the hole beneath it is square, making the fit impossible. At this point I wake up, feeling frustrated and demented.

After eight years of living under its tyranny, I've begun to look at the Dream like this: I either exorcize it by writing a book, or find a good psychiatrist.

The third reason for writing this book is connected with a phenomenon I've noticed enveloping me as I've passed into the second half of my twenties: a kind of crisis of cultural faith, involving a re-evaluation of the things I've held to be 'credible' for my entire adult life. You could say the process started some time back when I traded in a neglected pile of lo-fidelity seven-inch singles for my first Eagles album, moved on a pace when I found myself clearing out my wallet and replacing my membership card for Hothips Nightclub with a supermarket loyalty card, and slipped smoothly into fourth gear around the time I found myself wandering about the house in a pair of Totes wondering why *all* radio stations couldn't be as sensible and informative as Radio 4. Now I'm bracing myself for the next stage.

Am I about to realize that golf is cool?

Moreover, would this necessarily be a bad thing? Ironically enough, in the years since I abandoned golf in favour of rock and roll, there have been a glut of 'golf gets hip' features in the British broadsheet newspapers, suggesting that, in the aftermath of Tiger

Woods, Burberry street fashion, rock-and-roll golfers
such as John Daly and golfing rock-and-rollers such as
Alice Cooper, golf is becoming less bourgeois, more
working class, more open-minded. I'm not wholly convinced this is true – the last time I spent any time within
its iron borders, the golfing establishment had at least
a hundred years of evolution to go through before it
attained what most fashion editors and cultural
commentators would define as 'cool' – but something,
certainly, has changed. In chic secondhand shops and
boutiques, eighties Pringle sweaters sell for upwards of
forty pounds. Acquaintances of mine speak brazenly
of weekend trips to the local pitch and putt. For the
first time, I almost feel like it's safe to hold up my head
among normal human beings who have never taken a
free drop from Ground Under Repair or shown consideration for a dress code, and announce: 'Yes! I once
wore a ridiculous hat and a left-handed glove! And if you
have a problem with that we can settle it outside!' During
the conception of this book, I had the unique experience
of meeting an ex-greenkeeper at a night of psychedelic
folk music in central London, who revealed to me over
the course of an unusually passionate two-hour conversation that he, too, had once been a promising amateur
golfer, and still covertly believed that 'golf holds the key
to existential and spiritual peace'. Could there really be
more out there like me, hiding their secret histories
from the world? It's possible.

Nevertheless, by owning up to a golfing past, I realize
I'm putting myself at risk. After all, I'm telling people
that I *used* to play golf, when I was supposed to be
getting hip, not that I want to play golf *now*, when I'm
supposed to be getting boring. There's a big difference. Alice Cooper might spend his leisure time
working on his pitch and run shots *now*. But did he do
the same thing as a teenager? Of course he didn't. He
was much too busy corrupting his classmates or teaching himself the art of cracking a whip and singing with
an eight-foot-long python around his neck.

I fully grasp that, to many, the words 'golf' and
'credibility' are still approximately as compatible as the
words 'Thatcher' and 'breakbeat'. A book seems
the least painful way to put my confession out there – a
method, at the very least, of sidestepping those in-
credulous stares and that special tone of questioning
that's normally reserved for such tentative enquiries as,
'So. At what point exactly *did* you enrol at the
nunnery?' and, 'Precisely what kind of burning
ambition drives the collector of rare Nazi memor-
abilia?' On the few occasions that I have chosen to
disclose my golf life in public, I've regretted it.

'You? A former amateur golfing prodigy?'

'Yes.'

'You're winding me up!'

'No, honestly, I'm not.'

'But you like *After The Goldrush*!'

'That's true.'

'Did your parents play golf?'

'No. Could you keep your voice down, please?'

'What about the rest of your family?'

'No. Nobody.'

'So what made you take it up?'

'I don't know. It's a long story.'

'But I thought everyone who played golf was a right-wing bigot with no dress sense!'

'Not everyone.'

'Wow! You? I mean, I never would have guessed it, what with those sideburns and everything. Hey! You lot! Yeah, that's right – you over there, the coach party of impossibly gorgeous, trendy and intelligent fashion models! Come here. You'll never believe this. Guess what? My mate Tom took five years out of a normal teenage life just so he could hit a little white ball around a field with a big metal stick! For no apparent reason! And guess what else? The whole time, he didn't do any rude or sexy stuff with a girl, not once.'

If it comes down to a choice between the written word and a packed Soho bar, I'll take the coward's option every time.

Yet, simultaneously, I wonder if the written way isn't the most frightening way of all. I'm not just composing a teenage memoir here; I'm opening up the gates to a life that stopped feeling like my own several aeons ago, but which, at the same time, despite everything I've told myself in the past, might be the same life that formed a vast part of who I am. Once I begin coming clean, I wonder what kind of terrifying personal truths I might uncover. I embark on this mission fully aware that when it's over I probably won't be the same person I was when it began, and that I have no way of predicting the extent of the changes that might take place. Similarly, I'm conscious that while the first three reasons for writing about my life as a teen golf alien are logical and persuasive enough, it's the fourth and final reason that's the most visceral and dangerous.

And that's the fact that somewhere, somehow, I know I kind of miss it.

1

'If you could just drop me here, that would be perfect.'

'Don't be silly. You don't want to be lugging that great big bag all the way up the hill.'

'No, honestly, I could do with the walk. My head feels a bit stuffy, actually.'

It's September 1988, and I'm in my dad's car, trying to break it to him as tactfully as possible that I would prefer it if, from this point on, we weren't related. It's nothing personal, he has to understand. In fact, some people might say that his corroding 1975 Toyota Corona is quite a tasteful automobile. But not me. And certainly not the people I'm about to mix with. I'm praying that I won't have to resort to a 'tough love' strategy here, hoping that the grinding of my teeth and the sight of my hand hovering anxiously over the door handle will subtly yet vehemently transmit the message that if he doesn't stop the car within the next thirteen seconds he is going to render the rest of my life an abject nightmare.

'Are you sure? I mean, I don't see why I can't just take you up to the top of the road and drop you there.'

'I'm sure. *Please.*' The vehicle is still moving, but I am now inching the door open.

Two weeks ago, I was somehow granted membership at Cripsley Edge, one of the East Midlands' more exclusive golf clubs. My dad tells me he is glad about this, but knows nothing about golf – has never played or wanted to play. The game is probably as alien to him as an expenses-paid weekend at a Rotary Club convention. For two months, drawing on all my reserves of patience, I've just about managed to deal with these fundamental character flaws. He has unquestioningly taxied me up to my new Utopia for my weekly practice sessions, parked the main family car, a 1986 Vauxhall Astra, surreptitiously on the gravel behind the professional's shop, avoiding the members' car park and clubhouse, and kept interference into my golf life down to an acceptable minimum. But today is different. I can sense a change in him, a new curiosity. What's more, in a singularly unfortunate bit of timing, my mum has taken the Astra to the local garden centre, and we are travelling in the family's very own emergency vehicle, a tin-can-on-wheels known to anyone who has ever been intimately associated with it as the Sphincter – a car which, if driven at over 21 miles per hour, makes a noise suggestive of a giant, senile mechanical pig struggling to free a knot in its colostomy bag. All this would have been tricky enough on its own, but since today is the very day I am scheduled to play my first competitive round – the culmination of three months of coaching, three months of waiting and fantasizing from the vantage point of the course's practice ground – it is downright unacceptable.

'I mean it,' I say, unhooking my seat belt. 'I'm getting out now. *Now.* You may as well stop, because if you don't stop, I'm going to jump out anyway.'

'Well, if you insist. But I don't understand why. I was hoping that maybe I could stand outside the clubhouse and watch you tee off.'

'What?'

'You know – just quickly, and then go. I wouldn't try to talk to anyone or anything.'

'No. No chance. Please, please, please, could you stop the car now, and let me out.'

'Well, all right, but—'

'*Now!*'

Slamming the car door a little more forcefully than intended, I turn to check on my artillery.

One 1979 Slazenger golf bag, gut pink, passed on from friend of friend of grandfather.

One thirties seven-iron, custom-made – for a Smurf, judging by the length of its shaft.

One half-set of scuffed, randomly orphaned irons, on loan from junior coach.

One seventh-hand putter, closely resembling a boulder on a stick.

Sixteen and a quarter wooden tee pegs.

Two cartons of Happy Shopper orange 'drink'.

One 'Hollyhocks of the British Isles' tea towel, 'borrowed' from kitchen drawer.

Five second-hand two-piece golf balls, procured from undergrowth beside second green.

I appear to be all set . . .

The short ad in the local paper boasted 'Free Golf Lessons for the Under-fifteens', and nobody ever seems able to agree upon who spotted it. My mum claims I did, but I'm pretty sure the likelihood of me at thirteen reading a newspaper would have been about as high as the likelihood of me today putting on a pair of muddy jogging bottoms and nipping across the road with a football under my arm to ask if my 84-year-old neighbour, Clara Woodbridge, is 'playing'. My grandad claims that he placed the ad himself, but tends to undermine the authority of this statement by shortly afterwards claiming that he single-handedly overthrew Hitler's Germany. My dad, whose memory is the best out of the three, recalls the ad being pushed under the front door one morning by an anonymous source. It's the last explanation that seems most appropriate, but my own guess is that my parents spotted the ad together.

They needn't feel ashamed about this. They weren't to know that golf would be the One. I forgive them, and can totally understand their thought processes. It probably appeared to them that, between the ages of nine and thirteen, I'd worked my way through every sport in the average teenage boy's lexicon. I was good at everything, brilliant at nothing, and brilliant was the only thing I cared about being. The positive aspect of having an athletic kid, from my parents' point of view, was that it kept me away from the Village Gang. The Village Gang was something I drifted in and out of, depending upon whether I was just getting into, or just getting out of, a new sport. It was led by Sean Ryder, who not only had nearly the same name as Shaun Ryder, the lead singer of the Manchester indie dance group Happy Mondays, but nearly the same face as well. Several years after I stopped hanging around with Sean Ryder, I saw Shaun Ryder performing on *Top of the Pops* and was stunned to discover that my old friend had opted for a cooler way of spelling his name and made something of his life, but then I checked the chronology and realized that at the exact time Happy Mondays were mastering their 1988 album *Bummed*, Sean Ryder would have been engaged in dangling Mark Spittal off the Swingate bridge by his ankles in an attempt to bribe him into lending out his maths homework.

I imagine that around the time my parents saw the

ad, I was going through one of my dejected stages – I seem to remember it was the same summer I failed in my attempt to secure a place on the county table-tennis team – and spending a little too much time in Ryder's company for their liking. Golf probably seemed like a potentially effective distraction: a conveniently antithetical pastime that might keep me sidetracked while the rest of the gang were doing the Garden Fence Grand National or setting fire to one another's farts. I'm sure they didn't expect me to take it up with any real sense of purpose – even when I arrived back from the first lesson at Cripsley pledging to win my first British Open before my seventeenth birthday.

I, however, knew I was serious, right from the first nine-iron shot I hoisted above daisy-scaring level. There were several reasons why golf kept me hooked where other sports had failed to. It was the first out-door sport I'd played that allowed me to dress appropriately for the elements. Unlike other sports, it didn't just have its own stadium or court; it had its own *kingdom*. Even better than that, it had lots of *different* kingdoms, featuring an infinite number of architectural permutations and an infinite amount of words to describe them. None of the rigid oppression of the basketball court or the football pitch here. There seemed so much to learn, a baffling number of options requiring a mind-boggling amount of mental discipline. Unlike the times that I'd played other sports, I didn't get a discouraging inkling of what kind of an experience golf would be when I began to master it. I didn't *know* what it would be like. I just knew it would be mysterious and complicated and stimulating.

Suddenly, I was watching the 1988 US Open – surely one of the least remarkable major championships in golfing history, slogged out between two of the game's least punk-rock players, Nick Faldo and Curtis Strange – and seeing the future. At fourteen, I would become British Amateur Champion; at fifteen, the youngest ever European Tour professional, finishing in ninth place on the end-of-year money list. At seventeen, I would win the first of my seventeen US Masters titles, at the Augusta National Course in Georgia, and the first of my twelve British Open Championships, also at Augusta. The British Open has never been played at Augusta in Georgia, but I knew that I wouldn't have any trouble persuading the tournament organizers to change the venue, having done so much for the game at such a callow age.

I began to spend six days a week in a birdie trance – all my thoughts and energy turned towards my Saturday morning lesson. I stole copies of *Golf World* magazine from the waiting room of my dentist's surgery. I broke the greenhouse belonging to the lazy-eyed witchy woman next door with a sand-iron lob. I planned. I schemed. I visualized. Every week I improved. Every week Cripsley's assistant teaching professional, Mike Shalcross, dropped weightier hints about putting me forward for membership of the club. The fact that I hadn't played the course yet – I'd been settling for midweek games at the local pitch and putt – only made it twice as exciting. From the practice fairway, I gazed out towards the fifth and third fairways, memorizing the contours, projecting my own make-believe iron shots: the kind that would shoot up high over the flagstick, then attach themselves to the putting surface like Velcro. Right here, I saw the rest of my life roll out ahead of me like one infinite, luxuriant, green carpet.

After six weeks of dreaming, I was given a date for my trial for membership. At last I was about to find out what verdant delights Cripsley Edge held beyond the gigantic hedge separating the fairways belonging to the fifth and sixth holes. The trial was held by Bob Boffinger, Cripsley's junior organizer, and consisted of me hitting fifty seven-iron shots, being shown around the men-only bar, and nodding solemnly when Bob said things like 'absolutely imperative' and 'dress restriction'. I breezed it, offering what I still look upon as a favourable impression of 'Tom Cox, future Young Conservative sired by local textile magnate and county bridge champion', and betraying little trace of Tom Cox, future hippy slacker sired by inner-city primary schoolteacher and inner-city supply teacher.

'Does your dad play golf, Tom?' asked Bob.

'No. Only my uncle Rex. He took me up for a quick eighteen the last time we were at his place in the Cotswolds.' I'd learned phrases like 'a quick eighteen' from reading the biography of the golf commentator Peter Alliss.

'And what does Rex do for a living?'

'Oh. Er. He's a . . . barrister.'

Now, my thirteen-year-old powers of deception amaze me. I was an artist. Stage by stage, I was re-inventing myself, and my family were starting to pick up on the signs.

First, my mum, as I arrived home from my fourth lesson at Cripsley.

'Tom, what's that?'

'What?'

'That thing hanging out of your pocket.'

'It's a glove.'

'Looks like a dead bat.'

'Well, it's not. It's a glove.'

'Why do you only have one?'

'For grip, *of course*. Nearly all proper golfers wear them. You wouldn't understand. It would be like me trying to explain to you what "the honour" is.'

'The what?'

'The honour. It's what you get when you have the best score on the previous hole. You get the honour of going first. It's to do with etiquette. See? I knew you wouldn't understand.'

Then my dad, as he greeted me behind Cripsley's pro shop two weeks later.

'How's it going, man?'

'You're wearing jeans. Quick, get in the car. You're not supposed to wear jeans here. It's against the rules. And for your information I'm not "man", I'm Tom. People don't call each other "man" at a golf club.'

And lastly my grandad, as I arrived at his house for Sunday lunch, dressed in my first item of bona fide golfwear: a lilac shirt with meatcutter collars and embroidered 'golf bloke in midswing' design.

'Blimey! You could go flying with collars like that. Is that what you wear when you go down the school disco and pull all those hot bits of stuff?'

'Actually, I don't go down the school disco any more. And I don't "pull" – that's something that people in the sixties did. This shirt is what everyone at Cripsley Edge wears, so that shows just how out of touch *you* are.'

I began to speak in a whole new way, applying the terms I'd learned at Cripsley to everyday situations. 'Pushed it,' I observed, as my mum threw a balled-up piece of paper at the waste-paper bin and missed it on the right.

'What do you mean?'

'You pushed it. Got your hands ahead of the shot.'

'I don't know what the hell you're talking about.'

'You know – blocked it. That's why it pitched to the right.'

'"Pitched"? What the hell are you on about?'

'*God.* It means landed. Don't you know *anything*?'

For me, serving an apprenticeship as a proper rebel
would have come a bit too easily. On the occasions I'd
dipped my toe into it, with Ryder and his gang, it
hadn't felt much like rebellion at all. My parents might
have tried to distract me from it, but they seemed to
understand me a little too well. My dad didn't listen
to Val Doonican and Andy Williams; he listened to the
Ramones and the Rolling Stones. And while I'm proud
to say I was the first person at my school to wear Doc
Martens, I'm slightly less proud to say they were chosen
for me by my mum, after half an hour's dispute during
which she strived to persuade me to 'loosen up and get
with it' in front of a bystanding posse of four giggling
fourteen-year-old girls. By my thirteenth birthday, I
found myself somewhat anaesthetized to the effects of
sex, drugs and rock and roll. Well, maybe not the
drugs, but certainly the other two. My whole life I'd
had unlimited access to music that mud-wrestled with
Satan, yelped about fellatio and exulted in the benefits
of free love. Although I hadn't *had* sex, I felt like I knew
enough about it. My mum had relayed the facts of life
to me shortly before my sixth birthday, after which I'd
promptly taken them to school and made little Jimmy
McGuire burst into tears. By my tenth birthday, I could
recite entire subsections of *The Joy of Sex* word for word
to wide-eyed schoolfriends.

By my third year of secondary school, 92.5 per cent of the girls in my Geography class claimed to have 'done it' (the other 7.5 per cent having been decreed 'rough' via an unofficial class vote). Being the kind of thirteen-year-old boy whom girls intermittently tickle and tell all about their sex lives but never actually go on a date with, I certainly finished my school day *feeling* like I'd 'done it', then arrived home to a house in which few walls were free of black and white posters of naked existential German women leaning pensively over sinks.

For the moment, I could quite happily put delinquent teenage sex on the back burner.

Now – manners, sportsmanship, technospeak, repression: *these* I could use.

My dad might have been able to recite Monty Python sketches word for word, but did he know how to shake hands properly, or that sweatshirts should never be worn without shirt collars underneath? My mum might have dug Johnny Marr's guitar-playing on Smiths albums, but did she know not to keep her glass raised from the table for unduly long periods in the presence of the club captain, and that it was considered custom not to stand in the eyeline of your playing partner as he was taking his shot? I'd finally hit upon the only form of adolescent mutiny I could muster, the one thing that might leave my shockproof parents shaking their heads and pronouncing: 'I can't believe he's our son. I hope

he gets over it; it's probably just a phase.' The sensation
of power was overwhelming. I was James Dean in plus
fours. And, most worrying of all for my mum and dad,
I hadn't even had a proper game of golf yet.

. . . I turn back towards the Sphincter one last time and
check my reflection. Black trousers, bright pink polo
shirt from factory reject shop, slightly misshapen lilac
jumper. I'm essentially wearing a bastardized version of
my school uniform, but I figure that no one will really
notice and, besides, today, if all goes to plan, I'll probably be winning myself some *proper* golf clothes.
Through the window my confused, resigned dad waves
goodbye and mouths, 'Be brilliant,' but my pang of
errant guilt is drowned out by a mounting excitement
in my gut. I watch anxiously as the car makes use of the
full width of the club's private drive to perform a
U-turn, then begins to void its way back to Nocton, the
village we call home. Then, breathing out my relief, I
look beyond Cripsley's imperial gates, past judge-
mental pines and garden sheds that could be mistaken
for luxury dwellings, to the future: the birdies, the
blazer badges, the social functions, the soaring, drawing drives. This is it! I marvel. The thing I've been
living for for three months – a veritable lifetime. I
wonder what it will feel like: the opening divot,
the début sidehill putt, the first crashing drive. The
adrenalin surging through my bloodstream makes me

feel like I could fly, but only when the Sphincter is out of earshot do I begin the march to my destiny.

Tee off? I think, as I stride obstinately up the hill. Tee off? *Of course* he can't watch me tee off. Not even by telescope from a safely distanced asteroid.

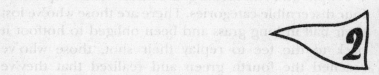

There's something uniquely liberating about running across a golf course. Everything you've been taught about dignity, grace and deportment tells you it's wrong, yet it feels so deliciously right.

Witnessing a running golfer is a bit like witnessing the class geek trying to chat up the prom queen. The humane part of you that wants to crumple up and hide battles it out with the diseased part of you that wants to keep watching. In the same way that a Mini Cooper isn't designed to be driven around a Formula One racetrack in second gear, a golfer isn't designed to gallop; he's designed to amble and ponder, stopping to sniff the heather and discuss the stock market along the way. Not only does the act of moving one's legs slightly faster than normal on a golf course seem to bring all the game's decorum and principles into disrepute, it has a way of making the runner look violently camp. Take the most macho, dynamic, one-hundred-metre sprint champion and put him at the mercy of the stopwatch on a dogleg par five, and he'll inexplicably mutate into Kenneth Williams.

People who run across golf courses tend to split into four discernible categories. There are those who've lost their ball in long grass and been obliged to hotfoot it back to the tee to replay their shot, those who've reached the fourth green and realized that they've left a tap on back at home, those who've crawled through a hole in the course's boundary fence for a dare involving ball theft, and those who feel like running for the hell of it. The third category has probably never come across the word 'etiquette' and doesn't even realize that running across a golf course is a perverted thing to do. The other three categories have one feature in common: they look like idiots. I fell into the fourth category.

The one thing you could say in favour of Ashley, Ross, Jamie, Bushy and me when we decided to charge down the fairway of Cripsley's seventh hole for no reason was that at least we'd made a *pact* to look like idiots. This agreement took a telepathic form. No one said 'Run!' after the last of our tee shots had torpedoed over the fried-egg-shaped bunker safeguarding the fairway, but we all somehow knew that's what we were going to do, as if we'd collectively heard a silent starter's gun.

'Your ankles are like a four-year-old girl's,' Jamie pointed out to Ross, as Ross crouched to tee up his ball.

'Well, at least I don't look like a lizard,' said Ross.

The next thing I knew, our shots were dispatched, and we were in flight: five whooping adolescents in polyester sweaters, each carrying several kilograms of rattling metal and wood on his back, doing the stampede of the swinging cretin.

It was April 1989 and I'd been a member of Cripsley for eight months. I'd met Jamie (12) and Ross (13) the previous summer at the junior lessons hosted by Mike Shalcross, and the three of us had been granted membership shortly afterwards, swiftly becoming friends and rivals. Jamie wore John Lennon spectacles, was tall for his age and had the quietly competitive aura of someone who might steal your girlfriend from under your nose without you noticing. Ross was more or less his opposite – undersized, high-pitched, and all out to prove he wasn't. Ashley (14) was a veteran Cripsley member of eighteen months with the physical characteristics and temperament of a hyperactive bull terrier, who'd long since outgrown junior lessons. I'd first encountered him a couple of weeks earlier, in Cripsley's pro shop, where I found him flailing desperately at inanimate objects, crimson-cheeked, while Nick Bellamy, one of the club's older, more sadistic juniors, swung him around by his knicker elastic at irresponsible velocity. Bushy (13), whom I'd also met at the junior lessons, was a dark, silent enigma, making up in premature stubble for what he lacked in words.

The friendship the five of us enjoyed was in its early stages, and over the last few months had often resembled the part at the beginning of a boxing match where each competitor weighs up his opponent for flaws. Nobody quite knew who each other was yet, with autobiographical factoids being eked out tentatively and strategically. I, for one, was still in the midst of my own reinvention, shining in the role of the all-round Respectable Boy – the kind who, given another arena in which to display his talents, might have made complimentary remarks about his auntie's Richard Clayderman album, delivered leaflets on behalf of his local Tory MP, and generally got the living crap kicked out of him a lot. Were my new friends putting on an act as well? Possibly. I'd learned, through overheard conversations, that Bushy's dad drove a ten-year-old Ford Cortina, Ross's mum lived alone with him and his sister and worked as a receptionist at the local brewery, Ashley's dad was a PE teacher, and Jamie had once almost been enrolled at a local independent, progressive secondary school. Did my mates, like me, come from homes where joss sticks smoked away on the mantelpiece and Bob Dylan croaked away on the turntable? It was difficult to tell. I was, however, pretty sure they didn't live in houses with posters of existentially naked German women on the walls.

What I did know for certain about Jamie, Bushy and
Ross was that, like me, they'd eyed the posh brats who
turned up at Mike Shalcross's junior lessons with unbridled scorn. Every week, there'd be five or six of
them, though never the same five or six: kids who
unlocked the rear doors of their parents' Granada
Scorpios to miraculously unveil lustrous high-tech
clubs that would probably double up quite nicely as
shaving kits, then sleep-hit their way through the lesson
in a style that suggested they believed they could tame
their personalized golf balls with sheer manners.
Together, the four of us would watch them gradually
vanish, for ever, back to their three-car garages and
private educations, and we'd sneer to one another in
the secret, satisfying knowledge that we were the odd
ones out – the ones whose parents didn't play, the ones
who turned up every week, the ones who were here for
the duration. We might not have known much, but we
knew we were impostors at the golf club. We'd known
it since the first day we stood side by side and contem-
plated one another's swings and clothes and packed
lunches. But we were going to take a little while before
we could admit it to ourselves.

It had been an interminable first winter – through
my eyes, six very limited golfing months, during which
I'd visited Cripsley as often as school and daylight
permitted, but emerged with very little to show for
it, other than a twenty-four handicap and nine

increasingly dark, rusty, ball-shaped indentations in the centre of my irons. With the evenings dark and use of the course restricted for new junior members, the practice ground continued to serve as the amphitheatre for my dreams. Meanwhile, I took a fifty-pence-per-round Saturday job caddying for the junior organizer, Bob Boffinger, which gave me an opportunity to test out just how robust my Golf Tom persona was.

I still consider Bob a friend today, and, equipped with what I know now, tend to believe that he saw right through my attempts to fit in and made me out for the lefty hippy spawn I really was. At the time, though, I was convinced I'd fooled him with Golf Tom almost as cunningly as I'd fooled myself. Under Bob's tutelage, Golf Tom learned the importance of a replaced divot, a firm handshake and a carefully read putt. Golf Tom held flagsticks, spoke when spoken to, laughed dutifully at the same jokes – 'Hey, Boffinger! Your golf bag's bigger than your caddy!' – he heard every week, and resisted the temptation to cough-mutter 'Miss it!' as hostile, patronizing opponents reached the top of their backswing. When Golf Tom sensed that the Red Sea had relocated to his lower bladder area during a mixed doubles match, Golf Tom made the noble decision to spend the next hour in agony, for fear that urinating in the vicinity of lady members might be perceived as discourteous. Golf Tom said things like 'Good shot!', 'I like your red, purple and yellow Pringle socks!' and 'See you again same time next week?', but not much else. Golf Tom probably gave his parents nightmares involving incubator swapping and small children with the head of Norman Tebbit. Golf Tom quashed everything inquisitive and imaginative in his nature. But what Golf Tom really wanted to do, if he was truly honest with himself, was drop all this protocol rubbish and get down to playing some golf.

In the spring, the hankering came to an end. In late March, Bushy, Jamie, Ross and I were permitted to play the course unaccompanied by an adult member for the first time, and from here things began to change. With the longer days, after-school golf turned into a golden reality, and we began to take full advantage of our new habitat. At four o'clock on any given weekday, you could find between three and five of us striding up the first fairway, screaming at our airborne Titleists – 'Bite!', 'Run!', 'Go!', 'Get down!' – as if they were disobedient guard dogs. Assigning famous alter egos for one another, we swung into the dusk and beyond, then said goodbye without asking if we'd be meeting at the same time in the same place the next day, because it went without saying that we'd be mad not to.

For more than half a year, to varying extents, we'd done a terrific job of pretending to be other people. We'd pulled our trolleys around the greens as mindfully as we'd instructed our parents to drive around the clubhouse car park. We'd replaced our divots after a shot on the course as neatly as we replaced our cutlery after a meal in the men-only bar. We'd spoken when spoken to in front of our elders, and always in the most cheerily uncontroversial manner possible. We'd talked to each other about brands of clubs, knitwear and wrist action, but not much else. Unsupervised golf didn't free us from these shackles, but it loosened them considerably. Gradually, we began to test for rebel credentials and talk to each other like friends, not humanoids.

'Have you ever been in a fight at school?'

'Might have been.'

'I was in one last week. Some twat who reckoned he did karate. I battered him.'

'How come your dad can't afford a better car?'

'I suppose cars just aren't important to him.'

'Have you heard of Curiosity Killed the Cat?'

'Yeah. They're shit. I prefer U2.'

As we set out on our round that night in April, it was with the fresh, thrilling insight that we were all normal, cursing adolescents after all, but with something else bubbling up inside too, a wriggling frustration that had built up over the winter months that we hadn't quite found a way of releasing. Running down the fairway didn't feel strange; it felt predestined. Nobody remembers who started first; it seemed to happen poetically, in perfect synchronicity. I've often wondered if other golf club's junior sections have had similar experiences, if a fairway sprint is a natural induction ceremony in the life of all teenage golfers. It certainly felt like it for us, because, after it happened, nothing was ever the same.

The seventh tee at Cripsley is shielded by a passage of conifers. Beyond that sits a gurning hundred and fifty yards of gorse, with a corridor of grass cut through it for players to walk along until, finally, the hole is governed solely by the colossal Georgian mansions which flank the right-hand side of the fairway. On a normal evening, a resident of these mansions would be able to look complacently out of one of the windows of their eleven bedrooms and admire a scene of utter serenity, punctuated by only the most infrequent, refined examples of human life. But not if they'd happened to be looking out of their window today, at just after 6 p.m.

'How good is this? We're running up the seventh fairway for no real reason!' Ross shouted, as we ran up the seventh fairway for no real reason.

'We're severely fucking about!' he observed, as we severely fucked about.

'Ashley's balls have dropped at last!' he continued, as Ashley, neglecting to check if the zip was fastened on his golf bag, allowed four or five brand new 'Go Further' ninety compression balls to scatter between his feet.

nice jumper

The initial impulse, while running on a golf course, is to break down laughing. In fact, it's possible that there are only two things funnier in life than running on a golf course. One is running on a golf course in tandem with several people you don't know very well. The other is listening to a running commentary on it as it is happening. I did both.

'We're almost at the bunker now. And we're still running!' shouted Ross.

I was the first to fall over, but the others soon followed: boys in pleated slacks, polo shirts and tight-fitting Slazenger jumpers, sprawled out panting like dogs rescued from a hot car.

It should, of course, have ended there. We could have picked up our golf bags, calmly executed our second shots, written the whole thing off as a freak occurrence, and resumed the rest of our lives as law-abiding golfers. But, in all probability, it was too late. You could feel it. The world was spinning, in that way it does just before something bad happens. I found myself running off a mental checklist as I lay gathering my breath in the semi-rough, a bit like the inventory you go through when you've left the house in a rush and have a chafing micro-suspicion that you've forgotten to put on your socks. I knew something was missing; I merely had to work out what.

Ashley, Bushy and Jamie: lying to my right, giggling asthmatically.

Gardens lining the fairway: deserted.

Adjacent ninth fairway: no sign of life.

Gut-pink imitation-leather golf bag: a few feet to my left.

Clubs: still in the bag, all intact.

I'd accounted for everything, apart from Ross. I'd just about had time to work this out when behind me I heard the '*thacckkkrunch*' of his three-wood making contact with his ball. I swung round, in time to follow the ball's majestic flight from my friend's clubhead, up over the boundary hedge, directly towards a glass conservatory belonging to one of the Georgian mansions to my right.

'Get up, ball!' commanded Ross, maniacally.

'Sit down, ball!' screamed the rest of us.

'Get up, ball!' commanded Ross.

'Sit down, ball!' screamed the rest of us, helplessly, wincing for the inevitable smash.

Nothing happened.

Defying the laws of physics and the building trade, the ball seemed to have located an invisible satin pillow in the midst of several thousand pounds' worth of glass-work. Either that, or an unusually agile pigeon had stolen it in midflight. Time seemed to freeze, as we looked where the ball had failed to land. We continued to wait, statue-like, sensing that the slightest twitch might cause the conservatory to be blasted to smithereens. I scanned the adjacent fairways for an

outraged Immediate Past Captain or Greens
Committee Official, but all of them remained deserted.
We looked. We waited. We waited and looked again.
Nothing continued to happen.

Over the following few days, we padded around the
course and clubhouse warily, half expecting some kind
of repercussion – a passing greenkeeper, at least, who
had witnessed the whole thing and reported it to Bob
Boffinger – but none arrived. Slowly, we began to relax
and believe our luck.

By running, we'd passed through an invisible door
into a new era. Before we ran, we'd been five spotty,
sporty adolescents doing our best to get to know one
another and convince ourselves we didn't feel adrift in
a world we weren't cut out for – a world of reserved
parking places, pedantry and stiff upper lips. After we
ran, we felt like five intimately correlated mavericks let
loose in a freshly mown promised land, where every act
of rebellion would be automatically amplified. Here
was a place with a unique, winning combination: a low
sense of risk combined with a high sense of danger,
something that was missing in the outside world in-
habited by our peers. If you could hammer a
penetrating, two-hundred-yard shot at a glass conservatory and come away unscathed, what else could
you get away with?

Even the most dedicated future British Open
Champion could be forgiven for laying his putter aside

for a moment and marvelling at the possibilities. Golf itself was fun – I'd known that from the first hedgehog-sized divot I'd torn out of my mum and dad's garden – but the stuff *surrounding* it being fun too? That was a prospect I'd never prepared myself for.

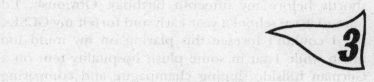

'And that was all it took,' Mike Shalcross explained to me. 'After I'd reduced my handicap to five and passed the arithmetic and handicraft test, I qualified for my card. I'm now an official member of the Professional Golfers' Association.'

'You mean that's really all there is to it?'

'Yep. You could be a pro, too, one day in the not-too-distant future, with a swing like yours.'

Coming from Mike, this was the best possible news. I'd had my suspicions all along, of course – my ability to out-hit men twice my age and point out the hidden flaws in the shoulder turn of Ryder Cup players had given me an inkling that I was in possession of a special golfing something. But now I had the concrete proof. In six months of competitive golf, I'd already reduced my handicap from twenty-four to fourteen, claiming first prize in such prestigious tournaments as the

Rabbit's Cup and the Crumpwell Charity Gong. Even if you took into account next winter's break and the odd mediocre performance, it didn't take a mathematical genius to work out that I'd be turning professional shortly before my fifteenth birthday. Obviously, I'd have to leave school a year early and forfeit my GCSEs, but I couldn't foresee this playing on my mind too much while I sat in some plush hospitality tent on a German hillside sipping champagne and comparing sand-wedge hosels with Bernhard Langer.

'Are you sure?' asked my dad, later that evening.

'Of course I'm sure,' I replied. 'I mean, Mike told me, and he's a pro. Of all people, he should know.'

Since a year previously, when he'd instigated the subterfuge that was my membership at Cripsley, I'd come to regard Mike as my rightful mentor. To me, he was Steve Pate, Sandy Lyle and Fred Couples rolled into one. With a Frank McAvennie haircut and the kind of blond good looks that you might have found leaning against a Ford Capri in an ad in a seventies issue of *Playboy*, Mike apparently had it all. His iron shots took off like scud missiles, browsed the sky, discussed the weather with a passing hot-air balloon, then finally agreed to come down, mechanized in their accuracy and spin. His drives, meanwhile, were a genuine concern to the RAF. In that I never questioned what such a finely tuned golfing animal was doing selling tee pegs to retired bookbinders in an East Midlands backwater, it now strikes me just how busy I must have been using Mike to boost my own ego. It also strikes me that much of the allure of Mike's game might have been down to its scarcity.

Mike, you see, didn't get out much.

At fourteen, I had yet to learn that 'professional' is the most misleading word in golf. While other sports clearly discriminate between mediocrity and excellence, golf frequently chooses to make them sound equally alluring. The clubhouse declaration 'I'm turning pro!' might sound exhilarating enough to a beginner or outsider, but the seasoned player knows it can often have all the life-altering significance of 'I've just got a job on the meat counter at Asda!'

In truth, there are two distinct types of professional in the world of golf: one who plays, and another who talks about it a lot. These – grouped under the headings 'touring' and 'club' – are about as far removed from one another as David Beckham is from a non-league supersub. In most cases, the touring professional – the kind you see on TV – competes at the top level of the amateur game for several years, then qualifies for one of the tours (European or American if they're exceptional; one of the inferior Eastern equivalents if they're anything less). The club professional, meanwhile, is seduced into ending his amateur days prematurely, by financial worries, ignorance or impatience, before he's had a chance to see if he's truly made of the same stuff as the big boys. He then serves an apprenticeship in small talk, psychotherapy and club refurbishment, all the time with the knowledge that, while he's sweeping up woodshavings, his amateur peers are perfecting their wedge shots. Finally, he might acquire his own equipment shop (attached to a club if he's lucky, attached to the local retail park if he's not) and get to play a little bit – by which time he's invariably too old to ever *really* become Steve Pate, Sandy Lyle and Fred Couples rolled into one, and all the ambition has been slowly and mundanely sucked out of him. Once a golfer turns professional he gains the right to earn money from his teaching skills but loses all his amateur privileges. Sometimes this can lead to fame and physical fulfilment. Most times it leads to a full-time position recommending practice aids in American Golf Discount. The difference between the top rung of the amateur game and the bottom one of the professional game can be compared to the difference between the fourth year of primary school and the first year of secondary school: the difference between feeling big and tough and feeling small and getting picked on.

In many ways, the professional's shop at Cripsley, overseen by the club's resident teaching pro, Roy Jackson, was like any other pro shop in Britain. That's to say, if you visited it at peak playing times, you'd find a patient young person (Mike), offering commiseration and encouragement, while anywhere between one and ten impatient old people ranted about their infinite golfing anguish in a manner that others might reserve for countrywide plagues and freak family tragedies involving heavy, serrated machinery.

'Why does nothing go right for me?'

'Is it something to do with the plane of my backswing or is God just out to get me?'

'I played absolutely brilliantly but still shot a hundred and thirteen for the front nine. Why?'

That sort of thing.

If the golfing rehab group was lucky, there would also be a middle-aged person (Roy) present as well, but more typically he would be out on the practice fairway teaching an improbably glamorous female pupil about the nuances of wrist cock, or performing some other equally urgent task, like discussing green irrigation over teacakes with the vice-captain, or taking a local sitcom star on a tour of the putting green. These activities would – along with his personalized number plate – represent his reward for enduring seven thousand, four hundred and twenty-seven conversations about 'the ball with the right velocity for you' with recently retired seventeen-handicap car dealers – the kind of conversations he could now leave in the capable hands of his assistant.

Forget social workers and shrinks; in the therapy trade, nobody works harder than assistant golf pros.

nice jumper

Mike's advice reservoir was inexhaustible. Problem with a slight hook? He was your man. Striving for more width on your backswing? See Mike. Having trouble persuading Sally Hodgkinson to come to her senses and dump her seventeen-year-old, XR3i-driving boyfriend? Mike had all the answers. I liked to see him as the David Leadbetter to my Nick Faldo. Together, I resolved, we were going all the way to the top – me on the course, coasting to a penultimate round of sixty-five at Valderrama in the Volvo Masters; Mike on the practice ground, ever poised to fine-tune the fluid Cox action – an action that would surely come to be known on the European PGA Tour simply as 'the Machine'. It was simple: here was a man who'd been perceptive enough to spot a rare talent which, if nurtured, could well come to define an entire epoch of professional golf, and he was going to do his best to hang on to it. Mike had never confirmed this to me, but from his eager, protective manner, it was pretty obvious that was the way he felt, and, if I was perfectly honest, I couldn't blame him. If I was in his position, I'd want to be in on me, too.

My problem was that a couple of hundred recently retired car dealers seemed to view their relationship with Mike in exactly the same way. If they could just hit upon that elusive, magical swing-thought, they too, accompanied by an acquiescent Mike, could make it to the first page of the leaderboard in the Volvo Masters, in spite of acute sciatica and a putting stroke better suited to the construction industry.

A few minutes seized with Mike in the murky pro shop began to feel like a stolen kiss in the dressing room of some modish, enigmatic movie starlet. The two of us would just be getting to first base, discovering the secret to the eradication of my narrow arc problem on long iron shots, when we'd be gatecrashed by Warren Ardle, wondering if the new rubber grip for his three-wood was ready, or Colin Allerton, enquiring if Mike had any thoughts on bump and run shots. Didn't these old men have jobs to go to? I wondered. Why couldn't they take their doomed quest for simplification via befuddlement elsewhere? Didn't they understand that Mike was mine?

It wasn't just the adult membership with whom I competed for Mike's attention. As an entire section, the juniors squabbled over him ferociously. There were around ten or fifteen of us now, all aged between twelve and sixteen, all playing golf regularly with a determination in our eyes that might remind an impartial onlooker of the time he was bitten by a rabid squirrel. Without Mike's encouragement, many of us might not have become members of the club at all, and now we took it for granted that he would continue to act as a mirror for the best side of our golfing selves. When Ben Wolfe, a thirteen-year-old with an unorthodox flying-right-elbow backswing, turned up on the first tee flaunting a graphite-shafted driver with eight degrees of loft, boasting that Mike had 'loaned' it to him, the rest of us felt as jilted as a child watching the birth of its first sibling. All of us felt we had a right to Mike's wisdom and equipment, yet none of us ever paid him for it.

Stealing time with Mike, I worked out, would require a rare level of cunning, and I soon learned all the tricks: the 'pretending to be practising my bunker shots a few yards from the shop while keeping one eye on the door' trick, which might lead to a free ten-minute putting lesson; the 'just happened to be passing as you locked up for the night' trick that might snatch me five holes together with Mike in the twilight; and the 'I was thinking of buying some clubs like these' trick, which might lead to a go with his two-hundred-quid driver. But hanging around the pro shop could be an intimidating business. The more time I spent around the place, the more I was convinced there was something strange going on there. Standing on the Astroturf in front of the practice net on the late summer evenings of 1989, Jamie and I would catch our breath as an Austin Allegro, bedecked with the Acid House logo, handbrake-turned its way into the shop car park, ejecting a lucky dip of characters as incongruous as they were terrifying. The gang was invariably led by Nick Bellamy – Cripsley's very own answer to Henry Winkler. My first-hand experience of Nick up to this point had been limited to the time I saw him swinging Ashley around by his pants, and a further fearful encounter in which he pointed out that he had been 'watching me', made a grab for my testicles, and snarled that my sort 'never learn'. I didn't know what he was talking about, but it sounded extremely daunting.

More often than not Nick, who occasionally helped Roy out in the shop, would be accompanied by Mad Terry. I usually managed to avoid Terry, and I didn't know what you had to do to make him mad, though legend had it that he held the East Midlands record for Headbutting the Wall of your Local Marks & Spencer Without Falling Over. Other bit players included a trail of skinny, pale girls wearing black lipstick and too much mascara, and Nick's techno DJ mate Trevor, a mini celebrity around East Nottingham since being caught urinating on a nightclub dance floor and making page seven of the local paper. To my knowledge, none of these people had handicap certificates or attended barbecues at the club president's beach house.

'What do you think they do in there?' I asked Jamie as we watched the shop door close, giving way to enigmatic giggles.

'You mean you don't know? Bellamy sits in the equipment room at the back and lets those goth girls *do stuff* to him, while Trevor and Terry watch. He has about five of them a week.'

'Bullshit. How would you know?'

'Mousey told me.'

'How would *he* know?'

''Cos he's Bellamy's slave.'

'Mousey' was our new name for Ross, who, despite (or perhaps partly because of) a burgeoning predilection for fairway vandalism and boasting about people he'd 'decked' at school, had by now established himself as the junior section's victim figure. Hindered by a voice that made the average seven-year-old girl sound like a movie trailer voiceover man, Mousey understandably felt a more profound need to impress than most. His favourite antic – saying 'HELLO! . . . *twat*' to senior members in a style which ensured only we, and not the senior, heard the 'twat' bit – required immense levels of voice control and timing and, in what must have been several thousand attempts, never backfired. But no matter how many balls Mousey fired at patio windows, no matter how vocal and risque his 'twats' got, he was always faced with two fundamental problems: a) that he sounded about as dangerous as Tweetie Pie, and b) that we would squeak his sentences derisively back at him every time he opened his mouth. The harder Mousey tried to cloak his emasculated rasp in an insouciant sneer, the more ridiculous he sounded. The more we squeaked back, the more obnoxious he got, graduating from 'HELLO! . . . *twat*' to 'HELLO! . . . *fuckwhippet*', and casting aspersions on the sexual preferences of the most benign adult members.

For Mousey, winning the favours of Bellamy's gang was the ultimate revenge. Already, a savage rivalry had grown within the junior section. With a handicap of 14.3, I might have been the best of the new generation of juniors, but Jamie, back up at 16.8, was closing in, and the Cripsley grapevine whispered that his mum was planning to buy him a new gold-shafted three-wood for his birthday, so I was watching my back. Mousey, meanwhile, had been admitted into the inner sanctum of the pro shop. Who knew what nuggets of advice my so-called guru Mike – not to mention Nick, whose prowess with a seven-iron was almost as lethal as his reverted Taiwanese bollock grip – was passing on to him?

I needed to know what was going on in there, and luckily I had a foolproof way of finding out.

The plan was simple. Earlier in the summer, I'd been to see the school careers officer and made it clear to him that I would merely be going through the motions for the remainder of my school life, and that my future was a bright thing that glittered in the opulent fairways of the European PGA Tour. After which I'd taken him through the specifics, from my first major amateur victory, to the securing of my tour card at La Manga in Spain, right the way to the attaining of my tenth Grand Slam. Clearly relieved at having his job done for him, he'd recommended without hesitation that I apply for some work experience in 'the golf area'.

The following day, I marched into the shop and demanded two weeks' unpaid work from Roy Jackson, who responded with the far-off look of a man forming a mental picture of extra helpings of teacakes and wrist cock. The conversation was left in mid-air when Roy broke off to greet a local second-division soccer player who happened to be approaching the putting green, but I took his remote smile to mean the deal was sealed. For two weeks, while my classmates destroyed plantpots at garden centres and stole Sony Walkmans from the Co-op, I would be leisurely swatting three-iron shots up Cripsley's practice fairway, intermittently pausing to serve an isolated customer or solder the head of a fractured sand wedge. Moreover, I'd have unlimited access to the Shalcross wisdom, and would investigate – and possibly usurp – Mousey's role as shop prodigy.

I might also witness some debauchery involving semi-naked goth girls, but, given the potential perks of working alongside Mike, I could write that off as a necessary evil.

The thing that really interested me about the pro shop, even more than the goths and Mike Shalcross, was the fact that I'd only seen half of it. If you can imagine a serial killer's tool shed masquerading as a village post office, you'll have a vague idea of what a curious, sinister vision it offered from the outside. The interior, meanwhile, was nowhere near as inviting. Customers had been known to make a special trip home to change into overalls before hunting for clubs in its more dingy corners. I've seen better illuminated medieval theme centres, and the place's aroma – old rubber, fur, petrol and something indistinguishable but defiantly deceased – was so powerful that even now a stroll past a slaughterhouse or tyre yard can send me into a nostalgic reverie. I found the shop's unchartered alcoves endlessly fascinating. It may as well have been Dr Who's Tardis. I'd been granted the privilege, a couple of times, of entering the room directly to the rear of the till, and discovered it had a lot of used pizza boxes and smelled even more strongly of fur. But there were at least five rooms beyond this, and, best of all, *the cellar*. What kind of hidden treasures lurked there?

On my first week of work experience, I found out: more pizza boxes, lots and lots of club shafts without heads, a couple of porno mags, and some wire wool. I found this out because my first job of the first day was to clear the place out – a task which, from what I could estimate after an hour of separating tee pegs from half-eaten Kit Kats, had last been attempted at some point during the summer of 1947. I half expected to find the skeleton of the last work-experience boy in one of the cobwebby cupboards, still glued to the fatal Kit Kat.

Next came my lesson in club design (Mike filed away at an ancient five-wood; I caught the wood shavings in a small bucket). But, finally, it was time to play. That is, Mike, Nick, Mousey and Roy went out to play the first eleven holes and the eighteenth, while I stayed back, manned the till and listened to the echo of their laughter as they strode euphorically towards the first green. I wondered how this was going to help me win the United States Masters.

Day two started with a jolt. Arriving with the intention of having words with Mike about my 'training', I was confronted with Nick, sitting on the counter, fingering a packet of Benson and Hedges. He seemed to be making a beeline for my crotch, so I, in turn, made a beeline for a set of Spaldings I'd been eyeing up on the other side of the room. 'Where's Mike?' I ventured.

'Oh, didn't he tell you? He's off for the next two days, playing in a tournament in Middlesbrough,' said Nick. 'It's my turn to be your daddy now,' he added with a cackle.

I did my best impression of someone whose heart wasn't making a dive for his stomach. How could this have happened? If Mike was going to Middlesbrough, why hadn't he asked me to caddy for him? With his powerfully coiled backswing and my astute course management, we could be an unbeatable team. Obviously there'd been some sort of mistake.

He couldn't do this to me, could he?

I checked Nick's face for signs of a wind-up. Nothing. Was that the trace of a smirk? No – it was just a malicious grin. Mike had let me down once and for all, and for the next couple of hours, until Roy rolled in for his 9.45 lesson, I was stuck here. I shivered.

'OK. Let's see it.'

Clearly he wasn't wasting any time. Resigned to my fate, I reached for my belt buckle.

'Your swing.'

'Eh?'

'Show me your swing, Tom. Show me your *swing*.'

For the rest of the morning, the two of us went at it tirelessly – in the practice bunker, in the cellar, in front of the shop, behind the shop. Me in front of the pro shop mirror, Nick behind me, making miniature adjustments to my hand action. Roy arrived, and swiftly departed for his ten o'clock teacakes, and we barely noticed. By lunchtime, my new swing was buffed to perfection: my shoulder turn was redoubtable, the club was no longer hooded on my take-away, and my wrists were working in unison, hitting against a strong left side. I had a new mentor now. I couldn't decide which was more wrong: the teachings of Mike Shalcross, or my assumptions about Nick. Without Terry and Trevor, Nick was about as dangerous as a children's TV presenter.

After four hours, I was finally permitted to hit a shot – though 'hit' isn't really the right word, taking into account how sweetly and lightly it glanced off the club-face. From what I could work out, the place it landed was somewhere between John o'Groats and Iceland. Elevated by the knowledge that if I could just remember thirteen swing thoughts all at the same time I could repeat this performance flawlessly, I was in a state of rapture.

Afterwards, while Nick nipped over to the men-only bar to prise Roy from an insistent teacake, I sat alone with a can of suspiciously chicken-vindaloo-flavoured Happy Shopper lemonade and drifted into a flawless reverie. My eight-iron to the final hole of the 1993 British Open came crisply into focus – the easy, wide backswing, the unhurried downswing, the compressed strike, the high flight . . . So crisply into focus, in fact, that I completely missed the tell-tale screech of the Austin Allegro's brakes outside. My first hint that I was in the presence of Mad Terry and Trevor came with the slamming of the shop door and the barked instruction, 'Hide!' Before I'd had chance to see the eight-iron shot's third bounce – the one where the backspin kicks in and it screws back down the sloping green towards the hole – I found myself hunching under the cash desk.

'Where's Nick?' hissed Trevor.

I told him.

'Give me the keys. Now!' hissed Trevor.

I reached up to the counter, found the keyring and slid it over to him. He locked the door. I scanned the surroundings, immediately registering four pairs of legs: mine, Trevor's, Terry's, and Greg Norman's. Greg Norman wasn't actually in the room with us, but his promotional cardboard replica was. Further inspection of the room revealed two more legs, pale and apparently female. Where had these come from? Had Terry sneaked them in in his voluminous ski jacket? I wondered if they were attached to a body, and, if they were, how I hadn't noticed it before.

If you ignored the sound of Terry chewing Greg Norman's cardboard ear and the distant thwack of ball against practice net, we were engulfed by silence. After what felt like several hours of this, I resolved, as acting shop manager and sole Cripsley member, to take decisive action. I did this by staying very still and silent under the desk while trying to stop my leg from shuddering.

'*Boyyys.*'

The voice seemed to come from outside the door.

'*Boyyys.*' Louder and more severe this time.

'Shit,' hissed Trevor.

'*Boyyys?* I know you're in there, *boys.* You forget, *boys,* that the professionals' shop car park is clearly visible from my upstairs window. I know this is where you go. I've seen the things you do here. Now, *boyyys,* come right out and explain to me why—'

'Go lay an egg, you old bag.'

'—you've just driven my wheelie bin several hundred yards down Cripsley Drive.'

There came a pause, during which I heard two sounds – teeth masticating cardboard, and something soft and squishy, up in my ears, drowning out rational thought: my heart. It just couldn't seem to find its moorings today.

'Now, *boyyys*, you may not know me, but I'm very dear friends with the club captain,' declared the voice. 'I know you're in there, and though I might not know all of you, I certainly know one of you. Richard Coombs, can you hear me? I know you're in there.'

At this, Trevor and the mystery pair of legs erupted into giggles. Richard Coombs was one of the junior section's posh kids – he attended the local private school, seldom took advantage of his membership at Cripsley, probably thought 'anarchy' meant turning up with less than the regulation amount of spikes on his golf shoes, and would probably spontaneously transmogrify into a lemon meringue if the likes of Terry, Nick and Trevor so much as exhaled in his general direction. Moreover, he definitely wasn't here.

She blabbered on. '. . . and you've got a choice, Richard. You can come right out here, pick my litter up off Cripsley Drive and return the wheelie bin, or I can tell the captain about your little game.'

Finally, we heard her retreating footsteps, followed

shortly by Nick's approaching ones. I picked myself up off the floor, inconspicuously, careful to be the last to do so, and properly identified Trevor, Terry, and the owner of the legs, a stick-like, blank-eyed girl with the translucent-yet-unremarkable complexion of an *Addams Family* extra.

'What the fuck was all that about?' asked Nick, as Trevor let him in.

What I had been witnessing, I discovered, was the aftermath of a game Nick had devised called Granny on Wheels. I listened as Nick, slightly miffed not to be included in his own invention, outlined the rules.

Granny on Wheels didn't actually require a granny on wheels, or even a granny. In fact, I couldn't really see where the granny bit came in at all, but I wasn't going to tell Nick this. Granny on Wheels, he explained, could only be played on a Tuesday, when the residents of Cripsley Drive, the affluent road that ran parallel to the course, left their wheelie bins out for that week's refuse collection. Wheelie bins, which had been introduced by the council the previous year as a fuss-free alternative to traditional, stationary bins, had already provided countless hours of revelry for the teenagers of the East Midlands, inspiring such games as Death Race 2000, Dalek Dodgems, and Drop the Local Sissy in the Wheelie Bin (Upside Down). Nick's game was considerably more sophisticated, since it required the competitor to edge his Austin Allegro up the pavement until its front bumper was resting on the bin, then, more carefully and slowly still, use clutch control and subtle steering techniques to edge it out into the open road. The rules, after this, became more open-ended. In order to complete Granny on Wheels successfully, the competitor could choose from a number of equally tempting options, including finding a steep gradient down which to release the bin, nudging the bin into the path of an oncoming vehicle, shunting the bin into a drive several yards away from the one belonging to the original bin owner, and – simple but classic – stamping your foot down abruptly on the accelerator and sending the bin hurtling down the road ahead of you. The winner was the one who came up with the most innovative way of dispatching the bin, or made the most mess.

In this heat, it seemed, Trevor, as designated driver (from what I could gather, Trevor, Nick and Terry shared the Allegro – I can only assume they 'acquired' it together, each assuming equal responsibility, and thereafter agreeing upon joint ownership), had manoeuvred the Granny on Wheels into the path of an oncoming cement truck, which had duly dispatched it into a ditch without so much as a swerve of wheels or shriek of brakes. Satisfied with their afternoon's work, Terry, Trevor and their gothic friend headed for the pro shop to bring Nick news of their triumph, but somewhere on the way found the bin's owner on their tail. 'It was bloody terrifying,' Trevor recalled. 'One minute, there was only a squirrel in my rear-view mirror. Next minute, there's that fat woman from *Carry On Matron*, waving a huge stick at me.' Whether this really was 'that fat woman from *Carry On Matron*' remains to this day very much up for debate, but Trevor's imagery left none of us in any doubt that it had been a wise move to duck into the pro shop as swiftly as possible.

As Nick and Trevor guffawed, Terry masticated enthusiastically and the goth did her best to look more cheerful than Christopher Lee's manic depressive granddaughter, I sensed a personal dilemma arising: one of those situations where, purely from partici- pating in group laughter, you've been half accepted into a social circle, but need that one final push, the perfect audacious comment or gesture. I quickly gathered some options. *So, Nick. That delayed wrist action you were showing me was really cool.* No. Nick was with his street mates now – he didn't want to talk about golf. *Trevor, baby. I hear you were caught urinating once in a nightclub. Can we be friends?* Come *on*. I told myself to think, quick. I thought. I came up with blank. I thought again. A brief anecdotal lull swiftly turned into a pivotal silence, all eyes on me to break the deadlock.

'I dare you to go back.' A voice said this, though it didn't seem to belong to Nick, Terry, Trevor or Gothilda. It sounded a bit like my voice. Or, rather, it emerged from the same place that the words I spoke normally did, but I didn't feel it come out.

Silence returned. Terry, for the first time, put Greg Norman's head to one side.

'Whaddayousay?' asked Trevor.

'I said, "I dare you to go back."' Definitely my voice this time: brittle, diluted.

'The little squirt's got balls the size of lemons,' said Nick, badass again now.

There was a pause, as a silent jury drank me in.

'OK, OK,' said Trevor. 'We'll go back. She doesn't scare me. I've seen scarier old bags in my tea. We'll go back, sure.'

'Yeah,' said Nick, reading Trevor's thoughts. 'But there's just one condition . . . '

'Right,' said Trevor. 'She wants her wheelie bin back, so I think under the circumstances, Tom, it's the least you can do to give it to her.'

From where Trevor, Terry and I crouched in the ditch with the wheelie bin, we were afforded a first-rate view of the driveway of the house belonging to the woman who might have been the woman from the *Carry On* film. From what we could see so far, there was no sign of life, unless you were of the opinion that three garden gnomes and a porcelain duck represented sentient beings. The wheelie bin rested in the ditch with us, where Terry and Greg Norman amused themselves by sifting through its contents. ('Wicked! This month's *Cosmopolitan*.') Nick and Gothilda watched from the pro shop, a hundred yards or so away. The five of us waited, as a dog walker faded into the distance. I didn't recognize him, but I felt I might have done. That was the thing about the residents of Cripsley Drive: even if they weren't members of the golf club, they always looked as if they should have been.

As I waited for the coast to clear, my attention kept returning to a concrete nymph at the front of Mrs Carry On's house. Something disturbed me about it – not just the fact that it was hideous and tasteless; something else, beyond that. Something about its out-stretched pose. The nymph – a singularly unhappy nymph – seemed to be searching with its arms for some invisible object: the very object, perhaps, that would restore its happiness.

Suddenly, I knew what I had to do.

I sauntered out into the open, looking about as cool as it was possible to look while dragging a four-foot-by-two portable refuse unit in your wake. I took a single look behind me – Trevor was giving me the thumbs-up, while Terry and Greg remained submerged in *Cosmopolitan* – but other than that, I was in a cocoon of concentration that even Jack Nicklaus might have found a little on the intense side. I peered down a mental tunnel at my target. My thoughts were occupied by two things, and two things only: nymph and wheelie bin. Nymph. Wheelie bin. Nymph. Wheelie bin. Two inanimate objects with gaping holes in their essential make-up that only I could simultaneously fill.

Five minutes later, as we performed a lap of honour in the Allegro, I admired my work. The bin had been too cumbersome to fit on the nymph's outstretched arms, but with it on its head the nymph looked somehow more human and contented. Returning to the scene of the crime hadn't been part of the original plan, but a slight uncertainty as to whether our adversary had witnessed my brazen vandalism led us back for fear of anticlimax: it was important that Mrs Carry On knew precisely who she was dealing with. You might not think it possible to fit five lanky, wriggling adolescents, a full-size golf bag, and a life-size cardboard tour professional into an Austin Allegro, but you'd be wrong, particularly if two of the adolescents happen to be sticking their legs out of the side windows. By the time we'd screeched up outside Mrs Carry On's drive, executed a handbrake turn, sounded Nick's customized Dukes of Hazzard horn and jeered obnoxiously (I don't remember what we shouted; it's not normally important in these situations, provided you shout *something*), she was probably quivering with terror behind her Laura Ashley curtains, vowing never to mess with *us* again.

'We underestimated you, Tom,' declared Trevor, as

we hurtled towards our next assault on the dreary adult society that sought to repress us.

Doing my best to blank out the image I'd seen a couple of seconds earlier through the rear window – of a rather confused elderly Asian gentleman puzzling over why anyone would want to adorn his prize statue with an oversized hat – I concluded that it would hardly be in the spirit of the moment (or, for that matter, of my burgeoning popularity) to bring up the likelihood that we had defaced the wrong driveway.

Once again, the Cripsley Law – commit a tiny misdemeanour and get severely bollocked for it, do something really mischievous and get away with it – prevailed. As Nick had predicted, we never saw Mrs Carry On again, and heard no sign of a repercussion from the direction of the captain and committee. Either the sheer unlikeliness of our behaviour was making us invisible, or the adult membership were making notes and stockpiling our crimes for rainy day retribution. Whatever the case, we decided there could be no harm in continuing to take advantage of the situation. Now we started to feel properly invincible. Two days after Derek Plunkett, a moonfaced ten-handicap electrician, nipped to the pro shop toilet and Nick replaced the dozen brand new Maxfli balatas in his bag with hollow practice balls, Plunkett arrived at the pro shop for his next game as jolly and credulous

as ever. When one of Mousey's 'HELLO! . . . *twat*' greet-
ings came dangerously close to becoming a '*hello* . . .
TWAT!', greens committee chairman Pete Churchley's
ear canal seemed miraculously to fill with cotton wool.
Then there was the day when the ladies' vice-captain
walked blithely through a daily pro shop game of Eight-
iron Tennis (objective: to throw your eight-iron hard
enough at your opponent to make them die) as if Nick
and I were ghosts that her rational golfing brain
refused to process.

My paranoia about Mousey's role in the shop hierarchy, incidentally, turned out to be premature. In the
end, the truth was disappointingly straightforward:
Mousey spent his school lunchbreak cycling down to
McDonald's for Nick, Mike, Trevor and Terry; as payment, he received their wisdom and personal
guidance. Granted, he got the odd free Chicken
McNugget, but I liked to think that my initiation rights
had involved a greater level of daring and ingenuity.

My 'work experience' continued. Over the remainder of it, I discovered that the pro shop is a bad
place to learn how to become a golf pro but a good
place to learn the art of fencing with snapped club-
shafts. The days were balmy and long, filled with
handbrake turns, Big Macs and apple fights in the
neighbouring orchard. Back from Middlesbrough,
Mike Shalcross, away from his role as club careworker,
was a less than effective disciplinary influence, and

quick to pick up the rules to such shop pursuits as Tarzan (a climbing and bombing game, involving concealing oneself among the club racks on the shop ceiling), Thief (one competitor attempts to take money out of the till before his opponent has the chance to shut his hand in the drawer), Catch, Fucker (one competitor belts two-hundred-yard four-iron shots while his opponent stands twenty yards in front of him attempting to catch them) and Meths Gun (a self-explanatory squirting game). Roy surfaced only intermittently, instructing me to clean an old set of clubs or sweep the doorstep, then vanishing in the direction of the practice fairway.* Goths were nowhere near as prevalent as I'd been led to believe from Jamie's estimation; when they did surface, Nick asked me to keep a lookout while he retired to the cellar with them to work on his 'follow-through'. After school, Nick and I were joined by Ashley, Bushy, Ben Wolfe, Mousey and Jamie. Alienated by the cold stares, rigid dress codes and stilted small talk of the clubhouse, Cripsley's junior section made the pro shop its official base.

The unruliness rarely stopped after that, but my work experience did. I signed off by breaking one of

---

*This behaviour was not exclusive to my work experience: even when I *wasn't* working in the shop, Roy had a habit of instructing me to sweep the doorstep, then vanishing.

the windows in the club repair room in a turbulent satsuma fight with Ashley. I knew I'd get away with it. Nick blamed the incident on 'a thick bird that flew into the window'. Roy, who was just on his way out, seemed to accept this, and then I was free. Estimating that Mike's decision not to pay me for my two weeks of graft could only have been an act of pure forgetfulness, I stashed a box containing a dozen Tour Edition golf balls in my bag, locked up, looked out onto another gorgeous evening in my adolescent Utopia, and homed in on a muffled desire on the back shelf of my mind. There was something I had to do, which I'd been forgetting to do for far too long. Something I knew was as essential to my everyday existence as eating and sleeping but which I'd somehow neglected.

I needed to play golf.

As a fourteen-year-old, I might have ceased caring about school, but I was still aware of the need for survival and the importance of an artfully chosen schoolfriend. I knew the rules, and I knew that, ultimately, all those hundreds of personalities I saw in the playground boiled down to two clearly defined categories: the kids who were good at football or fighting, and the kids who weren't.

With the kids who weren't good at football or fighting, I entered into a mutually beneficial business arrangement, where, in exchange for the vicarious thrill of sitting next to someone who was half-decent at football and fighting, they let me copy their homework, with the underwritten clause that I was allowed to pretend not to know them at breaktime. With the football kids, I tried half-heartedly to cling to some tenuous secondhand aura of cool as my credit rating dwindled

– I hadn't been in a fight since the second year, my interest in football had been on the wane since Mark Walters left Aston Villa and evening golf meant I found myself excluded from most after-school gossip – and my mates began to address the issue of exactly what they were gaining from their friendship with a golfing weirdo who couldn't quote from the best slaughter scenes in *Robocop*.

Gary McFarlane was different. Gary wasn't good at football, fighting *or* homework, and he hadn't even *seen* *Robocop*. Miraculously, though, the fact that he studiously avoided physical activity of any kind, and, when forced, indulged in it with all the élan of a mannequin with sunburn, didn't alter his status within the school hierarchy one iota. Gary was no one's hero, everyone's friend – one of those kids who just slid through trouble as if it wasn't there. It was hard to pin-point the precise root of his popularity, but I gathered it had something to do with his dad owning a Ferrari dealership and a rumour flying around school that his gorgeous, panda-eyed live-in au pair, Francesca, would let his sleepover mates watch while she showered.

Our friendship began when we both coincidentally sustained identical, fake leg-injuries during a school skiing trip. A day later, Gary ingenuously described to me an erotic dance Francesca and a group of scantily clad friends had performed for him during a bored Sunday afternoon, and the two of us became soulmates. Here was a new breed of friend: popular, well-dressed, rich, devious, crap at sport and never short of female attention. The other unusual thing about Gary, who wouldn't have known a pitching wedge from a garden trowel, was that he was one of the few schoolmates I could talk to about my golfing exploits without feeling like some kind of six-headed social deviant.

'In other words, if you play off nine handicap, that means you're expected to go round in nine over the par for the course?' Gary would ask.

'Yeah, but that doesn't really reflect how good I am. I'm a bit of a bandit actually,' I would reply.

'A bandit?'

'Yeah. In golf, a bandit is someone who's a better player than their handicap indicates.'

Another schoolfriend might have found it irresistible to use the similarity between 'bandit' and 'arse bandit' as an excuse to cast aspersions on my sexual orient-ation. But the ever inquisitive Gary would scratch his chin attentively and probe on. At last! I thought. Someone from the humdrum outside world who gets something approaching the true measure of how fascinating golf is – and by extension I am.

'I expect the clubs must weigh a bloody ton?'

'Yeah, but you get used to it.'

'And seeing as you are so good, you probably get loads of people offering to caddy for you in tournaments.'

The answer, in all truthfulness, was no. Thus far in my amateur career I'd found the levels of enthusiasm and loyalty among the caddy ranks to be little short of contemptuous. Upon being informed that he would be rewarded via the medium of my practice ball collection for his day's work, my first baghandler, eleven-year-old Paul 'Raz' Berry, had looked at me like I'd just stolen his favourite Teenage Mutant Ninja Turtle, before vanishing from my employ on a permanent basis. It wasn't as if he had even come close to fulfilling his obligations. On numerous occasions during the day I had rolled the grip of my driver around in my hands to find it hadn't been rubbed to the essential level of tackiness. Moreover, I felt his ideas about club selection covertly undermined my ability, and the recalcitrant look on his face when I requested that he retrieve my four-iron lob (I'd lobbed the four-iron, not the ball) from a holly bush to the left of Cripsley's sixteenth green hadn't exactly been a buoy for my confidence at a critical moment in my round. After Raz and I had gone our separate ways, I attempted to replace him with a couple of Cripsley's other eleven- and twelve-year-old members, but was barely met by the level of wide-eyed fervour I expected.

That left my grandad, who had burned his caddying bridges by putting the flagstick to the eighth hole in my golf bag by mistake, and Bob Boffinger, my regular caddy in Nottinghamshire junior and youth events.

The problem with Bob was that I couldn't help viewing his habit of running off, mid-hole, to offer assistance to fellow Cripsley juniors as an act of gross infidelity. I had, after all, been on Bob's bag for fifty pence a round during my first few months at Cripsley, and now, with our roles reversed, I wondered if there wasn't a little residual bitterness. Granted, Bob was fifty-eight. But I couldn't help suspecting that he nurtured his own small but perfectly formed dream of marching up the final hole at St Andrews in the 1990 British Open to a standing ovation with faithful little Tom Cox on his bag. By running off up the parallel fairway to find out how Jamie was scoring when, at two over par with four holes to go in the first round of the Midland Youths Championship, I needed him to help me find my ball, perhaps he was paying me back. Whatever the case, I made sure it was the only kind of payment that *was* happening.

Not that I was going to tell Gary any of this.

I could see what my new friend was driving at, and it required some serious thought. I played golf in an aspirational middle-class suburb, the kind of place where couples in sandals hold hands in front of estate agent windows; I went to school, on the other hand, in an evolutionary cul-de-sac with closed-circuit TV surveillance on its main street: a place whose principal form of boredom-prevention was an annual event involving semi-paralytic, eighteen-stone men racing prams down hills, seeing who could drool the furthest, then passing out. If my brain was a mansion for my interests, then golf luxuriated in the opulent master bedroom, while school was stuffed away neglectfully in the servants' quarters. The two passed one another on the stairs occasionally, but were on nodding rather than speaking terms. Sure, I gave my teachers and fellow pupils absolutely no doubt that they were in the presence of a legendary swinger-to-be and that they should be grateful I was magnanimous enough to attend the same classes as them. But when it came to actual interaction, I knew the two worlds should be kept roughly three solar systems apart. I had found this out, to my mortification, via an English oral assessment the previous term, during which, while dressed in a Lyle and Scott sweater, slacks and sun visor, I attempted to explain the intricacies of such golfing terminology as 'stiff shaft', 'rimming out', 'sweet spot' and 'tradesmen's entrance' to thirty fourteen-year-olds who viewed double-entendres as a synonym for comic genius.

Gary, however, was not one of them. He was always sprucely dressed – one of the few kids who wore trousers, not jeans, on Non-uniform Day – probably didn't find the word 'wormburner' the least bit amusing, and had the kind of haircut most of Cripsley's most eminent lady members would want to take home and feed teacakes to. These things convinced me that Gary would be the ideal caddie.

Well – these things, and the fact that he didn't expect to get paid.

Still, as a golfer, it's easy to forget just how bewildering the game's viper's nest of decorum can seem to a novice. Mindful of this, I made sure that Gary would make his début in the most innocuous of club events (the somewhat anonymous Monthly Medal), surrounded by the most tolerant supervisors (Jamie and me), during the quietest part of the day (late afternoon, when the majority of Cripsley's committee members would already have filed their cards and be tucked up in the clubhouse with a plate of steaming teacakes). In such an atmosphere, Gary could make the standard tenderfoot lapses – a mistimed cough here, a misplaced putter there, a badly situated trolley here – without causing any serious chaos.

On competition days, I made a point of arriving at the course ninety minutes before tee time, allowing myself ample opportunity to check on the day's early scores, slug a leisurely fifty or so shots up the practice fairway, develop a feel for the pace of the greens, and receive a good-luck dead leg from Nick in the shop. My pre-round routine was planned out in the finest detail in a notebook the night before under such headings as 'Alignment', 'Exercise', 'Relaxation' and 'Mental Adjustments'. I was, after all, due to turn professional in just under a year's time.

Today was a Sphincter day, so I insisted my dad drop

me half a mile away from the club in the car park of the local Texas Homecare superstore. Given a choice between humiliation at the hands of newly-weds buying woodchip or humiliation at the hands of members of the Cripsley league team, I opted for the DIY enthusiasts every time.

As I walked up the club's winding drive, a familiar figure came into focus, sitting by the first tee, wishing a foursome of octogenarian Irish doctors good tidings for the day. 'Morning, Seve!' shouted the figure. He was wearing a Pringle sweater, identical to the one Nick Faldo had donned to win the World Matchplay Championship the previous year. The crease in his Farahs would work equally well as a culinary aid and samurai weapon. As I got closer and my gaze moved down his immaculate figure, I tried to ignore my stunned face looking back at me from a pair of spiked Footjoy shoes that had been buffed to within an inch of their life.

'I did say I was teeing off at two forty-seven, didn't I? Not one forty-seven?' I asked Gary.

'Yeah, I've been here a while.' He sounded chirpy.

'You managed to find the club OK, then?'

'Oh, easy. I took the liberty of scoping out some of the pin positions. Checked some yardages as well. My dad whizzed me up in the Testa Rossa an hour or so ago. It's just his runabout for weekends. Your club captain seemed to like it. I thought he was going to make my dad an offer.' He chuckled.

Speechless, I surveyed my own attire for the day: £2.99 jumper from factory seconds shop, school trousers, cheapo polo shirt handed down from Dad, £13 all-weather golf shoes replete with ill-concealed hole in left toe.

'Hi, Gary,' hollered a passing Mike Shalcross, ignoring me.

'Right, buddy. Are we ready to kick some arse, or what?' said Gary, turning to me. But I hadn't caught up with him yet. I was still a good forty seconds behind, my mind attempting to process the fact that he really had used the phrase 'scoping out some of the pin positions'.

The first hole passed tidily if uneventfully, Gary silently observing as I racked up a couple of model tee-fairway-green-putt-putt par fours. The trouble began on the third, as my squirty seven-iron approach tailed off into the greenside bunker.

'I've been thinking about something quite obvious that's wrong with your swing,' said Gary, as we left the tee.

I allowed him to continue, poised to crush him like you might crush a caterpillar that had misguidedly crawled beyond the spectator ropes at the British Open.

'Well,' he went on, 'John Jacobs, the golf teacher, whose book I was reading last night, says that a strong left-hand grip can leave a player guarding against a destructive hook shot. I've noticed that your left hand shows four knuckles when you grip the club, which is very strong, and leaves you trying to compensate at impact. You kind of got away with it on the first two holes' – here he began to demonstrate – 'but it crept up on you on this shot.'

The guy had spent a couple of hundred quid on golfing paraphernalia and suddenly he was Tom Kite.

'Really?' I replied, doing my best 'you-have-much-to-learn-young-Skywalker' voice.

The problem was: he was right. My grip *was* too strong. And, if I gripped a club now, I'm sure it would still be too strong. It's the least conventional thing about my game, and leaves me holding the club awkwardly through impact so it remains square to the target, in much the same way that you see Paul Azinger, the American touring professional, doing. I've had a go at correcting it over the years, but it has never felt right, and I've come to the conclusion that if Paul Azinger can use it to win one major championship and come second in two more, I should be able to live with it.

That's not to say, however, that it doesn't bug the shit out of me.

'Shut your face and carry the bag, Gary,' I told Gary.

By the difficult dogleg par four seventh, relations had fully deteriorated. Having been advised that I had a treacherous 'spinning right foot' on my follow-through, warned about the dangers of a 'decelerating putting stroke' and reprimanded for 'hitting from the top', I'd made a deal with Gary: if he stopped playing junior golf doctor, I'd resist the temptation to fling him by his head into a nearby bunker.

How on earth had he learned so quickly? He must have been up all night, every night, since he'd offered to caddy for me, memorizing every instruction manual on the market. In golf, there's not quite such a thing as a 'textbook' style. Even a photogenic swinger, like, say, Fred Couples – who always seems to aim twenty degrees left of his target and can look as if he's poised to keel over like a skittle at the top of his backswing – has the odd defect. But Gary's ideas were about as orthodox as they come. Lowly baghandler or not, he'd planted malignant seeds of doubt deep within my hitherto reliable methods – the kind of flaws that the quality player shouldn't even concern himself with during a competitive round when, between that big-lipped sandy deathtrap on the right and that gorse bush on the left, there's no room for technical tinkering.

This probably went some way towards explaining why I was eleven over par after ten holes.

Jamie, on the other hand, was hot. At one over par, he was already seven better than the score his handicap suggested he should be achieving. I watched as, gradually, Gary gravitated towards him. I didn't mind since, although this meant I occasionally had to fetch my own seven-iron, it also meant I could remind myself what it felt like to play while not under a microscope. Besides, it had been fun to watch Jamie assault Ross a couple of weeks ago with the extra-long, bendy flagstick from the twelfth hole, and I had a feeling that if Gary kept making those adjustments to Jamie's hands at the address position he was in for similar treatment.

But then a very strange thing happened: Jamie started playing *even better*. He birdied the thirteenth and fourteenth, holed a bunker shot at the fifteenth, and from tangled rough at the sixteenth hit a three-iron shot further than most helicopter pilots travel in a year. By the seventeenth, I was lagging behind the two of them, like a sulky child being dragged on a country walk. By the eighteenth, Gary was carrying Jamie's bag as well as Jamie's swing secrets, and the pair were crouched studiously over a putt for a round of seventy-one, while over in a copse to the left of the green I poutingly attempted to locate my ball, unassisted, and salvage a miserable eighty-nine.

I saw less and less of Gary after that. The nods we exchanged in school corridors went from courteous to imperceptible to non-existent. It was the sad end to what might, without my strong left-hand grip, have been a beautiful (I never did get to see the au pair in the shower) friendship.

Or almost the end. In 1994, as a very different kind

of golfer, I handbrake-pirouetted into the car park at Stoke Rochford Golf Club in Lincolnshire, fifteen minutes before my teeing off time in the Midlands Youths Championship, and noticed a crowd shielding the first tee almost as effectively as the cloud of dust I had disturbed was shielding the Sphincter. Keen to see what the commotion was – it was a big event, but not *that* big – I put off changing out of my 'Never Mind the Bollocks' T-shirt and hoofed it over to the tee. I arrived in time to see a faultless grip, followed by a swing which only one word would do justice to. 'Conformist'? Almost, but not quite. 'Textbook'? That was it.

'Still sticking rigidly to that warm-up routine, I see, Tom,' said Gary.

As his playing partners teed off, the two of us caught up on our edited highlights of the preceding half decade. Gary had packed in college and, supported by his dad's Ferrari business, was dedicating his life to the amateur golf circuit, with a view to turning pro. I, on the other hand, had packed in the amateur golf circuit and, supported by the state, was dedicating my life to drinking myself stupid, punishing my eardrums with discordant rock music and chasing after girls in Nirvana T-shirts, with a view to getting laid and having an extremely good time.

I walked down the fairway of the par four opening hole with Gary and watched his second shot rocket towards the flagstick. I said goodbye, and watched from

a distance as he strode resolutely towards the green –
even his walk was textbook – and couldn't help
wondering if he was as hard on himself as he once was
on me. Then, gently encouraged by a greying admin-
istrator in a bottle-green suit, I moved the Sphincter
out of the space marked 'Club Captain' and changed
into some more appropriate attire for the day's events.

5

My first impression was that it was a shelter for ailing guinea pigs.

The configuration of twigs and branches before us, where we hunkered in the bushes to the left of the eighteenth fairway, could also have been mistaken for a latent bonfire, but it was doubtful that even the most highfalutin arsonist would have had the patience for something of this complexity. There was the additional suggestion of an animal's nest, but what animal, bar the most overdeveloped chimp – of which you didn't get a lot in suburban Nottingham, and which, besides, didn't nest – was this dexterous? No: this was art. It had layers, meanings. If you bumped into it on a black night, while camping on an ancient burial site for Indian warriors, you would be very, very scared.

As it was, we bumped into it in broad daylight, a few feet to the right of an ancient burial site for pet cats, hence weren't very scared at all. It didn't take us long to work out who was behind it.

'I'm going to boot it down,' announced Jamie.

'No – don't. He might have set a trap in there,' I said.

'It's probably where he lives,' mocked Ashley, relishing the snap of the first twig.

'Does he really think he can keep us away by building these?' I said.

'He' was Stig. And this was one of his masterpieces: an edifice designed entirely, it seemed, to trap lost golf balls – though not particularly effectively. It was far from the first example of Stig's creations we had encountered, and it had all the hallmarks of his postmodernist style: the 'portcullis' formation of twigs on the roof, the big diagonal branch across the entrance, the overall sense that anyone over the age of three would be able to destroy the whole thing with one swipe of the hand. This was the third piece of Stigart we'd destroyed in the last three hours, and we were starting to wonder why he bothered. If he was *really* trying to keep us away from the stray balls of Cripsley's members, surely he could have used a more effective contraption – a rabbit trap, say, or a twenty-foot-deep viper pit with a net and some leaves over the top of it.

Stig, who looked like Norman Mailer might do if he took baths in the local pond and tailoring tips from the skip to the rear of Allied Carpets, was one of Cripsley's greenkeepers. This meant he was paid somewhere between seventeen and ninety-four pence per week and naturally inclined to supplement his income. He did this with a sideline in balls. The system worked something like this: Roy Jackson sold brand-new, expensive balls to the members, who hit them in the direction of Stig, who sold them back to Roy Jackson, who sold them back to the members as practice balls. The members, of course, didn't know they were hitting their balls in the direction of Stig; they just thought they were hitting them in the direction of undergrowth. But Stig and undergrowth were more or less synonymous. He seemed to spend two-thirds of his life in it. He knew all the angles: the conifers to the right of the seventeenth, the gorse to the left of the sixth, the tangled rough to the right of the ninth known to us as Snakeland. There was a rumour that he even kept a snorkel and goggles handy for use in the pond at the eleventh. Someone must have been tipping him off, since he was permanently in six places at once. If you went down to the practice fairway to ease a destructive hook out of your swing, Stig's molecules would miraculously materialize among the enormous pine trees on the left. I once thought I saw him mowing a green, but now I come to think of it, the sun was low and I had the beginnings of a hazy headache at the time.

Life must have been great for Stig until we came

along. A thousand members losing an average of two balls per round is a big load of balls, whichever way you look at it. And previous junior sections, by all accounts, had been far too well-heeled and complacent to waste their time crawling through wet grass in search of a Titleist balata. We, however, had a burning desire for free missiles, and, in our opinion, an awful lot more right to them than a pungent old man who didn't even know what a Howson Hippo was. Ball-hunting expeditions took place early on Saturday evenings, straight after that week's competitions, and probably saved us a good tenner of pocket money per fortnight.

The architecture began going up about a month after our first expedition, and gave us the eerie feeling that we were being watched. There was always something portentous about destroying one of Stig's creations. As mere barricades, they were so ineffectual that it was hard not to suspect something occult backing them up. The accuracy of the location for these erections, too, was astounding, and hardly to their creator's advantage. Invariably we'd kick back the branches to be confronted with a dozen shiny white Titleists and Maxflis. More often than not, one of these was a cunningly situated dummy (a hard-boiled egg, usually), but the others certainly seemed authentic enough when we blasted them down the first fairway later that evening. None of it made sense. Here was a man who probably kept an entire database on the behaviour of errant shots, who could plot the average landing area of a slice from the fifth tee to the inch. Yet he was naive enough to imagine that a few elaborately arranged twigs and a dairy product constituted some kind of fearsome deterrent to a bunch of adolescents who habitually smirked in the face of danger and danced with the devil in the pale moonlight. It wasn't even as if returning to his handiwork and finding it snapped and scattered persuaded Stig that a change of plan might be in order. He simply rebuilt it – not more robustly, just more elaborately. There was always the chance, of course, that he was deliberately trying to *help* us find the balls, but why would he want to do that? It all defied logic. Like that of Stonehenge or the Colossus of Rhodes, the precise meaning of Stig's creations could probably only be elucidated by their architect.

After a typical Stig-enhanced ball-hunting expedition, we divided our takings into three categories: onions, rocks and spuds. 'Onions' were the soft, balata-covered balls that the pros use, 'rocks' were the more solid, surlyn-coated, everyday hacker's equivalent, and 'spuds' were the *really* cheap and nasty models, deployed by only the blind, the stupid and the senile. Golf-missile technology has now progressed to the point where even a budget ball gives a modicum of feel, but in those days the difference between hitting an onion and a spud was the difference between walking on air and wading through clay. Onions went straight into our golf bags, while rocks were added to the practice ball collection. Then came the exciting part.

Like all the best games, Ching! evolved haphazardly out of boredom, instinct and a pioneer's spirit. Provided there were enough spuds to go round, it could involve any number of players, but I think the most I ever saw participate was eleven. It was invariably played on Cripsley's second practice fairway, a juicy eight-hundred by one-hundred-yard strip of grass out of view of the clubhouse, shielded by tall trees and backing on to a peacefully middle-class Legoland housing estate. The rules were simple: five points for tarmac or tiles, ten points for automobile, twenty points for glass, zero points for silence, and minus ten points for tree trouble (i.e. if your ball got snagged in the branches and didn't make it to the housing estate). Anyone with a driver and an appetite for destruction could take part.

Of course, in the absence of a referee standing beyond the trees and marking the results, the points system could be somewhat ambiguous. It was generally agreed, however, that 'Thunk!' meant your ball had landed on a road or roof, 'Clang!' meant it had made contact with a car, which you naturally hoped was moving at the time, and 'Ching!' meant you'd hit the jackpot and smashed someone's window. The most astonishing thing – although we were starting to get used to this now – was the utter lack of repercussion. Ching! probably took place forty Saturdays per year for three years, and not once did we look around to see the vice-captain storming down the fairway, hands on hips, in our direction; not once did we witness an aggrieved resident storming into the clubhouse demanding to know who owned the Penfold Ace which had just inadvertently fitted his Rover 2.4i with a miniature DIY sunroof. Every game started with the crackle of revolution in the air, and ended with nothing more than the sound of a wood pigeon woo-woo-wooing in a nearby tree. Did the folks who lived between Rolleston Close and Aldman Road accept broken windows as a consequence of living within four hundred yards of a golf club, or were they glad of the free balls?

It was certainly a mystery to Jamie. If you took the necessary measuring equipment and pinpointed the archetypal landing area for Ching! contestants, you'd probably find yourself in Jamie's front drive. The extra challenge of trying to break his own bedroom window always meant that he played even more enthusiastically than the rest of us, yet in three years he didn't even manage to hit his back lawn.

Still, no one hurled himself into a game of Ching! quite like Stig. Stig obviously didn't know what Ching! was, and probably still doesn't, but it's a testament to the self-discipline of the man that every week, without fail, he would arrive on the dot to witness the first shot go sailing over the trees.

'He's just there – over near the silver birch. I can see his wellies,' Ashley would point out.

'OK, after three, let's all hit our spuds over his head at the same time,' I would command.

If you crouched beneath the level of the branches, it was possible to see Stig's breakdancing feet simultaneously pulling him in five contradictory directions as our impromptu air raid rattled the trees above his head. He probably thought we were rich, wasteful brats, but that didn't stop him from chasing our crossfire as if his next set of rubber footwear depended on it.

Like most of Cripsley's greenstaff, Stig wouldn't communicate with us in normal human terms, to the extent that we speculated whether he had the mental facility to do so. Yet it's quite possible he felt the same way about us. The warfare between the junior section and the Cripsley greenstaff took a spontaneous, primal form redolent of an early battle for territory between Neanderthals. It wasn't something that began with any particular incident or argument; it simply evolved, as if purely by instinct or smell. You could say the whole thing was the result of an intuitive clash of collective personalities: we thought they were subhuman trash; they, on the other hand, thought we were spoilt little fuckers with too much time on our hands. Looking back and reconsidering the intricacies of this intellectual debate, I tend to see the greenkeepers' point. If I had been haughtily instructed to reconstruct a piece of grass in the style of a billiard table, in the pissing rain, been paid the price of a Tracker Bar for the privilege, then looked on as two shiftless fifteen-year-olds destroyed it in a game of Divot Lacrosse, I think I would take a dim view of the situation too.

At the time, though, the greenstaff often seemed like the one thing keeping Cripsley from graduating from occasional adventure playground to Garden of Unlimited Pleasure. We couldn't understand why, when they could have been building a picturesque lake next to the seventh green, they always seemed to be throwing pointless sand on a green or digging an unfathomable trench in the rough bordering the fifth tee. More than that, though, we couldn't understand why they were always *there*. Members weren't our problem at this stage: they didn't *expect* someone to be re-enacting the climactic scenes from *Zorro* with the flags from the practice putting green and so they could suspend their disbelief and not actually see it. But the ubiquitous greenkeepers were more perceptive. With them around, we could still sling clubs at each other and hide ornamental tee markers in one another's bags, but always with the tottery knowledge that the weeping willow might be watching, that the pampas grass blowing harmlessly in the breeze might have *ears*.

Whether it had a mouth was a different matter altogether. Verbal consultation between juniors and greenstaff was conducted on the most economic scale. Most garrulous of the bunch was Rod, a man whose head, we reckoned, came as close to resembling a cauliflower as a human feature can without looking edible. Rod, who had acquired the nickname 'Farmer' after one of the adult members had joked he was attempting to grow peas in the seventh green, was the sole member of the team with whom we might attempt to conduct a conversation. Our encounters with him were brief and to the point. 'Hello, Rod!' we would say brightly. At which point Rod would mutter the words 'juniors', 'bloody' and 'you' in random order, then chunter off into the distance – presumably to plant some more peas. This would tell us he was in one of his more upbeat moods.

Rod's cohorts were nowhere near as talkative. In addition to Stig, they included Rog, a mysterious hunch-shouldered creature whose stubble grew furiously high on his left cheek but remained un-fathomably barren elsewhere, and Reg, a human battering-ram who communicated through the medium of snapped gardening implements. We would hear them from over the fence as we approached the tenth green, a gently rising lunkhead chorus of grunts building to a lilting nimwad crescendo which sounded distinctly like, 'Go home, Juniors!' Whether they did this to break up the tedium of the daily grind or purely for our entertainment wasn't clear, but we thought it only fair to respond by devising our own comparably drongoish response: a series of Quasimodo chants and spaz-wit groaning noises, punctuated with cries of, 'My brain hurts!' and, 'Stop hitting it with that shovel, then!' We would top this off with an impromptu game of Ching!, this time with the greenkeepers' tool shed performing the function normally reserved for the trees to the left of the practice fairway – what, in a more sophisticated sport, might be referred to as the 'net'.

This ritual would go on for anywhere between five and twenty minutes, after which the groaning would fade out, Stig, Rod, Rog and Reg would get bored and move away – back to their half-open copies of *Gravity's Rainbow*, presumably – and we'd celebrate by jumping into one of the bunkers that our enemies had just raked and holding Mousey down while we filled his golf bag with sand. Mousey never complained at this and seemed to understand that it was an essential part of the ritual. We all pictured ourselves as satirical wunderkinder audaciously mocking our unenlightened dogsbodies – rather than the puffed-up, confused milk-sops we really were, betraying our future selves by crossing swords with men who, very soon, might have served as useful allies. Once again, we would get away with it all and feel indomitable and invisible to our superiors, but, in our collective heart of hearts, we probably suspected the truth. And that was that even on a half-deserted golf course where cacophony and high jinks seem to be sucked up into the great big silence, you don't spend ten minutes shouting, 'Ohhhh . . . the bells! Fucking hell, the bells!' at the top of your voice without *someone* of influence overhearing you.

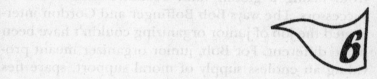

The period surrounding my fifteenth birthday represents my peak as a golf maniac – the moment when teenage pleasure-seeking and sporting excellence came together and briefly coexisted in seamless harmony. I might not have turned professional and left school, as I'd hoped, but that summer I compensated by shooting my first sub-par round – a (more innuendo) sixty-nine in the Crossman and White Shield – and became the first under-eighteen to win Cripsley's hallowed club championship (though, I suspected from the way Jamie, Ashley, Mousey and Bushy were playing, not the last). By the autumn, I had a handicap of three, shelves groaning under the weight of silverwear, a regular slot in the Nottinghamshire county team, and the captaincy of the strongest junior league side Cripsley had ever boasted.

Gordon Willard said I was lucky.

Until recently, Gordon had been Cripsley's oldest junior member. Gordon had passed beyond the official age for junior and youth tournaments a short time before I joined Cripsley, but he hadn't let that stop him from taking a gloomy and obsessive interest in his successors. The ways Bob Boffinger and Gordon interpreted the job of junior organizing couldn't have been more different. For Bob, junior organizer meant providing an endless supply of moral support, spare ties for prize-givings, free lifts, petty cash, imaginative fundraising events and competitive holidays. For Gordon, it meant arriving out of nowhere at a singularly unhappy moment in your round, admonishing you with an inane golfing proverb – 'Fairway wood, fairway dud' – then vanishing until the next time you dunked an elementary pitch shot into piranha-infested waters. I'm sure Gordon must have contributed to our cause in some other, incredibly beneficial behind-the-scenes way, but we never saw any evidence of it. He appeared to have been created purely to revel in our misfortune. In the thirty or so rounds he witnessed me play, I don't think Gordon ever saw me hit a good shot – which was remarkable, since I hit an awful lot of them. His disappearances between the outset of a perfectly executed backswing and the final revolution of a ripping drive were as confounding and sudden as his arrivals at moments of extreme golfing doom, violence and frustration. When Gordon decided to step down from his self-created post, by an apparent coincidence a golden era dawned for junior golf at Cripsley. This might have been viewed as a piece of prodigiously unfortunate timing for Gordon, but not by anyone under eighteen who had ever squiffed a bunker shot in his presence.

Our relief, however, was short-lived. As we improved under Bob's guidance, Gordon became, contrary to our hopes, a more, not less, central figure. He remained invisible for our searing long irons and masterful lobs, continued to take little to no interest in our ever more encouraging away results, still couldn't growl the words 'good score' without sounding like he was extracting an unusually obstinate chunk of mozzarella from the side of his mouth. But Gordon's role now had far more definition. In our eyes there was no longer any pretence of supporting the juniors. To us he was, quite brazenly, Hell's Trucker.

Accompanied by five or six obsequious goons, Hell's Trucker stalked the fairways in the late summer evenings, a bit like Robert Duvall might have stalked the beach in *Apocalypse Now* if he'd been six inches taller and spent too much time with tarpaulin. With a haulage company inherited from his father, a fondness for Yorkie bars and a hairstyle which was more a cheek-style that happened to creep up onto his head, his mere presence provided a chilling warning to us all about the dangers of arrested golfing development.

According to the general rules of golf, sevenballs are strictly forbidden, but Hell's Trucker and his mob didn't care, and – moreover – knew that no one would dare question them. As the sun began to set, you would see them swaggering over the ridge on the tenth fairway, the last gang in town, and you would make yourself scarce.

For a whole year, Hell's Trucker eyed us on the greens, hunted us in the rough, and hounded us in the clubhouse. I'd wondered in my early years at Cripsley why the adult members were so tolerant of junior shenanigans: were they simply an unusually charitable group of people, or had we just been lucky? Hell's Trucker answered my question once and for all. Our luck had run out. We wondered how he found any time for trucking at all, since he seemed to be on the golf course every minute of the day, making our lives a misery.

'Tom, what are they?' he demanded, as I attempted to take a short cut through the clubhouse to the locker room.

'They're trainers,' I said.

'I know they're trainers. What do you think you're doing wearing them in the men-only bar?'

'I thought I could just nip through to get my clubs out of my locker and change into my golf shoes.'

'Well, think again. This isn't a bloomin' sports stadium, you know.'

The climate had changed. One moment it was possible to smash an adult member's greenhouse and ride home in the Sphincter a free hooligan, the next you couldn't walk around with your trouser zip down for fear of being summoned to the competition room for a disciplinary hearing. Whether it was Mousey petulantly hurling his club into a pond after a missed three-foot putt, me pulling my trolley inside the line of the bunkers by the sixteenth green, Jamie wearing shorts with ankle socks, or Bushy failing to place his knife and fork together after a clubhouse meal, you could guarantee Hell's Trucker would know about it. He couldn't have been more vigilant if he had installed miniature spycams in our tee pegs and manned every bunker with a surveillance dwarf.

The fundamental problem was that Gordon had been made Tournament Chairman. While that might have meant squat to the hunks of monosyllabic sinew that drove his lorries, within the boundaries of Cripsley it meant he was the closest thing to Maggie Thatcher, or at the very least God. Clearly, the adult members viewed Gordon slightly more positively than the juniors did. Tournament Chairman's privileges included such luxuries as a reserved parking spot, a reserved tee time for Saturday competitions, being referred to as 'Mr Tournament Chairman' by fellow members and . . . well, that's about it, really.

'Hello, Gordon,' I would say, upon seeing Hell's

Trucker emerge from his Ford Sierra Cosworth in the club car park (he didn't drive any of his trucks up to the club), and he would stare me down, his swastika eyes noting my insubordination. The reprimand always came later on, from a messenger – Jim Prescott, or Clark Allydyce. 'You must call the Tournament Chairman "Mr Tournament Chairman", Tom,' I would be informed. 'Oh – you mean Gordon? He's the Tournament Chairman now? Oh, right. I didn't realize,' I would reply, feigning innocence. 'I'll remember in future.'

'Hi, Gordon,' I would say to Hell's Trucker, the next time I saw him.

But he knew he would have his sweet revenge.

When the shit hit the fan, the people who had been striving to get cool were invariably Robin and me. We weren't the oldest juniors, but since those who were older were either part-time golfers or Ashley – who, despite being the most senior in age, was still only the size of Bob Boffinger's leg and eternally nine in the head – we were looked upon, oddly, as the ones who should be 'setting an example'. It had taken a while for the two of us to become friends – Robin was the son of a member, and I had originally thought he was a bit on the sniffy side, but all that changed after he was kind enough to share with me a bottle of Thunderbird he'd stashed in his locker. The other notable detail about Robin is that he looked a bit like Chesney Hawkes, the one-hit-wonder ego-rocker of the late eighties, but I decided that, since he seemed like a good laugh, I could let that go.

Disciplinary harangues took place in the little white scorer's room, to the rear of the men-only bar. As Bob Boffinger and Hell's Trucker used phrases like 'absolutely imperative', 'correct colour slacks', and 'local rules', Robin and I nodded obediently, promised to be more civilized young men, and tried not to break out in hysterics at Bob's constantly gurgling stomach. Bob probably saw through Hell's Trucker's bullshit just as clearly as we did. He never told us as much but it was clear to us that, forty years earlier, Bob had been the kind of teenager who liked nothing better than leaning out of slow-moving cars and making constipated sheep noises at passers-by. With Bob on our side, these bollockings were something to be weathered with good grace. 'Yes, we will wear collars under our jumpers next time.' 'No, snapping your seven-iron across your knee is not a good example to set younger members.' 'No. Hiding the greenkeeper's Flymo is not big or clever.' Two minutes after being let back out into the fresh air, Robin and I would be over at the pro shop, throwing full, frothed-up cans of Fanta at one another – assured in the knowledge that we were in the one place to which Hell's Trucker's doomwatch didn't extend.

Just once in the Trucker's reign did we get caught for doing something *truly* horrible.

A lot of people have taken credit for the act over the years – Jamie, Ashley, Mousey – but I would like to say, for the record, that it was me who put the mouse in Rick Sweeney's shoe. It was just too tempting. The Sweeney was a speccy weed who looked like a ginger version of the Milky Bar Kid – one of the few private-school sprats who'd come through Mike Shalcross's junior lessons and maintained enough enthusiasm to join the club itself – and it was our avowed mission to heap misery onto his nervous, paranoid existence until he left the junior section for eternity. It certainly wasn't that we were threatened by his ability: he was consistently last in every competition he played in, and his swing had all the elegance of a giraffe getting its neck trapped in a filing cabinet. In fact, I cannot quite remember our precise reasons for the incessant bully-ing, but I seem to recall it was something to do with his dad having a beard.

The previous week, the Sweeney had withdrawn from the Waldman Carr trophy at Bullwell Forest Golf Club, clearly rattled by hearing seven people simul-taneously whistling the theme to a well-loved seventies TV cop show as he began to unwind his first backswing of the day. After that, you might have expected him to be on his guard, but on this particular day he had been downright negligent: leaving your brand-new Adidas shoes sitting out in the open, in the locker room, while your auntie treats you to teacakes in the clubhouse was never going to be a good move with Ashley, Jamie and me in the vicinity. As for the mouse, it hardly looked dignified, sitting there in the cellar of the pro shop, its forehead glued to a seven-year-old Kit Kat. I surmised it was the least I could do to honour it with a proper burial. The prank was an act of common sense more than anything else, and when it resulted in no immediate outcome – the Sweeney was far too cowardly to report us, we assumed – none of us were particularly surprised.

Three weeks later my mum arrived in my bedroom, wearing a look on her face I was well acquainted with. I'd seen it on the local news, on the faces of parents of teenage drug-dealer rapists. 'I'm ashamed of you, Tom,' she said.

I racked my brain for recent transgressions. Dirty socks left under living-room sofa? Grade E in Business Studies coursework? British Home Stores glass lampshade smashed with three-iron? 'What now?'

'What do you think? Putting that poor bird in that poor boy's shoe. I can't believe you could do such a thing! Bob Boffinger's just been on the phone, and he's horrified. He says he wants to see you and Robin in the competition room tomorrow at four o'clock. And take that ridiculous smirk off your face.'

I couldn't help smiling. It had been *three sodding weeks*. I'd assumed, quite logically, that I'd got away with it. What had the Sweeney been *doing*? I knew for sure he'd played at least three rounds of golf since the mouse's interment. Had he been walking around the course, wondering why his left shoe seemed to fit just that bit more snugly than the right one? Did he mistake that slightly moist, decomposing smell for that of his own socks? And what was all this bird nonsense?

At school, I had a foolproof method for seeing myself through punishment with a straight face. I thought about the back of Beau O'Dowd's head. Beau O'Dowd was the boy who sat in front of me in Maths, and treated me to a view that was a miracle of vapidity and uncomplicatedness, even in the notoriously vapid and uncomplicated arena of backs of heads. If I focused on it intensely enough, I could remain poker-faced under even the most extreme didactic pressure. I can picture it now: its lacklustre yet neat arrangement of hairs, its overwhelmingly underwhelming sense of sheer *headness*. I've even been known to call on it in more recent times of real crisis – when I'm in danger of losing an argument, say, or finding Mark Lamarr funny by mistake.

I'm ashamed to say, however, that that time in the white room with Bob Boffinger, Robin and Hell's Trucker, even Beau let me down.

'This is really unforgggivabbble,' stressed Bob, who had an endearing habit of reverberating on his 'b's and 'g's upon becoming riled. Not quite a stutter – something more guttural and impressive.

'May I ask if either of you boys know who's responsible for this blatant victimization?' said Hell's Trucker.

'Haven't got a clue,' I said, shaking my head in horror.

'I really don't know, Mr Captain,' pleaded Robin, somehow making the note of sarcasm in his voice audible only to me.

'Gruuurgggle,' said Bob's stomach.

'I mean, a dead bird in a boy's shoe!' said Hell's Trucker. I felt a nudge from Robin. 'Rick Sweeney might not quite fit in with the other juniors, but he's got as much right to play golf, peacefully and undisturbed, as anyone else.'

'This is really unforgggivabbble,' stressed Bob.

'And I suppose you killed the bird as well?' asked Hell's Trucker.

Another nudge from Robin, followed by an uncomfortable silence. One of two things was going to break it.

'Blllurgle,' said Bob's stomach.

Beau O'Dowd's head, Beau O'Dowd's head, BeauO'Dowd'sheadBeauO'Dowd . . .

A piece of paper had arrived on the table in front of me from the direction of Robin. I tried not to look at it. I didn't try hard enough. It contained a rough sketch of a boy with glasses, running away from a tiny sparrow. Next to it was a speech bubble, which said,

'Keep away from me! I don't like toads.' I let a grin escape.

Hell's Trucker clocked it, and pounced.

'This kind of thing has been going on too long,' he said. 'It's not as if these boys haven't been warned. My feeling is that they spend too much time at the golf club.'

'But why are you blaming Tom and me?' pleaded Robin.

'Because you're the ones the younger lads look up to.'

I dwelled on this for a moment. Earlier in the day I had suggested to Jamie, the 'baby' of the junior section, that the two of us go out and play some serious golf for a change instead of what we were doing, which was hanging around in the pro shop, using the *Yellow Pages* and the shop phone to order a random selection of dog trainers, landscape gardeners and thatched-roof specialists for people we didn't like at our schools. Jamie had duly outlined to me that he 'couldn't be arsed'.

'If these boys realized there was a bit more to life than golf,' said Hell's Trucker, 'and weren't permitted to come up here seven days a week, then perhaps they'd have a bit more respect.'

Hold on a minute, I thought. We – well, our parents – were paying membership fees here. Not as much as the adults, true, but not exactly a matter of a couple of groats, either. We were *supposed* to have unlimited access to the golf club. It was the middle of the summer holidays. We were young. We were enthusiastic, which, from what I could gather from Bob, was more than any of the Cripsley junior sections of the past had been. We were also getting *good*.

'These boys think they own the course . . .'

Er, excuse me, Mr *Sevenball*.

'. . . and unless we show some discipline I can only see this getting more and more out of hand . . .'

Christ. Had this guy no idea whatsoever what it was like to *dream*?

'. . . so the only option seems to be a two-week suspension.'

What!?

'Clllurrrrble,' said Bob's stomach.

'Gordon, I think that's a bit extreme,' said Robin beseechingly.

'Under the circum—' began Hell's Trucker.

'No,' interrupted Bob, 'I agggree that *at the most* a suspension should be imposed, and that at the least, it's abbbsolutely imperative that the bbboys should be bbbanned from visiting the gggolf clubbb on Mondays and Tuesdays.'

Robin blurted out the opening consonant of a protest, then sank back into his chair. He didn't want to be suspended. He was also well aware that Bob wouldn't dream of doing anything to jeopardize our golfing futures.

Hell's Trucker had a notoriously short memory, as evinced by the astonishing amount of junior tournaments he forgot to attend as organizer, and Bob and Robin were perhaps postulating that this would be the kind of ban that would stand as Big News only until HT's next social function as captain.

I, on the other hand, silently wondered how the hell I was expected to operate on only five days' golf per week.

It didn't make sense. For years Cripsley's elder statesmen had yearned for a junior section that would venture forth and make the club famous with its crashing drives, metronomic irons and honeyed putting strokes. Now they'd got them, they seemed to be overwhelmed with feelings of ambivalence. We didn't misbehave any more or less than we had before we became accomplished players, but we were certainly reprimanded *miles* more frequently. You couldn't help wondering what was really going on. Was Graeme Finch, for example, *genuinely* upset when he reported me to the committee for failing to repair that pitchmark on the seventh hole? Or was he simply pissed off that two days before, during my six and five defeat of him in the club's matchplay championship, I'd been routinely outhitting him by ninety yards? Was Gerry Cummings *truly* bothered that Jamie had played his shot out of turn in his league match against him, or was he jealous at the height and backspin that Jamie got on his pitch shots?

Whatever the case, Robin's conjecture about the ban was right. Three Tuesdays after its instigation, we were tying Mousey's shoelaces together in the pro shop. Two Mondays after that, we were sneaking out to the fifth hole and dropping a bag of practice balls in one of the greenside bunkers.

We were on our guard, however, and feelings of victimization – ours – did our golf no end of good. Rarely a week went by without Ashley, Jamie, Robin, Bushy, Mousey or me reserving a spot at the prize table. The more oppressed we felt, the more we won, the more our actions fell under the spotlight, and the more risqué and enjoyable our games of Ching! and Eight-iron Tennis became.

Somewhere in the middle of all this, I won the club championship by five shots from an elusive adult member named Terry Titterton. This made me abruptly, immensely popular – more popular, perhaps, than you'd have any right to expect to be having just beaten the best players in a modestly ranking East Midlands golf club. Titterton had held the championship for the previous five years, the members greeting his victories with an increasingly bilious stoicism. He was a 'country member' of Cripsley – which, in this case, meant he came to the club once a year, won its most prestigious event, then vanished back to his 'proper' club in leafy Surrey, leaving Cripsley's shell-shocked league team sitting around with steam coming out of their ears. Hell's Trucker probably had fantasies about driving over Titterton's golf bag in one of his juggernauts.

Titterton seemed like a nice enough bloke to me, but for the captain and many of the other low handicap players, his ability annually to bring *their* course to its knees in just two rounds mocked their failure to do the same thing over the course of a year, and his easy temperament and Home Counties charm while he was doing it seemed to undermine everything from their swings to their sex drive. Obviously, I wasn't their ideal choice to do the dethroning (I suspect they would have preferred someone with a few more Pringle jumpers – or even one, for that matter), but, in the absence of any other candidates, I would have to suffice.

Moments after I'd signed my winning scorecard, the clubhouse grapevine began to whirr. Titterton had 'left in disgust', 'couldn't even be bothered to stay for the prize-giving'. By the time I had made my way from the clubhouse to the locker room to change into my blazer, my back felt raw. If you had removed the polo shirt I'd borrowed from my dad, you would have found a patchwork of bright red hand marks.

'Well done, Tom. You sure socked it to him,' said the man with the glasses who once told me off for looking for balls in some gorse near the seventh green.

'You scared him off, kiddo,' offered the camp man with the long putter whom Jamie had christened 'Puff Legs'.

Who the fuck *were* these people?

As I wrestled my way towards the prize table, there, waiting – grinning – was the tournament chairman, poised to shake the winner's hand and present the trophy. Earlier in the year when I had been triumphant, he had been sure to undermine my victories with backhanded compliments, such as, 'Enjoy it while it lasts, Tom,' and, 'I see by your dress sense that your mum makes good use of her old curtains,' whispered beneath the shelter of applause. This time, though, he just glowed: 'You've done us proud, Tom.' It didn't matter that he hadn't been the one to break Titterton's stranglehold; what mattered was that it had happened in his year as captain.

Finally, at long last, the two of us were poised to be united. Here was my chance to initiate a future of peaceful adult–junior relations, maybe opening up some career opportunities in the transport industry in the process. I have gone back over the scene countless times over the years, and there are a lot of things I would have liked to say as Hell's Trucker passed me the trophy and I stared, dry-throated, into all those eager faces who pretended to know me, and wondered whose victory it was. But, in the end, the two I used – the only

two that I could find at the time – probably did the job
as well as any.

'Thanks, Gordon,' I said.

If someone tells you that golf isn't a dangerous game, the chances are they've never been hit on the arm by a three-wood shot that hasn't bounced.

Don't be suckered in by TV golfing injuries. Those spectators you see grinning and rubbing their ankles after John Daly's ball has clattered into the gallery are putting on a brave face for their heroes. Two minutes later, with the TV cameras elsewhere, they'll be reverting to their baby voice and pleading for a hot-water bottle, a comfort blanket and an ambulance. Golf balls *sting*. I found this out in 1990 during the annual Notts county juniors *v.* county police match, when Sergeant John Trevanean propelled me into a bunker with his hooked fairway wood shot. One second I was standing thirty yards in front of him, forty-five degrees to his left, in what I assumed was a safe position. The next I was prostrate in forty feet of sand, with a tangerine-sized lump trying to work its way out of my arm.

The first sensation, upon getting hit by a golf ball, is a mixture of dizziness and extreme pain. Then comes the easy part: a prolonged, malevolent throbbing. Finally, you feel like something is growing inside you, directly beneath the point of impact – a spherical thing, yes, but at least twice the size of the missile that hit you, and fitted with rotating teeth. I'm still thankful that I put my arm up in time. The ball had been heading directly for my temple.

But golf is a man's game. Trevanean's apologies were sincere, but businesslike – I was disappointed; I'd hoped I'd be offered at least a free guided tour round the local CID for my misfortune – and we moved quickly onto the next hole. First aid? First schmaid. We had a match to play.

Don't let the long johns and umbrellas fool you; golfers are *tough*. The balls are the least of it (although the legendary club player who had to have his legs amputated after licking the poison from the inside of one might beg to differ). Additionally, there are unruly, flailing swings, loose clubheads, water hazards and – in the case of the Cripsley juniors – flying killer apples and Mars Bars to think about. By the time I was sixteen, I'd been stabbed with the jagged metal shaft of a five-iron, almost decapitated by a low-flying Braeburn thrown by Jamie, pushed into a pond, subjected to witchcraft by a manual labourer, intimidated by a red-neck trucker, buried to my neck in leaves, and tripped over by an errant flagstick. At the 1991 British Open at Royal Birkdale I had stood two hundred yards up the fairway, listening helplessly to the terrible snapping sound as a tour professional – England's Richard Boxall – broke his leg *just by swinging*. I knew the risks, but I carried on regardless.

What I hadn't bargained for, however, was just how much damage a wooden tee peg could inflict.

This particular tee peg had been dozing innocently in my golf trousers, a remnant of my round earlier that day. Like most of its breed, it was about an inch and a half long, with a less than threatening appearance. Sure, it had a pointy end, but if you wanted to use it to commit an act of violence, you'd have to go to extreme and fairly pointless lengths, such as attaching a chain-saw to it.

Put it this way. If I had been looking to cause some trouble that night, it wouldn't have been my weapon of choice.

Accompanied by Mousey, I was staying over at Ashley's place, which was only five minutes' walk from the course. The golf trousers were an unfortunate by-product of a last minute sleepover invitation. I was sure, though, that if I wore my shirt loose, put my hands in my pockets, and introduced a slight strut into my gait, I could just about pass myself off as a non-golfer.

Having tired of ordering pizzas and pest control for Ashley's unwitting neighbours, we'd decamped a mile down the road to Stablebridge, where Ashley's uncle lived. Ashley didn't call Stablebridge 'Stablebridge'; he called it 'Stabbo', just like every other affluent Beeston kid who went there to convince himself that he was three times as tough as he really was. 'Stabbo' was Nottinghamshire's answer to the Bronx, but without the swagger – the kind of place teenagers visit under the illusion that it is 'happening', and the rest of the world visits only to buy secondhand cars, and only if nowhere else is selling them.

Ashley's uncle, Lanky John, lived dead in the heart of Stabbo, on a street (I noted silently) where my dad claimed he had been thrown into a hedge during early sixties gang warfare. It's not beyond the boundaries of possibility that Lanky John was the person who pushed my dad into the hedge. My parents, who'd grown up in places like this, had warned me about 'Stabbo' and people like Lanky John – which of course was exactly why I was here.

No one seemed to know what Lanky John did for a living, but Ashley, Mousey and me could only imagine it was something important and exciting. His place was a council house masquerading as a theme park. Our guided tour of his home entertainment began with a television set the size of a small cinema screen, took in a cellar full of brand-new sports equipment (all mysteriously still in its boxes), bypassed a 'Scalextric room', took a couple of detours via a mini bar, and finished up in a heated swimming pool. An hour later we were back on the street, unanimous in the notion that we were going to be just like John as soon as we were old enough to get a driving licence, a Filofax full of underworld contacts and a fast getaway van.

I wondered why my parents couldn't be more like John. Why didn't *we* have a pool room and four hi-fi systems? I didn't understand my mum and dad. Their working-class youth had been spent in places like Stabbo, surrounded by the salt of the earth, but having been to teacher training college and circulated among Nottingham's hippy community, they had moved to more affluent, middle-class areas where people wouldn't beat you up for owning a copy of *Jean de Florette*. What was their problem? Why did they have to go and make me middle class, when it was clearly much more fun to be working class? Stabbo wasn't so bad. If they lived in a cheaper house in an area like this and bought fewer books, they too could afford a Super Nintendo and a globe-shaped drinks cabinet.

Well, I decided, I was going to be different. I wasn't going to make the mistake of thinking that I was 'above' Stabbo. So its housing estates looked like good places to go and get murdered? So what? Pierce the surface of these monotone buildings and you found proud, ace-laugh blokes like Uncle John, with their infinite supply of games rooms and goodwill.

Yes, I mused. This was *my* place, populated by *my* people, and if I did happen to get thrown into a hedge while I was there, I wasn't going to let it make me feel any different. Sure, I thought, as I double-checked my polo shirt was untucked, you might get into a few scrapes while you were in a place like this. But that's the law of the jungle. That's what it's like in the *real* world. Some of us can hack it. Some of us can't.

Golf Tom had worked for a while, but the persona was starting to have its limitations in terms of parent-bothering, in the same way that trying to out-amplify my dad's Rolling Stones records with Bing Crosby would have its limitations. This, though, this – the very thing my mum and dad had been part of, and fought to get away from – could work. Right here, in Stabbo, I might have found the very thing that would unravel my infuriatingly placid parents. I looked across at my friends, swaggering along beside me: Ashley to my right with his polyester jumper sleeves drooping over his arms and a pitchmark repairer between his teeth, Mousey to his right with his sideways-on baseball cap. Oh, yeah. We were heavyweight. And we knew it.

The funny thing about the tee peg was that I didn't feel myself take it out of my pocket. I don't even remember the act of flicking it being a conscious one. Even when it made contact with the window of the terraced house to our right, I'm not sure I even noticed, it all seemed so inconsequential – mere static in the background of whatever conversation the three of us were having at the time.

This perhaps accounts for my decision to stand my ground, two minutes later, when the large man with steam coming out of his ears began charging down the road after us.

'Tom, run!'

Why did we need to run? We hadn't done anything.

'Come *on*, Tom!'

With the passing years, the image of his face has blurred into that of generic primate, but I remember his acid breath – a fusion of Special Brew, burning tyre and senile dog – as if I was in its fragrant presence today. To say he was a heavy man wearing the clothes of an even heavier one, he arrived in my face alarmingly quickly.

'*Tom!*'

'Right, you little fucker, you're coming with me.'

'Oeeeeoooowwww!'

Everyone has seen the classic cartoon image of an adult dragging a bothersome kid by its ear, but they assume that's exactly what it is – a cartoon image, not something that happens in real life. I, on the other hand, know better. I couldn't work out which was worse: Dog Breath's dog breath, or his lughole lock. One thing was for certain: I wasn't wriggling free without seriously jeopardizing my future as a music lover.

With the world spinning and my head at right angles to its customary position, I wondered at first why Dog Breath was leading me back to Lanky John's house. Then I remembered that all the houses on this road looked the same; we were going back to *his* place. His unrelenting grip suggested coffee wasn't on the agenda. I could live with that – it probably smelled of dog anyway.

After being dragged roughly through a room that didn't even hint that it might contain a Scalextric track then up a flight of stairs, I found myself locked in Dog Breath's bathroom, alone. From a cursory glance, I took the colour scheme to have been inspired by a large, diverse meal and a particularly bumpy fairground ride. As I got intimate with the rubber ducks, I strained my remaining good ear to pick up snatches of conversation from downstairs.

'Lock all the doors.'

'He's only a kid, Barry.' This from a considerably less ominous, feminine voice.

'That little bastard threw a fuckin' brick at our window.'

'Now, Barry, I doubt if it was anything as big as a brick.'

'I ought to take my belt to the little pissbag.'

'Now, Barry, remember what the doctor said about your ticker.'

A couple of moments later, the bathroom door

swung open, revealing first Barry then, cowering behind him, a woman offering me the kind of nervous smile that suggested she was sorry her sadist husband was imprisoning me in her bathroom but there honestly wasn't too much she could do about it. I took this to be Mrs Barry.

'So – what have you got to fuckin' say for yerself?' enquired Barry.

That it's illegal to hold innocent people captive in badly decorated bathrooms. 'Not much.'

'What do you think you're doing, going around throwing bricks at good people's windows?'

Well, we guessed from the stonecladding on the front of your house that it was a bad person's window, but we obviously got it wrong. 'It wasn't a brick.'

'Fuckin' sounded like a brick. Nearly bloody smashed the bloody thing.'

'It was a tee peg.'

'A what?'

'You use them for golf.'

'Are you taking the twating piss? I ought to pissing smack you one. I'm calling the fucking police.'

I would like to say that I sprung into decisive action at this point, attacked Barry with the loofah, slipped nimbly around Mrs Barry, then escaped to the safety of Ashley and Mousey, emptying the remaining tee pegs from my pocket onto the hall floor and offering an insouciant, 'That's what you get for messing with the

Golf Boys, you fat prole!' on my way out. I would *like* to say that, but the somewhat more cowardly truth is that for the next thirty minutes or so I remained locked in Barry's bathroom, intermittently quivering and re-enacting the most gripping scenes from the 1989 US Masters with the help of the rubber ducks (I assumed these belonged to Mrs Barry; something told me Barry wasn't a duck kind of guy). During this period, the doorbell rang twice. Firstly to announce the arrival of Ashley and Mousey, who'd finally worked up the courage to try to rescue me. Secondly to announce the police.

Eventually, after what seemed like several hours of muffled exchanges, the bathroom door opened.

'Oh . . . hi, Tom. How's your arm?'

Sergeant John Trevanean certainly looked more imposing in uniform than he did in his Slazenger pullover, yet somehow less ominous than he did with a fairway wood in his hand. I'm sure he was as surprised as I was to be meeting up with his ex-golfing opponent in a bathroom in Stablebridge, but no one was more taken aback by this development than Barry. It's per-haps a measure of the severity of his disorientation that his reaction managed to exclude the words 'piss', 'bastard' and 'twathead'.

'You two acquainted, then?'

From here Barry's case, not that strong to begin with, began to lose more steam than a just-opened dishwasher. I was amazed and proud at how quickly Ashley and Mousey – who'd been detained in the spare bedroom after trying to persuade Barry to set me free – and I turned on our Frightened Golf Kids personas, as Barry began to look more and more like an irrational old slob. Trevanean, whose twenty-three years on the force had obviously never prepared him for homicidal tee-peg hurling, was remarkably professional about the whole thing, and his poker face as Barry revealed the offending missile – 'They threw . . . *this!*' – was a testament to his self-possession under extreme pressure. Having assured Barry that we would be dealt with 'appropriately', he – with the assistance of his constable – did a good job of getting us out of there as quickly and tidily as possible.

The journey home in the panda car was a quiet one, the three of us in the back still reeling from Barry's body odour, the two officers in the front finding it hard to summon the appropriate words with which to tick us off. With thoughts of sleepovers a thing of the past, we were dropped back one by one at peaceful, tasteful houses with the faint aroma of Shake N' Vac and potpourri. Mine was the final call of the night, and I was struck by how welcoming my home looked. I also found myself experiencing the hitherto unknown emotion of not dreading the prospect of being forced to watch *Manon des Sources* by my mum and dad. As we pulled up alongside the Sphincter, Trevanean finally voiced something that clearly had been bothering him for some time.

'You're all nice boys, from nice homes. You love golf, and it's not as if you're struggling for ways to spend your time. What I can't understand is: what on earth were you doing walking the streets in a place like Stablebridge?'

While one part of me pretended to think it was a narrow-minded thing to say, somewhere deeper down I was asking myself a similar question.

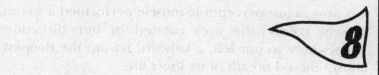

Even in the days before his petulance became legendary, it didn't take a trained nursery nurse to deduce that Colin Montgomerie was a stroppy so-and-so. While his fellow European Tour players milled contentedly around Wentworth's practice putting green, efficiently carrying out their pre-round warm-up routines or sharing the odd 'witty' observation ('If Clarky keeps chipping like that he'll be deep-fat frying by the end of the day!'), Colin stood disconnected, on the edge of the action, hands on hips, shooting that I-flipping-dare-you stare at some maddeningly inconsiderate object in the middle distance – a ladybird which had presumed to use the line of his shot as a runway, perhaps, or an umbrella displaying a colour scheme not quite to his liking. He was definitely pissed off. Or perhaps he always looked like that. Whatever the case, Mousey and I made a snap decision not to like him.

'What's the matter with that mardy git?' I asked my friend.

'I think someone's stolen his pram,' peeped Mousey. Then, a little too loud for my liking: 'Don't cry, Colin!'

Somewhere between Colin's left jowl and the edge of his nose, a just-perceptible muscle performed a spasm. Slowly, coldly, the eyes rotated in our direction. Somewhere to our left, a ladybird let out the deepest, most relieved breath of its short life.

'D'you reckon he heard you?' I whispered.

'Do you think I give a shit?' said Mousey, picking up the pace of our escape.

For Mousey, spitting insults at European Tour professionals was the logical extension of saying 'HELLO. . . *dickwit*' to Cripsley's adult members. By the time he warned Colin Montgomerie not to cry at Wentworth, he'd already urged Jesper Parnevik to 'Get a new hat!' at Fulford, squeaked insensitively about Eamonn Darcy's jelly-limbed backswing at Woburn, and – perhaps most boldly of all – honked 'Good shot!' after watching Sam Torrance plonk a straightforward iron into a lake at the Belfry. Some of us thought we heard Sam mutter 'fuck off' under his breath, but on the whole the most Mousey would get would be a fleeting arctic stare or exasperated sigh. In terms of player–spectator stand-offs, though, that was the golfing sphere's equivalent of Eric Cantona kung fu-kicking his way into the family stand at Selhurst Park.

'We're severely fucking about!'

Puberty might have finally left its mark on Mousey's scrawny physique, but it had somehow managed to overlook his vocal chords. Now that he was almost as big as the rest of us, his voice's similarity to that of an orphaned sparrow seemed more apparent than ever. His impudence made us cackle malevolently along with him, but it didn't stop me, Robin and Jamie from derisively cheeping 'Don't cry, Colin!' at him all the way back up the M1 in the back of Bob Boffinger's executive sports car.

In all fairness, it wasn't surprising that the professional arena was a place where Mousey felt the shackles of his runt status more keenly than ever. His introduction to European Tour spectatordom had hardly been dignified. During our first pro tournament, the 1990 PGA Championship, five of us had cut across Wentworth's deserted east course in an attempt to bypass the crowds and sneak a seat by the eighth green on the west course, where the nub of the tournament action was taking place. 'Last one to the green is Steve Rider's bastard love child!' Mousey had cried, and streaked off up the fairway – at which point, obviously, the remainder of us had stopped dead in our tracks and watched, waiting to see precisely how long it would take him to realize he was on his own. He had progressed about seventy yards when the lower half of his body abruptly disappeared from view.

It took only two of us to pull him out of the swamp in the end, and he claimed that the leeches on his leg didn't hurt all that much, but his day's misfortune wasn't quite over. Two hours later, on another illusory short cut through Wentworth's scrubland, we encountered a brook: not a particularly wide brook, but nevertheless the kind of brook that demands you to engage your brain before you hurdle it. In theory, Mousey's idea of lobbing his bag over the water first as a precaution had been sensible enough, but the throw itself was pitiful, executed with the level of brute force one of the railway children might have summoned in an encounter with an abnormally persistent feather. Mousey had watched, open-mouthed, as the bag rolled and bumped its way down the far bank in comic slow motion, before finally plunging into the water with an emphatic 'plop'. The rest of us, true friends that we were, waved goodbye sarcastically as rucksack and current became one and began to meander their way in the rough direction of Heathrow. We knew the rucksack didn't contain Mousey's house keys or wallet, since Mousey kept all his valuables tight to his waist in a bum bag.

It did, however, contain the sun visor that Mousey had gone to great lengths to get Seve Ballesteros to autograph earlier in the day.

I couldn't help feeling some of Mousey's pain, in this instance. I'd been with him – and several other over-eager teenagers – earlier, behind the eighteenth green, waiting for Seve to emerge from the scorer's hut, and I'd seen how my friend's behind-the-ropes bravado had mutated into unsophisticated awe upon being plonked within a five-yard range of a bona fide legend. No sooner had we seen the flash of Seve's Slazenger logo in the morning sun than we were on him, Mousey leading the chase.

'Seveseveseveseveseve! Pleaseseveseveseve! Pleaseseve pleaseseve pleaseseve pleaseseve pleaseseve!'

You had to give the Spaniard credit. For a man with sixteen rabid adolescents hanging off his back, he made an impressive attempt at walking in a straight line. Baseball caps, pens, giraffe-shaped headcovers, visors and tournament programmes were thrust towards every one of his orifices. He moved quickly but signed neatly, in his own capsule of calm. I now realized where he developed the composure to hole all those pressure putts.

'Seveseveseveseveseve!'

The poor bloke was going to be lucky to swing a club at all after this. It was disgusting and barbaric, I remember thinking, as I kicked a nerdy-looking blond kid out of the way and made a desperate grab for the star's earlobe.

'Seveseveseveseveseve!'

Unlike Mousey, I still have my signed visor. I force it on bemused house guests occasionally, and can never decide which I'm more proud of: the autograph itself, or the bloodstain – my bloodstain – alongside it.

Every so often, during our day trips to these tournaments, we stopped mucking around and remembered that we were there to watch some golf. When we did, it always made me wonder why I ever spent my time doing anything else. Without exception, every professional we saw close-up – even those who appeared to swing the club like a born lumberjack on telly – made the game look effortless. 'How on earth can they hit it so far,' I wondered, 'when their arms seem to be moving at the pace of a doped-up turtle?' Even the quick swingers looked like they were hyper-aware of the club's position at every point of its vortex. The slow swingers, meanwhile, were pure show-offs, with deft hands that seemed to linger with the ball at impact, savouring the compressed succulence of the strike. If I was more subdued than my friends on the journey home from a long day at Wentworth in Surrey, or the Belfry near Birmingham, it was because I was trying to retain that sense of ease so I could still reach for it in my back garden later that night. 'I've found the answer,' I would announce upon my arrival home, brushing past my parents in the hallway, declining their offer of some suppertime couscous. Then, with the perfect mechanics of my backswing illuminated by the patio floodlight, I would spend the following three hours undergoing a religious affirmation of everything I believed about the game and my innate ability to master it. Golf was life. Life was golf. God was in the swish of blade against freshly clipped turf. Around midnight, my swing, freed up immeasurably by the mental image of the player's swing I'd seen earlier in the day, would reach its ultimate groove. It was all so *easy*.

Imagine how good I would have felt if I had actually been able to hit a golf ball.

The next morning, it was never quite the same. Sleep, I concluded, was the big problem. If I could somehow keep swinging all night, the next morning I would be able to flash it around Cripsley like Greg Norman's kid brother. But four reluctant hours of Rapid Eye Movement – four reluctant hours of Rapid Eye Movement during which I dreamt about nothing but the first one and a half feet of my golf swing – would kill the feeling. I'd still play better than ever the next day, shoot some of my lowest scores, but I knew in my heart of hearts that I wasn't the all-embracing golfing beast who'd been under the spotlight the night before.

Then there was the lawn to contend with. It looked like it had recently doubled up as the venue for a Monster Truck rally.

'That's it,' my mum would announce, 'no more

divots. There are clods of earth everywhere! You could at least have replaced them!'

'I think, actually,' I would reply, 'if you ask any professional greenkeeper, you'll find that divots should not be replaced; they should be filled in with sand and seed.'

'Well, *fill* them in with sand and seed then!'

'Haven't got any.'

'I'm going to put my foot down this time, Tom. If you want to swing your clubs, you do it at the golf course. New grass costs money, and until you make it onto the professional tour, that's the one thing you haven't got.'

'What – grass?'

Grimace.

'Look – if it makes you feel any better I'll just swing with my three-wood. When you're playing with a wood, you use a sweeping action. It's not steep, like an iron, so it doesn't take any divot.'

'No. I've had enough.'

'Don't you want me to become a professional?'

'Don't try to bribe me. No more swinging in the garden. That's my final word on the subject. Why don't you come inside and think about something other than golf for once? Listen to some music. Remember? You used to like music. It might help you swing better and relax. Me and your dad bought the new Lou Reed album the other day. It's a bit dark in places, but track five's an absolute killer.'

Whoever Lou Reed was, I was pretty sure he wasn't going to help me rediscover the sense that my forearms were made out of elastic.

Feeling thoroughly misunderstood, I would slink off to Cripsley, where I'd console myself by hosting a game of Who's This?. I might have lost the Swing – the all-conquering, strangely personal (yet classic) amalgam of all the smoothest techniques I'd observed at the PGA event the previous day – but I hadn't lost my mental image of the handiwork of the pros themselves. Who's This? was a game for two or more players, and required them to assume the roles of THE MASTER and *the minions*. THE MASTER would swing the club in the style of a well-known professional, and *the minions* would be required to guess who it was in as little time as possible. A variation on this was Who's This (Tramp)?, which was limited to impressions of players with average annual earnings of less than eighty thousand pounds.

I invariably got to be the host of Who's This?, owing to my ability to execute, at a moment's notice, a technically perfect impression of any swing in the top two hundred of golf's world rankings. You name the action, I could replicate it, whether it was Payne Stewart's 'rolling wrists', Jack Nicklaus's 'backwards sway' or Eamonn Darcy's 'just killing this shrew – be with you in a minute'. If there had been a captive mainstream market for physical golf parody, I would have been in the top league, Phil Cool in plus fours. (Pulling faces was *easy*. Converting your hands from a 'cup holding' position to a 'door knocking' position in 0.2 of a second? *That* was hard.) However, as things stood, I was naturally blessed with the world's most useless party trick. Have you ever tried bellowing, 'Hey, everyone! Watch! Here's my Davis Love III!' to a packed big city bar?

My golf friends, however, were absolutely floored.

'Wow! You really captured that way Faldo has of driving the club into the ground like it's a big hammer.'

'Tom, do your Christy O'Connor Junior. Go on! *Please.* I love it when you do Christy.'

'How cool! Do another! Your impressions are so good. Have you ever thought of actually swinging that way on the course? Wouldn't you be just as good as the pros, if you did?'

It was a good question, and one I'd considered at length. Well, sure, I *could* use my 'Fuzzy Zoeller' in this week's Midlands Youths Championship. I *could* use it to shoot my best score ever, and win the tournament easily, and be incredibly popular among my peers. I *could* make my path to the European Tour qualifying school a hell of a lot easier. But it just didn't feel right. By borrowing someone else's swing, I'd feel like a fake. I didn't want to be a body double; I wanted to be the

Best. Compromise was death. I had to do this on my own terms, even if they were frustrating, masochistic and unpredictable.

I knew, if I could just be patient, that the dream back-lawn action would be back for good. It would have helped, though, if I could *get* on my back lawn. My mum's ban became even more stringent after I caught a microscopic fragment of gravel on the downswing of my 'Ben Hogan' and propelled it through the patio windows, rudely interrupting her in the final stages of some heavy baking in the kitchen. I thought she was overreacting, to be honest, but looking at the strength of her grip on her egg whisk, I judged that it might not be a good idea to say so, and opted to take my crusade indoors.

Living-room golf was less messy, at least. Divots were no longer a problem (although if you lift up the arm-chair in one corner of my parents' living room it's still possible to see the scuff mark left by my seven-iron), there were no strong winds to distort my swing, and it was always dry. What's more, unlike back-garden golf, missiles were permitted. In most pro shops you can buy a certain kind of hollow practice ball, designed to go approximately an eighth of the distance of a normal ball. For the serious golfer, these items are a joke – until, that is, that same serious golfer is stuck in his parents' living room, desperate to work on his delayed hand action, with his local course closed and a small yet fearsome middle-aged woman blocking his exit to the back garden with a potentially lethal kitchen utensil.

By the simple act of closing our heavy living-room curtains and clearing the furniture into the corners of the room, I would construct my own practice net. I doubt the curtains would have withstood the venom of a proper ball constructed with balata-coating and elastic innards, but with my Airflo balls I could bash away as fiercely as I liked, and within an hour had usually worked myself up into a rare sweat. If my parents objected, they didn't say so, or perhaps they hadn't clocked what I was up to.

My major mistake occurred not during one of these practice sessions but en route to a half-time break. I had been feeling pretty pleased with myself, having pummelled the curtains with a hundred perfect 'Craig Stadlers' in a row, and was heading to the kitchen for a well-earned glass of Coke when I heard the ripping sound. I knew it couldn't have been caused by me because, though I still had hold of my three-wood and it was trailing freely behind me, any imbecile knew that a three-wood head – which is rounded and smooth – couldn't make anything rip as destructively as that awful noise had suggested. It had been more of a fully realized tear than a rip: a spiteful cleaving sound, the sound that something jagged makes when it is working its way through something soft and precious and relishing it.

I scanned frantically for the family cat, eager to assign the blame, but was pretty sure I remembered seeing Woosnam (What? You didn't expect me to name him after a professional cricketer, did you?) passed out in the airing cupboard half an hour before, and besides, his blunt, out-of-service claws had long since become a running joke with neighbourhood mice. Then, very slowly, I allowed my eyes to follow the shaft of my three-wood from my hands, past the rubber grip, along the smooth shiny metal, down to the clubhead.

Which wasn't there.

In its place was an ugly, serrated metal stump. On the end of the stump was some stuffing, and a gash. Hosting the gash was my parents' art-deco sofa. On the far side of the room, at the foot of the curtains, was the head of my three-wood.

It had flown off during my last shot. Lost in the narcissistic daydream of my performance, I hadn't noticed. It was understandable, really. But potentially not to my parents.

Acting quickly, I restored the room to its former state, opening curtains and rearranging chairs and tables. It looked like the kind of living room you find in a Habitat catalogue, if you ignored the fact that its centrepiece had its guts spilling out all over the place. But that was a problem that could be solved, too. On the chair on the far side of the room, I spotted the cat blanket. Folded in half and placed carefully it covered the entire rupture. Who could tell? I thought. The old fools might not even move it for weeks. If I could just get the cat to sit on it and never move again, I had no need to worry.

It was astonishing: with a bit of quick thinking, I'd fully reversed my earlier mistake. I rewarded myself by going to get that Coke.

I remained a free man for approximately seven and a half minutes.

I could tell from the portentous tone of the knock on my bedroom door that I was in trouble. A voice followed.

'Tooooommm?'

There was an important decision to make here, one which could change my life, if not the entire future direction of professional golf. Confess, or concoct an elaborate excuse? The decision wasn't as easy as it sounds. A straight confession would seem far-fetched enough on its own: would my mum really believe that the clubhead just happened to fall off as I was swinging, and that the tear happened not during a golf swing but during a mundane stroll across the living room? More to the point, would she care? No: she would simply come to the conclusion that I had ripped her sofa because of golf, that golf was inherently dangerous and – horror of horrors – that golf was in control of me, and I wasn't in control of golf.

Slowly, silently, by the collar of my Le Shark polo

shirt, she led me to the scene of the crime. With the blanket gone, it was a thousand times worse than I remembered.

'What's *this*?'

It was final decision time. Confess, or pass the blame? Take my medicine and a few weeks without living-room swinging until she begins to forget it ever happened, or jeopardize my career and, moreover, be wrong in the arena of golf?

'Oh no! That's awful. I can't *believe* that cat!' I said.

That left only the videos.

There were around three hundred of them in total – a few purchased from WH Smith, the majority taped off the telly. You would find among them every single moment of BBC golf coverage broadcast between January 1989 and August 1992, with the heart-rending exception of the final two shots of the 1991 Benson and Hedges International, which my dad had erased with an episode of *The South Bank Show*. It was a more appropriate replacement than I realized at the time: I didn't merely consume televised golf; I turned it inside out, upside down, then subjected it to the kind of in-depth analysis normally reserved for cubism or the complete works of Alberto Moravia. When the BBC's soft-spoken swing expert Alex Hay observed that Tom Watson was hitting a six-iron, even though it was blatantly obvious that he was hitting an eight-iron, he probably had no idea that he was undermining a Nottingham teenager's entire faith in humanity. Anyone who watched golf with any sense of purpose, watched it again, memorized it, dreamed about it, then watched it again with his finger on the freeze-frame button, would know that Tom Watson hit a typical eight-iron in calm weather conditions one hundred and fifty-one yards.

Nothing of this seemed remotely unusual to me: not the filing system (alphabetical *and* chronological, naturally), not the list of past British Open winners on my bedroom wall, not the obsessive note-taking during the final round of the US Masters. From the first time I entered the pro shop and overheard Mike Shalcross and Roy Jackson having an inscrutable conversation about a tour professional who was 'changing to graphite', I resolved not only to know what phrases like 'changing to graphite' meant, but also to know everything and anything it was possible to know about the professional game. It was only later, when I began to invite golfing friends up to my bedroom and watched their mouths form silent question marks as they saw the endless rows of filed and numbered tapes, that I began to get an inkling that my behaviour wasn't run-of-the-mill for a wannabe pro. And it is only recently, having met a few thousand too many *Star Wars* fans, that I have started to realize that my habit of forcing guests to watch repeatedly the BBC's coverage of the 1989 Suntory World Matchplay final and miming along with my favourite bits of Bruce Critchley's commentary – 'And that is *miles* past Nick Faldo!' – might have been a touch on the irritating side.

In an unofficial poll conducted among everyone I've ever known who has never played the game, golf has been voted the Worst Television Sport in the World, outdulling – among others – horseracing, bowls and (I can't believe this) darts. The people who have decided this are quite clearly misguided, if not psychologically disordered. Admittedly the camera's habit of lingering on birdlife for periods of up to ten minutes doesn't exactly serve as an advertisement for the game's sex appeal, and the commentators don't do themselves any favours by letting slip political leanings of the Ottoman era, but golf has a spectrum of environments, permutations and inside knowledge that no other spectator sport can begin to match. Anyone can thoroughly enjoy a football game. It takes imagination and perseverance to get the most out of a golf tournament.

I have worked out the exact amount of time I spent watching golf as a teenager but won't list it here, since it cripples me to think just how much of it I could have spent having sex or listening to Three Dog Night's greatest hits. Let's just say if you took the amount of hours I owned of golf on video, multiplied this number by ten, and added an extra hundred hours to allow for tapes borrowed from friends, you'd be fairly close to the mark. I saw professional golf as my own version of the magic potion in Gosciny and Uderzo's *Asterix* books, which I could drink (watch), then carry inside me in order to fight (play) better, before going back to my druid (telly) to replenish my supplies (tapes) every day or two. The fresher the potion was in my system, the better.

My final act before setting off for an important round wasn't to check I'd packed my waterproof bottoms and flat cap; it was to rewind my British Open tape and watch Payne Stewart butter that three-hundred-yard drive one last time. I'd then carry the image around for the rest of the day, with its accompanying commentary ('And that's right down, over the bunkers, through the gap . . . He really snorked that one, Bruce!'), and pit it against my friends and *their* favourite images. While other teenagers heard the jangle of the Stone Roses in their heads while they swaggered, we heard the whisper of Peter Alliss in our heads while we swung. Tame or not, it had exactly the same effect: it momentarily lifted us out of our frustrating adolescent predicament and allowed us to see ourselves as something far more stylish than we really were.

These images made us better players and more desirable people, we imagined. Merely by humming the easy-listening theme tune to his Fred Couples instruction video ('Chck-Chck-Chck-Chckkk-Duh-Duh-Dah-Duuuhhh'), Ashley could inspire me to crunch fifty flawless five-irons in on the trot up the practice fairway. By assigning one another the names and characteristics of famous professionals on the first tee and saying things like 'Good one, Ray' in a ridiculous Kentucky accent, we knew we would reach a higher standard. If I pretended that the monthly medal was the British Masters, and that asthmatic old Ron Schofield, my twenty-one-handicap partner for the day, was actually Jodie Mudd – 'a three-time winner on the tour this year, Bruce' – it would stoke my competitive fire immeasurably. None of this embarrassed me in the slightest. Why should it? I was only rehearsing for adulthood, wasn't I? In a matter of a year or so, when I'd reduced my handicap to scratch, I'd gain my PGA tour card and I'd no longer need to pretend. All this would be normal: the person standing next to me on the tee really would be Fred Couples; an American man called Bob really would be yapping hysterically about the 'air brakes' on my sand-iron shot. I just wished it would all hurry up and happen – that hormones and furniture and windows and general rules and the temptations of Ching! would stop getting in the way. I wanted the professional golf world to come along, swallow me, and seal me off from the outside one. And if that seems weird, don't laugh – it wasn't. You would have felt exactly the same way if you had three hundred golf videos and no girlfriend.

In a household consisting of two schoolteachers, a schoolkid and a self-sufficient cat, July is traditionally a time of liberation and harmony. For years, my family's ritual would be very simple. A few days after breaking up from school, we'd all hop in the car, leaving Woosnam to survive on dilatory rodents and next door's prawn salads, and drive vaguely in the direction of Italy in our battered Morris Marina, assured in the knowledge that, wherever we wound up, it wouldn't be too far from a swimming pool and a man selling some crushed, sticky ice stuff in a tub. Six weeks later we'd come back, several shades darker, able to impress our friends by knowing the Italian word for 'arsehandle'.

This arrangement worked wonderfully well right up until the late eighties, when I unaccountably turned into the spawn of Satan.

Of *course* I couldn't stop playing golf and go to *Italy*!

Completely out of the question. France could swivel, too. And, no – I couldn't stick it out for 'just a fortnight'. I had tournaments to play. *Work* to do. Who knew what kind of havoc two weeks in a foreign climate might play with my muscle memory. Besides, August was the height of the season. Couldn't my parents see what kind of a head start I'd be giving my competitors? If I was going to win that first major championship before my teens were out, I couldn't go flouncing off to the Mediterranean whenever I felt like it.

'But think of it this way,' my ever patient mum would reason. 'Surely you're going to spend two weeks of this summer messing around with your mates in the pro shop. Why not just devote that time to practising instead, and come on holiday with us?'

'You just don't get it, do you? Being in the pro shop *is* all part of practising. I'm soaking up the atmosphere and learning when I'm in there.'

As a peace offering, out of the living-room cupboard would come the British bed and breakfast guide. And, in reply, as a war offering, out of my bedroom would come the guide to golf courses in Britain and Ireland.

'What about Aldeburgh in Suffolk?'

'Erm, I think you'll find the nearest decent courses there are Aldeburgh and Thorpeness, the longest of which has a total yardage of only six thousand three hundred and thirty yards. Now, I don't think that kind of length is going to *challenge* me, is it?'

'Now here's a nice-looking little farmhouse, on the Yorkshire Moors.'

'The moors? I've never heard of any golf courses on the moors. And that thick heather isn't going to do my wrists any good.'

'This looks nice, though. Hangstead Hill Golf Course – it's only about seven miles away.'

'He-*llo*! It's a municipal course. They probably only mow the greens once a month. Do you know what kind of damage that could do to my competitive putting stroke?'

Eventually, a reluctant bargain would be struck. In exchange for a minimum of three games of golf on a quality course, I would agree to spend a week in the company of my parents at an isolated farmhouse, being fed free-range eggs by a rotund, welcoming lady called Jackie who probably couldn't name the winning 1985 Ryder Cup squad.

While my mum and dad traversed the local peaks and valleys (walking without hitting shots – how idiotic can you get?), I would wait impatiently on the first tee of a nearby course called something like Hillycliffe or Wickledale until an amiable yet lonely member arrived on the first tee and enquired if I would care to join him for his day's play. Invariably this would be a man in his late fifties or early sixties, searching for the secret formula which would get him playing off a handicap of fourteen instead of eighteen. After three or four holes, he would start to quiz me on my formula for hitting the ball so straight and far – at which point I would mischievously advise him to do the exact opposite of what he should be doing. 'It's all about keeping your left arm completely rigid,' I advised Peter Fortnam, a twenty-one handicapper who moved with the ease of a man who had woken up to find his arms had been stolen in the night and replaced with steel girders. 'Golf is a game all about the legs,' I preached to a man I remember only as Mr Invisible Football.

When it came to local juniors, I showed slightly more respect. But after a visit to Rotherley Golf Club in north-west Yorkshire, where I was followed around by three fifteen-year-olds who gasped at my every shot as if I was some kind of fearsome proto-John Daly, it was hard not to assume an air of superiority. It's amazing how much mightier 250-yard drives can feel when punctuated by noises like 'Cor!', 'Bloody 'eck, yoth!' and 'Ohmyfuckinggodlookhowfarit'sgone!' My wife won't thank me for this, but I don't think I will ever again feel as loved as I did for those three hours when, Ian, Mental Ian and Smithy jostled to get the best view of my sophisticated technique. For a tiny, perfect pocket in time, I was as good as I thought I was.

Back at Cripsley, a new, more exciting type of golf holiday was being orchestrated. Like virtually everything that benefited the Cripsley junior section, the idea came from Bob Boffinger. For a fortnight of our summer holiday, Cripsley's juniors would play host to the juniors of Oporto, a golf club in northern Portugal: they would play in our competitions, sleep in our houses and pretend to eat our food. A year later, we would visit their home city, and do the same things, but with slightly less solicitude.

Meeting the Oporto plane at East Midlands Airport, each of Cripsley's six junior team members was allocated a Portuguese 'equivalent'. Robin got Pedro, who was serious-minded, swashbuckling and tall. Jamie got Carlo, who was icy and insolent. Mousey got Ricardo, who was defensive and underdeveloped. Ben got Jason, who was eccentric and goofy. Bushy got Mario, who was dark and enigmatic. And I got Alfonso, who wore ridiculously short trousers.

It was hard to work out whether Portuguese golf fashions were ten years ahead of British ones or ten years behind them. Looking now at a couple of photos from the period, I can see that Alfonso could quite easily pass for the singer in a late-nineties American art rock band. But at the time we were pretty much agreed that our Latin counterparts, with their bucket hats and drainpipe trousers, were sartorial cretins – a view which becomes all the more questionable when you consider the prevailing Cripsley penchant circa 1990 for bright green flecked slacks and pink polo shirts.

The summer of 1990, anywhere from thirteen to

twenty of us – Bob Boffinger, the Portuguese, the Cripsley junior team, and an assortment of other juniors not usually including Rick Sweeney – would ride around the Midlands in a minibus, learning Portuguese swear words and ransacking alien locker rooms. These were afternoons of parched fairways and stolen baseball caps, evenings of repeat screenings of the 1987 US Masters, and mornings of unusual eating habits.

The staple breakfast in my house over this period was cornflakes. Or, in Alfonso's case, three cornflakes. Each morning he would eye me mistrustfully as I filled my bowl with Dr Kellogg's finest then added the correct amount of milk to moisten the cereal without making it soggy. Thereafter he would shake his head, smile to himself and tuck into his own creation – to all intents and purposes a bowl of milk with cornflake croûtons.

Still, at least he liked my mum's sandwiches. Every morning without fail, the two of us would be packed off to the golf club with wholemeal doorsteps containing all manner of exotic delights from the Sainsbury's deli counter. And every lunchtime, without fail, Alfonso would order a huge lasagne from the clubhouse kitchen. 'Don't be silly. He's obviously just got a good appetite,' said my mum, when I aired my suspicions about this. 'I wish you'd eat as well as that sometimes.' A month later, when I looked out of the spare-room window onto the roof of the extension and my eye chanced upon a fortnight's worth of clingfilm, pastrami and bread, I didn't have the heart to tell her.

If that summer seems relatively uneventful now, it is perhaps because it will forever stand trial next to the return leg the following Easter. Bob Boffinger should have seen the portents at Heathrow – Ben very nearly getting arrested for pulling the stuffing out of a chair in the departure lounge, me getting searched at Customs then discovering that a bottle of shampoo had exploded in my rucksack, Bushy almost eloping with a stewardess – and admitted defeat. But if there was one thing Bob Boffinger wasn't good at, it was admitting defeat. We were his boys. We were going to do our club and country proud.

If ever there was a look that said, 'Yes, I have heartlessly disposed of your mum's homemade lunches, and I know you have now found out about it, but I hope we can still be friends,' then Alfonso, upon greeting me at the airport, exhibited it. He displayed his gratitude for my tactful circumlocution of the whole sandwich issue by treating me to a 'moving' rendition of 'Hey, Jude' on his Bontempi organ, an interpretation whose only true flaw was the substitution of 'you' for 'Jude'. I couldn't work out if this was because the song was directed at me, or because Alfonso didn't know the words, so decided it was best to grit my teeth and mime enjoyment. However, these festivities didn't provide any guarantee that Alfonso's family wasn't going to pay me back for poisoning their son. Until I stayed at Mr and Mrs Alfonso's place I hadn't realized that the real point of fondue was to kill the offending animal *in* the fondue set, while deftly keeping it as pink as possible. From here, things got progressively rawer, until I half expected the final supper of the holiday to be staged in the local zoo, with spears substituted in place of forks.

While it is the golf courses in the south of Portugal that attract the tourist trade, not their more barren northern equivalents, Oporto's local links was opulent enough, with lush, serpentine fairways and billiard-table greens. Oporto's corpulent businessmen members had the best of both worlds: on one side of the course was a private beach, providing unlimited sunbathing; on the other side was a shanty town, providing un-limited greenstaff. I've never seen so many dark faces surrounding a golf course, and might have found this refreshing had they been holding putters and not shovels.

Alfonso's dad, much like mine back home, provided a tireless taxi service to and from the club. I was grate-ful for the lifts, but slightly less grateful for the stops he performed en route. It was always the same. 'My father is going to stop here for five minutes. We will wait in the car,' Alfonso would explain, on the way back from another long day at the club. Four hours later, Mr Alfonso would emerge, with the sunny demeanour of a man who had no idea it was three fifteen in the morning, and we would proceed home, me feeling like the only person who thought there was anything unusual about this. The alternative was hitching a lift with Alfonso's friend Rico, who drove a Renault Five with one of its back passenger doors missing, thought red lights were for girls, and had only one tape in his car stereo, which consisted of Supertramp's 'Dreamer' recorded, as far as I could work out, twenty-four times.

'You like Supertramp in England, Tom?' Rico asked, hurtling over a level crossing, looking at me, in the back seat, rather than at the school bus looming in his windscreen.

It was all too much. Before I'd even got my bearings in Portugal, I found myself in a state of sleepless, half-starved, nervous delirium. This shouldn't serve as an excuse for my irrational, incautious behaviour over my fortnight there, of course. But I'm going to use it anyway.

It was her swing that drew me to her initially. Long. Rhythmical. Suggestive. From three fairways away, it whispered through the grass to me. I'd fallen for her long before I set eyes on her face, but the fact that her face was framed by a bob of fair, silky hair and had a look that was earthy and slightly naughty didn't exactly discourage me.

'Who's that?' I asked Alfonso.

'That's Shue. She is a – how you say in England? – "big girl". Ha, ha. You want to meet her? Ha, ha. I sort it out.'

Shue was Oporto's star girl player. Why no one else in the predominantly male Oporto junior section had already snapped up this nine-handicap beauty was one of the great mysteries of the western world to me, but I gladly took up the offer of an introduction, and acted quickly on Alfonso's suggestion that I should offer to caddy for her in a local girls' tournament the following day. Shue's English was patchy, so the two of us communicated almost exclusively through the language of club selection. She was exactly what I was looking for – which, during this point in my life, meant she had a solid swing, blonde hair and bigger-than-average breasts. Although she never told me in words we were an item, she seemed fairly happy in my company, flashed me plenty of shy smiles and was clearly impressed with my all-round technical knowledge and course management.

Now I simply had to get a job, learn the language, and find a flat to rent in the locality. But – no hurry – there was a good week and a half yet to sort all that out. For the moment, I was happy to watch her hit shots on the Oporto practice ground.

Five days of the Portuguese holiday were to be taken up with a trip to Lisbon. Under normal circumstances, this would have meant the opportunity to test out my swing on some of the most intricate and pampered courses in Europe. With the chance to make my virginity a thing of the past, however, golf was rapidly losing its significance. Besides, these courses had buggies for hire, and – let's face it – that was infinitely more exciting than any number of carpet-like fairways, elevated tees and triple-tier greens.

At Lisbon's handsome Aurora golf course, Robin and I worked out a fuss-free way of deciding who would drive our buggy. Every three holes, the two of us would race from the previous green to the vehicle, while simultaneously punching one another in the leg; the one who reached the steering wheel first got to drive. We came out about even over the full round. While Robin, ever the one-trick pony, perfected the art of driving *extremely fast* at pine trees then swerving out of the way *right at the last minute,* I opted for the less conservative approach, slinging our vehicle at full speed towards anything and anyone in our path, then attempting to figure out how to use the brakes. Not content with running over the feet of Bob Boffinger's wife Marjorie, I then proceeded to make Aurora the only course equipped with seventeen and a half ball-cleaning units. Ball-cleaning units, for those who don't know, are circular metal contraptions, mounted on plastic sticks, containing a brush and soapy water: labour-saving devices installed on the tees of your better class of golf course for individuals who find the act of spit 'n' polish uncouth. The ones at Aurora were particularly futuristic in design and particularly solidly made, but evidently not quite solidly enough to stand up to a fifteen-mile-per-hour wallop from a golf buggy. What's most memorable about the incident is not the satisfying 'Snap!' of the collision so much as my decision to bail out four yards before impact, leaving my passenger alone and frozen in terror.

From that day to this, Robin has never travelled in a car driven by me. This, I sense, is no coincidence.

During the evenings in Lisbon, we were served barely dead animals and cheap red wine at a mysterious hut a couple of hundred yards from our hotel. This was better than having to pay to wait an hour for a bowl of chips in the hotel – the lone meal we'd ordered there we'd had to march into the kitchen and rescue from the hot plate ourselves – but far from ideal. The meat (horse? baboon?) we pushed doubtfully around our plates. The wine we necked theatrically. Then we headed back to monopolize the second floor of the hotel and find out more about one another than we probably wanted to.

Robin, who, while sober, was about as near as any of us came to responsible, lost all pretence of fatherliness under the influence of alcohol, and thought nothing of singing along to Madonna's 'Borderline' at the top of his voice at 2 a.m. The rest of us, in turn, thought nothing of joining in at the top of our voices, despite the facts that a) most of us didn't know the words, and b) the song was being broadcast through the miniature headphones of Robin's personal stereo. After two Bacardi and Cokes Jamie, who could be cold and backbiting, became everyone's easiest-going confidant. Ben, entrepreneurial and off-the-wall normally, stayed more or less the same but only talked about Pringle's latest range of sweaters three times per hour, instead of the customary seven. Mousey became even more desperate to prove himself than usual, but typically passed out before he had done so. I'm not sure about myself, but going on my current drunken persona, I'm pretty sure I shouted a lot more than usual, told complete strangers I loved them and viewed the act of hiding a pint glass in someone's bag as worthy of a Bafta for comic innovation.

No one went through a more dramatic character overhaul, though, than Bushy, who, possibly dissatisfied with his role as the 'quiet one' in our group, took to leading the charge of the rabid ape warrior through the corridors of the hotel. The beauty of Bushy's drunken marauding was that it didn't matter whether the remainder of us were part of it or not; he was off in his own magical land of self-discovery. If I never sit alone on a Yorkshire moor under a full moon, that first night in Lisbon is probably the closest I'll ever come to seeing a man get perceptibly hairier in a matter of minutes. For every glass of rancid red wine Bushy downed, his stubble seemed to grow an additional centimetre until, finally, he became Jack Nicholson in *The Shining*.

Several times on one particular night I rode up and down in the hotel's lift with Bushy. Bushy's favourite thing about the lift was that it had a huge mirror stretching the length of its rear wall. 'Oh, it's you again!' he would growl at his own reflection, mesmerized. This was funny the first time but even in my inebriated adolescent state had started to wear thin by the time the two of us embarked on our eighth journey up to the fifth floor, so I left Bushy and his alter ego to it. He was last sighted at around midnight, by Ben, who remembered seeing him running off into the bushes, making tormented but strangely overjoyed howling noises.

Ordinarily Bushy returned to the room he was sharing with Mousey at around 4 a.m. and promptly puked in the bidet. No one, least of all Bushy, can account for his whereabouts in the preceding four hours, the only clue being the faint smell of pig lingering on his Lyle and Scott sweatshirt.

It wasn't until the final night in Lisbon that I located the room that Shue, along with two of the other Oporto girls, was sleeping in. While a normal person might have opted for a more direct manoeuvre – say, asking the question, 'Shue, what number room are you staying in?' – I decided that the best way to locate her room was to crawl, accompanied by Mousey, along the hotel's air vents until I saw something resembling a female leg through the wire grid. It strikes me now that, having gone to this convoluted effort, it might have been a good idea to stick around and make the most of the view, but in the event it only took the faintest glimpse of a bra hanging on a chair to send the two of us scurrying back to our friends, anxious to reveal our discovery.

The two hours that followed this are a blur of hormones, crap wine and cowardice, but I can say for certain that at around midnight I found myself alone, rounding a corner in the hotel corridor, and discovering a disconsolate Shue, arms folded, leaning on the wall opposite the door to her room. Why I happened to be rounding this particular corner – this corner, which led only to Shue's room and concluded in an emphatic dead end – is unclear to me now, but suggests a) that I might have been in the area for some time, and b) a general lack of coincidence.

'Shue, what's the matter?' I said to Shue.

'Oh, Tom, it is terrible. I have lost my key and my friends, they are sleeping. I do not want to wake them up and I do not know what to do.'

This was too good to be true. 'That *is* terrible,' I said to commiserate.

'I will have to sleep out here in the corridor.'

Yes! And I will too! 'Don't be silly. We will find a way to get back in.'

'Oh, but how?'

'Well, I don't know. I suppose, er . . . Well, you could always come back to my room.' What was I thinking of? My room had two single beds, and Robin was in one of them. We weren't going to get up to anything in there, and, anyway, Shue didn't look like a Madonna kind of girl.

'I don't think I should.'

So, instead, we stayed where we were. We sat in that corridor together in perfect harmony (sexual frustration) for what felt like hours (ten minutes). Side-by-side, hand-in-hand, then – eventually, inevitably – mouth-in-mouth. We kissed as only teenagers can, or – more accurately – as only two people can who believe there is a hidden sexual organ located to the rear of the tonsils.

What can I say? It was intense, it was sloppy, it was . . . quick.

Then, very quietly, Shue knocked on the door of her room, and I skipped back to my room in a daze, already garnishing the encounter in preparation for my friends.

I didn't kiss Shue again. Not properly. She said she found it hard to express her true feelings in English but that she 'needed time'. Unfortunately, time was what I had least of: I had to catch a plane back to Heathrow in three days. Comprehending that the situation was a lost cause, I made the noble decision to spend each of these three days mooning around and kicking my heels in the rough vicinity of her apartment, while my friends raced buggies and hid the golf shoes of ingenuous Portuguese stockbrokers.

To his credit, Alfonso did his best to lift me out of my fug, taking me out on the town and introducing me to a succession of local teenage lovelies, all of whom had one fundamental shortcoming: they weren't Shue. I do question his motives, however, on introducing me to Michaela, a six-foot-one, fourteen-stone neighbour of his who'd clearly won at least three heavyweight titles, then unsubtly nipping around the corner to 'buy some chocolate' – for forty-five minutes. Michaela couldn't have looked more pleased with her day's catch if she'd been sitting in front of a human-size spider's web, rubbing her hands together.

There's a photograph of me with Shue, taken on the final night in Portugal, just before our farewell dinner at the club. Decked out in my dark blue blazer with its Cripsley Edge badge, I look like I'm blushing for the camera, flushed with young love, as my friends grin politely in the background. The truth, though, is that my face is red because twenty minutes earlier, I had been in the Oporto club's tiny sauna with all my clothes on. I did this because Robin and Ben shouted, 'Last one in the sauna is gay!' and, in an at the time highly important attempt to cast aspersions on the nocturnal activities of Mousey, Jamie and Bushy, I valued hetero-sexuality over comfort.

What the picture also fails to reveal is that eleven minutes earlier Shue thwarted me in my attempt to put my hand on her thigh, seven minutes earlier I punched Carlo, the most insolent of the Portuguese juniors, in the chin for making kissy noises at me, and three minutes earlier Shue handed me a letter, which she made me promise not to read until I was back in England.

You could say it looks like a normal kind of golfing picture, hinting at a normal kind of golfing romance, at the end of a normal kind of golfing holiday.

But then you could also be the kind of idiot who says the camera never lies.

I read the letter on the plane home, in the toilet – chiefly because I didn't want Robin and Ben reading over my shoulder and finding out that I had been lying about putting my hand down Shue's shirt. The standard letter from dumper to dumpee is usually cushioned by ambiguity, with lots of statements like, 'I'm not looking for a boyfriend at the moment,' which actually mean, 'I'm looking for boyfriend, just not one like you.' But clearly not in Portugal. In unnerving sentences worthy of a grade-A English student, Shue informed me in no uncertain terms that she had a boyfriend already but had smooched with me because she thought I 'might

be a better kisser than him'. She went on to admit she
had been proved wrong in her assumption, and that
the feelings from the night in Lisbon had not been
strong enough, and, besides, she had decided she
fancied Jamie more. She signed off by saying that
she didn't mind if I wrote to her to 'ease my pain', but
only on the condition that I told Jamie to write too.

I had snogged an ice queen.

Assuming an expression of zero emotion, I returned
to my seat, where Mousey and Jamie were dividing the
tee pegs they had stolen from Portugal's locker rooms
over the course of the fortnight. I regarded Jamie for a
moment: he was two years younger than me, with the
looks of a young John Lennon and a handicap of seven.
If pushed, I'd have to admit I thought his swing was a
bit on the loose side to hold up under pressure. I could
understand, though: Shue was a capricious girl, uncertain of what she wanted out of life, but sure it was
something she couldn't have. If she'd snogged Jamie, I
was sure she would have written him a letter confessing
that she couldn't go out with him because she had a
crush on me. At least, I thought I was sure.

As I sat there dodging the tee pegs flying over my
seat, I took a moment to weigh up the evidence, which,
in no particular order, went something like this: 1) I
felt heartbroken. 2) I was fifteen. 3) I had been led on
and messed around. 4) I had a picture of a golfing
goddess in my wallet who was too far away to tell my

friends that my anecdotes about her weren't true. 5) She had preferred Jamie. 6) I could beat him in the county championship next Tuesday. 7) I felt sad. 8) In five minutes, I was going to be giving Mousey a dead leg.

It seemed I was going to live through this, after all.

'We nearly lost him for ever,' Bob Boffinger told my dad, who was waiting at the airport to drive us home in the minibus, as we came off the plane. 'But I think his mind's back on the job now.'

I never did get round to telling Jamie about Shue's letter. I was naive, but I wasn't stupid, and I certainly didn't want to give Jamie any help finding people to make him feel good about himself. He and I had started playing golf at Cripsley on the same day, and over the years, as Cripsley's two best junior players, we'd developed a seething, cloak-and-dagger rivalry. That is to say, Jamie's rivalry towards me always seemed seething and cloak-and-dagger; I was always completely up front about my intentions to thrash the pants off him.

When I played against Jamie, I didn't just play against Jamie: I played against his mum, his dad, two thirds of the Cripsley membership, the Nottinghamshire Union of Golf Clubs, his brand-new titanium-shafted driver, and the ever-fluctuating age difference between us. Jamie was born in August 1977, two years and three months after me, but not if you were a regular reader of the local paper's sports page. At one point during 1991 the paper seemed to carry headlines in the manner of 'Embryo Reaches out of Womb to Win Golf Tournament!' almost weekly. Jamie's fellow Cripsley juniors couldn't decide which to be more baffled by: the way the paper seemed determined to chronicle the most minor of his golfing achievements, or the way he got progressively less pubescent in every article.

Jamie's parents made a gallant attempt to pretend their son's sporting future didn't represent their pension plan, but it didn't take a sports psychologist to see through them. You'd spot them greeting him on the eighteenth green in the wake of the rare competitive rounds he fouled up, their mouths offering bland sympathy, their eyes offering piercing disbelief. 'What was that? That was shit!' I once heard Jamie's dad say to his son in a quiet, leafy corner of the course during a county boys event. Jamie's dad didn't play golf, and to any other non-aficionado the tee shot his son had hit – far from a pure strike, certainly, but long and straight and high enough to be well clear of trouble – would have looked nothing less than spectacular. To him, though, it was the closest thing to a family bereavement.

I always managed to keep a nose ahead of Jamie in handicap terms. A week after he came down from six to five, I would come down from five to four, and so on. In the eyes of the rest of the world, though, it seemed that I was permanently holding his coat-tails, particularly since, at any given time, I was between two and five years older than him. 'Boy Wonder' other members of the Cripsley junior section called him, somewhat scornfully, but not scornfully enough to stop them desperately wanting to be his friend and get a go with his top-of-the-range, graphite-shafted four-wood. Whether Jamie was eleven, thirteen or three, he had the preternatural power to make individuals several years older than him turn into sycophantic wrecks with a flash of his copper beryllium sand wedge.

My relationship with Jamie is perhaps best encapsulated by our coaching session with Gavin Christie and Pete Boffinger in the winter of 1991. Pete, Bob's eldest son and Cripsley's finest player at the time, had decided to do a good turn by taking his two most promising understudies to the local driving range to meet his teacher, who, we all hoped, would offer us a jumpstart on the road to stardom. Christie, who allegedly once turned down the chance to work for a beseeching Seve Ballesteros, worked regularly on the practice grounds of the European Tour, offering swing tips to a quarter of the European Ryder Cup team. Ian Woosnam, Howard Clark and Mark 'Jesse' James had all worked with him and, uncoincidentally, possessed the most arid senses of humour on tour. To describe Christie's manner as 'blunt' would be like describing Mount Everest as a 'hillock'. Picture a less optimistic version of Frazer from *Dad's Army* ('We're doomed!'). The thing that amazes me most about my meeting with Christie is not that I was brave enough to carry on playing golf but that I have recovered from the psychological scars of the confrontation and gone on to become something roughly approaching a self-confident human being.

Here follows a transcription of our encounter. The dialogue begins with me standing in the driving range bay, hitting shots with my five-iron, feeling somewhat self-conscious and wondering why the stubble-flecked vagrant in the trenchcoat behind me is watching so intently.

Stubbly trenchcoat man: What's this?

Me: What?

Stubbly trenchcoat man (swinging arms in the manner of *Thunderbirds* cast member): This.

Me: It's you, doing an impression of my swing.

Pete Boffinger: Sorry. Hello, Gavin. I didn't see you there. Tom, this is Gavin. Gavin, meet Tom.

Me: Hello, Gavin. Nice to meet you.

Gavin (removing trenchcoat): The problem is that you've got no flex. There's no flail in your swing. It's craaap. You look like you're rowing, not playing golf.

Me: Oh. Really? I'm not very good at rowing.

Gavin: I don't expect you would be, if you row with the swing you should be using for golf.

Jamie: Ha!

Gavin (picking up my five-iron and hitting a powerful, straight shot with wristy, springy motion): You got to do this, you see.

Me (retrieving five-iron and imitating him): Wow.

Gavin: That's where all the strength comes from. The flail of the wrists. Effortless power, not powerless effort. If you don't do that, you'll always be craaap.

Me (feeling simultaneous need to cry and shout for joy): I see what you mean. I think I felt something once on the practice ground.

Gavin: Yeah, but thaaat was your girlfriend.

Pete: Ha.

Me: This is amazing. I'm hitting the ball twenty yards further. The strike's more solid, too.

Gavin: Of course it is. (Moving on to Jamie's bay.) He's got it. Tom, look at your mate. He flails it. Waaatch him. (To Jamie.) Now, move your thumb a centimetre to the left.

Jamie (moving thumb and hitting an even straighter, better shot than the ones he'd hit immediately before): Nice!

Gavin: Of course it is. What do you think they pay me for? Now, Pete, I'd love to stand around chaaaatting all night, but, well . . . I wouldn't. And, besides, a coach has got to eat.

Pete (opening wallet): Thanks for this, Gavin.

Gavin: No problem. Remember, boys: flail. Jamie, you've got it, naturally. Tom, you can learn it, if you work aaat it.

See what I was up against? Here was the eternal battle of the gifted golden child and the plucky outsider. T-Rex *v.* Slade. Manchester United *v.* Wimbledon. What I identified in myself as the swaggering radicalism of the insouciant misfit, everyone who mattered seemed to see as the plodding perseverance of the determined underdog. I couldn't win. If I practised, I was showing the world just how hard I had to work to reach my friend's hereditary standard. If I didn't practise, I was admitting defeat.

It seems to me now without a sixteen-year-old brain to obscure my judgement that Jamie and I could have pushed ourselves to the top had we conducted our rivalry in a different manner and fully appreciated the value of it. Instead, we squandered what was meant to have been nurtured. Rather than seeing who could work on their game most, the race was on to see who could appear to work on it *least*, who could get to the tee latest, who could pretend to be entering the least amount of tournaments, who could demonstrate to the other just how many more things in life were more important than golf. It's impossible to overemphasize the futility of this little mental game, when you take into account the fact that we were playing it from the standpoint of two people who spent their every waking hour at their local golf course. *Of course* we both wanted to be the best! *Of course* we loved golf!

What were we scared of? Why were we ashamed of being so damn dedicated? For a pair of kids who were rarely apart for five years and would play between ten and thirty-six holes per day in their summer holidays, head-to-head practice rounds between Jamie and I were rare. When I look back and see myself at fifteen, striding down the fairway, laughing, on another irresponsible sunny day, I don't see myself with Jamie: I see myself with Robin or Mousey or Bushy or Ashley or Ben. Jamie's there too, but a couple of bunkers' distance away, never truly with me. Yet on the few occasions when the two of us *did* go out alone, with serious golf on our mind, there was nothing more invigorating, and it represented the one time when we truly seemed to admit to ourselves that this was where we belonged.

In only one environment, though, were we truly united.

Our inductions into the county junior team arrived – like so many new frontiers for the two of us – within a few weeks of one another. Jamie probably felt the same way about the rest of the county boys as I felt about him, and somehow this brought us closer. If Jamie had this year's state-of-the-art equipment, our county teammates had next year's. (I, meanwhile, was quite content with a mish-mash of 1967's, 1981's and 1987's.) If he was worshipped by the powers of the Nottinghamshire Golf Union, they were worshipped harder. No longer was he the youngest, the most spoiled, the most natural, the best dressed, the most born for the role . . .

Nottinghamshire golf at this point could be summarized in a single word: Worksop. 'Golf does take us to some beautiful places,' the legendary British professional Henry Cotton once observed, but clearly he had never driven along the A57, bypassing Manton, in the direction of Belph. If he had, what he would have said was, 'Golf does take us to some beautiful places, in the middle of some *absolutely fucking abysmal* places.' Four types of people end up in Worksop: those who are born there, those who get lost there, those who go to clandestine right-wing rallies there, and those who are extremely good at golf. Worksop Golf Club itself – like all the very best courses in Nottinghamshire, strangely enough – was a sporting fantasyland within pitching distance of an urban nightmare. A stunning mixture of woodland, heather, gorse, sculptured fairways, enormous wire fences, adjoining dual carriageways and tower-block vistas.

Worksop's juniors were the only golfers who appeared in their local paper more frequently than Jamie did in his. If they weren't on the back page, grinning toothily with the county championship trophy, they'd be somewhere closer to the front, heroically displaying the abandoned infant they'd discovered in the bushes at the back of the green belonging to their course's sixth hole. Worksop was that kind of course.

You might have heard of one of Worksop's junior team from this period. He's called Lee Westwood, and, for the last half decade, along with Darren Clarke and Colin Montgomerie, he's shouldered Britain's brightest golfing hopes. Then, as now, the arrival of Westwood on the first tee was a proper event, replete with everything bar a bugle. I did manage to score lower than him in the odd tournament when he was really off form – admittedly one of these was the Kedleston Goose, where I only played seven holes due to sunstroke – and my name is engraved after his on the list of winners of the Lindrick Junior Open trophy, but as a mortal I knew better than to try to make friends with him. Besides, in order to do that I would have had to break through the bottle-green forcefield of kow-towing county officials which permanently surrounded him. We spoke only once, although I use the word 'we' in the vaguest sense. Lee spoke. I did something which was a bit like speaking, but with more saliva.

The setting was Shifnal Golf Club, in Shropshire. The event: I can't remember for certain, but it's likely it was the Shifnal Junior Open. Westwood: lacing up his Footjoy shoes in preparation for his afternoon teeing-off time. Me: returning, rosy-cheeked, from a gratifying round in the low seventies, somewhat startled to find myself alone in the same room with the Midlands' nearest thing to Tiger Woods.

'Good round today, Coxy,' said Lee.

The comment threw me off balance on four counts. Firstly, he had made it without looking up from his golf shoes. Secondly, in the twelve minutes it had taken me to hole my final putt, sign my card, put my clubs in Bob Boffinger's car and neck a can of Happy Shopper drink, Lee had managed to gain the knowledge that I had shot a 'good round'. (This was unbelievable! Did he see me as a *competitor*?) Thirdly, he was aware of my existence. And finally, he was aware of my existence enough to *make up his own nickname* for me. I was impressed! So impressed, in fact, that I said this:

'Thuaaankhghgsds, Lee.'

I've been fortunate enough, over the years, to meet several of my heroes, and brave enough to insult some of them. I've telephoned the New York rock-and-roll icon Dion and told him that he isn't 'always the best judge' of his own work. I've implied to The Who's Pete Townshend, six minutes after meeting him, that the follow-up to *Tommy*, *Lifehouse*, might be a load of pretentious old codswallop. I've hinted to the original punk rocker, Jonathan Richman, that he should spend less time talking about cement. But to a boy two years older than me who happened to be quite good at hitting a ball around a field with some holes in it, all I could say was 'Thuaaankhghgsds'.

Which should give you an idea of how big a deal Lee Westwood was in Nottinghamshire junior golf in the early nineties.

Westwood was by no means the only one. Around 1991, it seemed blindingly obvious to everyone on the Midlands golf scene that the Worksop team of today was the European Ryder Cup side of tomorrow. They probably could have sent out their under-thirteens team and still beaten, say, Lincolnshire. It didn't matter how well the rest of us were playing: as county team members from rival clubs, we always felt a little like charity cases, third-reserve goalkeepers called up for a friendly match but only because the top man 'couldn't be bothered' and his immediate understudy had a partially fractured thorax.

Many were the hours when Robin and I and even Jamie puzzled over what exactly gave the Worksop boys their edge. It wasn't as if their techniques were flawless. Danny Parfitt, one of the youngest and most universally bum-sucked of their ranks, looked to have the wrist strength of George from *Rainbow*, and Westwood himself had an unusual swing where, mid-impact, he appeared to nod at the ball as if he was encouraging it to go closer to the hole.

With hindsight, though, it's quite obvious where we were going wrong. While we were trying to banish our less impressive rounds from memory by retiring to a nearby copse to throw pine cones at one another's heads, the Worksop contingent were compensating for theirs by trudging back to the practice ground to iron out the kinks in their backswings. While we saw the act of being in the vicinity of the golf course morning, noon and night as dedication enough in itself, they weren't satisfied until they'd hit enough shots to put blisters on top of their calluses. North Nottingham-shire boys in general were taller, wider, grittier and less imaginative than their southern rivals. I might have spent my early childhood in a mining village not far south of Worksop with people who substituted the word 'sery' for 'man' in their everyday dialogue, but I played my golf further south, and in the eyes of Westwood and company that made me virtually a Londoner. Subtle signs – the outmoded nature of my equipment, my complete lack of friends called Justin, the absence of the phrase 'got my putting boots on today, yoof' in my repertoire of humorous quips – gave me away.

But what really set me apart was my parents.

Don't get me wrong here. My mum and dad couldn't have been happier that I spent my wild years hitting golf balls towards flagsticks rather than throwing dogs off pedestrian footbridges like most of the other boys from my school did. But the curious archaic rituals of the game, the sheer grasp it held over my life, bamboozled them.

They gave it their best shot, it has to be said – even if, as far as my mum was concerned, it was at a distance. She never spent too much time watching me in competitive play after the occasion, in the aftermath of an early Cripsley junior event, when she recklessly stepped over the painted white line dividing the unisex area of the clubhouse from the men-only bar and received a 'talking to' from the club's snotbag steward. Thereafter her support was offered telepathically, usually from the safe haven of a nearby garden centre. My dad, on the other hand, stayed right by my side, no matter how many Immediate Past Captains commented on the inappropriateness of his corduroy trousers or bristled at his enquiry regarding whether the furry headcover on their putter was 'real otter'. It was either that or the garden centre, after all.

I'd witnessed the kid-bashing that went on on the fairways of the Midlands. I'd seen Darren Cheeseman's dad stalk after him down the fourteenth at Retford, repeatedly chastising him for his morally objectionable choice of club off the tee, and I'd heard about the sunvisor-flinging scene in the car park that erupted afterwards. I knew all about what John Chittock's mum thought of her son's putting stroke. ('Bloody pathetic! You'd of thought we hadn't trained him!') That headdown, cocooned look of the north Notts boys arriving on the tee wasn't concentration; it was *fear*. I didn't want any of that.

That said, a bit of gentle encouragement every month or two wouldn't have gone amiss.

'Did you see that?' I would ask, turning to my dad and frothing as my five-wood shot sailed over a giant oak tree, two bunkers, a lake and several potentially murderous amphibians to within four feet of the hole.

'Yes!' he would reply, looking through his binoculars, in completely the opposite direction. 'Jackdaw, wasn't it? Terrific.'

'I meant the five-wood.'

'Oh. Fine. Can't say I was watching. Go get 'em, kid. Great birdlife around here!'

It was only on the bad rounds, however, that I found this *really* hard to deal with.

'Fuckin' 'ell. That's three long-iron shots I've sliced today. What the shag's wrong with me?'

'Oh well. Just think: your mum's cooking pepper sausage pasta tonight, with that nice basil sauce she does.'

It seemed, at times, as if he was having a conversation with his other, more mellow son, who just happened to be standing behind me, and invisible.

I'm sure the other golf parents felt even more bewildered in his presence.

'Mr and Mrs Case, who pick the county team, say our Wayne might get called up for the England squad this year.'

'Oh, really? Some lovely wildlife in this part of the world, don't you think?'

'He's really done well this season, and that coaching he's got from Steve Loach has worked a treat. He's shortened his backswing. Can you see? And that low hand position? It's really helped. But I just wish he'd stop trying to hit those long shots out of the rough grass and take his medicine. I've told him a hundred times, wood in the rough, wood in your head.'

'Mmm? Well, never mind. We're having pepper sausage pasta for dinner tonight. *Look at the size of that buddleia!*'

My performances in county events were a constant disappointment to me. Away from Cripsley, where I could often idly knock the ball round in two under par in practice, the game seemed more complex, and I found myself unable to relax.

'Concentrate,' advised my mum, which worked for a while, but essentially left me concentrating on concentrating, as opposed to on getting the ball in the hole in as few strokes as possible. I couldn't have tried much harder. My preparations – whole hours devoted purely to playing holes in my head – bordered on the catatonic. Yet my away results – the away results that *counted*, anyway – never reflected the golfer my pragmatic self knew I was, let alone the one my hot-headed adolescent self hoped I was.

On 21 August 1991, I found myself standing on the first tee at Church Brampton Golf Club in

Northamptonshire, playing for the biggest prize of my career: my legs, and possibly several other vital body parts.

That morning, just before I set off for Northampton, an envelope had arrived, containing my GCSE results. 'Do you mind if I open it this evening?' I'd asked my parents, nonchalantly. 'I don't want the results to put me off my game.' I said this, but what I'd meant was: 'I am going to open this envelope, but first, in order to demonstrate the insignificance of my exam results, I'm going to win this golf tournament and prove to you just how great I am at golf, so you don't shout at me quite as loud.' I knew I'd messed my exams up. My revision had amounted to a half-arsed half an hour per subject between putting practice on my bedroom rug, and I'd made it perfectly clear to my teachers that, nice though their subjects were, they weren't going to help me loft a blind nine-iron over trees to a postage-stamp green in the Sun City Million Dollar Challenge. During my multiple-choice Biology exam, I picked answers at random in order to leave more time for designing dog-leg par fives in the margin.

Golf was going to save me. I could sense it.

At Church Brampton, however, I came a mediocre twentieth, then sat very quietly in the back seat of Bob Boffinger's car on the journey home to my doom. 'Don't worry,' said Bob. 'I'm sure you can make it up to your parents.' I was sure I could make it up to them, too. I could shoot sixty-eight in tomorrow's event, the Kibworth Open, for starters.

I was putting *miles* too much pressure on myself. If I went around the course in eighty, I didn't think in terms of how I could ameliorate with a seventy-three; I thought about how I could ameliorate with a *sixty-*three. Every time I teed the ball up, I betrayed myself by shouldering the expectations of a miracle-worker, yet somehow simultaneously not realizing how good I really was.

I now know I could have done better. With more realistic standards, I might have been playing off one handicap instead of three; I might have won the county boys championship; I might have been the one who got younger every year. But then again I might not have. I won't kid myself that my starry-eyed standards were the only excuse for my inability to perform. In all honesty, I don't think I *wanted* to win enough. For all my dreaming and planning, the idea of stepping up to the prize table in my jacket and tie, in front of all those golf parents, never really appealed to me all that much. On the rare occasions when I was in contention with a few holes to play, I would instantly begin talking myself out of a potential victory. Think about all those expectant, gormless faces, the coward part of my brain would whisper to me. Do you really care about impressing them? And what about the speech? Can you cope with the sheer monotony? Just how much do you *want* to be bum-scratched by hundreds of people who aren't really your friends?

I don't remember ever blowing a good round deliberately, but it was slightly alarming how often I would wake up from the spell of my Coward Demon to find myself on all fours re-enacting a scene from *The Texas Chainsaw Massacre* using my ball, my three-iron and a nearby holly bush as props, when just a couple of holes previously I'd been challenging for the tournament lead.

Junior amateur golf speeches are all the same. And by that, I do mean *exactly* the same. If your most boring, cardigan-wearing uncle had been feeling particularly shiftless and uninspired one dreary bank holiday afternoon and decided to pen a few verses in tribute to his local Inland Revenue office, he couldn't have come up with something more flat and insipid than the anticlimactic declamations I witnessed in the clubhouses of north Nottinghamshire. It wasn't long before it got to the point where me and Robin, standing at the back of the room fidgeting, could mime along.

'I'd like to thank t' greenstaff, for t' condition of t' course,' that particular week's austere north Notts winner would begin, with all the effervescence of a boy who'd spent the last four hours coaxing otters into a cage with a large stick. 'And t' catering staff, for t' food. And . . .'

Come on! You can do it!

'And . . .'

Now, now – no peeking at that copy of *The Marshall Brickman Guide to After-dinner Anecdotes*.

'. . . And t' organizers, for putting on t' event.'

At which point, to a chorus of 'Well done', the winner would shuffle back to his seat to give his powers of mental agility a well-earned rest, and the whole event, the thing we'd spent so many hours preparing for and bitching about and living for, would just kind of . . . die.

Was that *it?* I used to wonder, no matter how many times I saw it happen.

Bushy was the only one I ever saw handle matters differently. As the surprise winner of the Waldman Carr Trophy at Bulwell Forest Golf Club, he subverted the rules entirely. Bushy didn't care about the green-staff, the clubhouse's steak and kidney pie wasn't a patch on his mum's paella, and he probably didn't know who the shag the two hundred inane faces grinning at him were, much less want to know. What Bushy said was short and to the point, and did that rarest of things: it reflected his true feelings at the time. It also ensured that his name was a talking point on the Notts golf scene long after the hormonal whims of the pupils of Nottingham Girls High School had trans-formed him into a part-time player.

All Bushy said was: 'Bad luck, lads.'

Bushy never *was* selected for the county team, funnily enough.

Unlike Bushy, though, *I* never won a county event – not a *proper* county event, under the gaze of Big Brother. I never got to stand there, look out onto that monotone sea of propriety and say, 'Look! My clubs aren't as good as your clubs, my clothes don't have labels on them, I drink Happy Shopper ginger beer on the course, and my parents don't even play or like the game, but I've still beaten the lot of you!' Or something which said the same thing in a more witty, concise manner and concluded with the phrase, 'So, neh-neh-neh-neh-neh!' I'm still slightly bitter about that, but I'm learning to deal with it. At least now I can hold up my hands and say, 'Look, I wanted golf to be fun off the course, as well as on, and it wasn't, so I couldn't quite give it my all, and – you know what? – that's OK.' At least now I can say, 'Perhaps I simply wasn't *made* to be a proper county golfer. Perhaps I was made to be a good golfer, but one who likes to throw pine cones and hide large pieces of wood in his fellow players' lockers. And – you know what? – that's OK too.'

Back then, though, I had a long way to go before I could be so philosophical. Somewhere inside, an illogical mid-adolescent war was raging between the hormones that wanted desperately to be part of something and the ones that wanted to tear that something down. I loved golf. I hated it. I was supposed to be winning the British Open in just under a year. It all mattered so, so much.

11

If I wanted to be a better player, I concluded, I needed a better golf course to practise on.

I first saw Par-adise as a spectator, but the sensation that we belonged together was as immediate and overpowering as it might have been if I'd won my first PGA Tour event there. Ever fallen in love at first sight? Remember the feeling? The twittering innards. The blancmange legs. The freakish, intuitive perception of a complete stranger's soul. Now, take that same enchanting stranger, and imagine their body stripped naked and magnified to a size of five square miles . . . picture every hump and hollow exaggerated, enabling you to examine them in a manner you never believed possible. Imagine them with not only bumpy bits and crevices but *pine trees*. Imagine a four-hour hike across their surface, with the result that, no matter how hard you tried to get to know them, there would always be more to explore.

Sneering bunkers, marble-slick greens, 'Come and have a go if you think you're hard enough!' rough, pine-patrolled fairways which seemed always to be lurking in mist, and a regal, ghostly clubhouse conspired to make Par-adise the greatest golf course I had ever seen. What made it something more than that, something *carnal*, was the way it revealed itself: slowly, teasingly at first, then – without warning – ostentatiously and imperially. One second you'd be tootling through some bog-standard Robin Hood country, counting off lumberyards, one eye on the road, one eye on your *Good Golf Course Guide*. A moment later, you'd take a right turn down a dusty track, pass through a corridor of woodland, and – blam – there it was, letting you look right down its top.

Par-adise was set in a deep bowl, hemmed in on all sides by monolithic Forestry Commission land, and gave the impression of being an entire, separate country, never mind merely a golf course. Par-adise didn't have houses backing on to it – not even big, stately ones – for fear, presumably, that a quirk in the tastes of their residents might taint its majesty. Where most clubhouses had strict dress codes, precluding the wearing of things like jeans, trainers and Sigue Sigue Sputnik T-shirts, Par-adise's probably had a different underwear by-law for every one of its umpteen chambers. Par-adise knew it was gorgeous and enigmatic, and asked you what precisely you were planning to do about it. Par-adise – let's face it – wasn't *really* called Par-adise, because that would be crap and tacky. Its actual name was something proud and evocative. If Par-adise knew that I was calling it Par-adise, right now, it would be utterly affronted.

Good.

Par-adise broke my heart.

I should have known it was too good to be true.

Par-adise, it seemed to me, didn't have junior members. While it might have mutated into a leering, gnashing host during big tournaments, for the majority of the year it sat there two-thirds deserted, admiring itself and licking whatever it had where mortal golf courses had wounds. It didn't seem to manufacture star players in the way that most of the north Nottinghamshire courses did, and, on the odd occasions when it did, these too were solitary, enigmatic (and, I assumed, unusually rich) creatures. So when Ted Anchor offered to help me gain membership there, I was somewhat taken aback.

Ted was one of the junior section's chief allies at Cripsley. A measure of the immense respect reserved for him among us juniors is that not once – publicly or privately – did we think to add a 'W' to the front of his surname. A former champion pentathlete, he represented everything that was good about the people you can meet at a golf club. If your entire experience of social golf amounted to Ted's good manners, selfless sportsmanship and irrepressible sunniness, it might be enough to convince you that dress restrictions, xenophobia and plus fours held the combination to a rosier world.

There were only two ways to make Ted stop smiling: tell him about a misfortune, or pull on his jowls. He was a beacon of optimism for everyone who knew him, the kind of rare man who seemed to be above day-to-day niggles, yet reserved a deep sadness for the properly tragic. Bob Boffinger was the brains, soul and legs behind the Cripsley junior section. Ted was the heart.

It's a special golfer who can be totally in love with the game yet smile beatifically after futzing six successive eight-iron shots into a stagnant pond, and Ted was that man. Unlike his contemporaries, Ted knew he couldn't lick us at golf, and didn't waste his or our time trying. 'That was one mighty drive,' he would gasp, whether the tee shot I'd hit was awe-inspiring, decent, or downright ordinary. I might have started to nourish my own doubts about my ability to win that British Open, but Ted was always unequivocal about my potential. On my less upbeat days, I would sign up to play with him, just for the sheer confidence boost.

If there was anything frustrating about Ted, it was that he believed *all* of us were going to win the British Open one day – something even we, deluded as we were, knew to be highly unlikely. He probably never realized it, but we squabbled over him terribly.

'I'm playing with Ted in the Naylor Cup on Saturday.'

'Ted gave me twenty quid yesterday.'

'Ted said he thought I was favourite to win the club championship this year.'

Ted probably didn't put a tenth of the thought, effort, money and time into the junior section that Bob Boffinger did, but he made us feel better about ourselves – better, probably, than we had any right to feel – and because of that he was perhaps the more sought-after patron. His praise, whoreish though it was, *mattered*. He might have slipped Mousey a tenner early in the day (Mousey's mum had to support two unruly teenagers alone on a small income, and, learning of this, Ted had stepped in as clandestine benefactor) and signed up to tell Jamie how great he was tomorrow, but when he approached me on the practice ground that day, *I* felt like the special one.

'How's the swing, killer?' asked Ted.

'Ah, pretty good,' I replied. 'I just don't seem to be able to score, though. I creamed it round here in seventy-one yesterday and made four birdies, but I played in the Girton Junior Challenge the day before and stubbed it round in thirteen over. How crap was that?'

'You've got to stop blaming yourself, my boy. You're

doing all you can, and it's obvious you should be scoring better with that kind of swing and the distance you hit the thing. It's this course: it's just not difficult enough for you. And that gives you a disadvantage against those Worksop boys straight away.

'I'm heading up to the clubhouse now to order some teacakes. Now – you finish hitting those balls, and I'll meet you in the men's bar in twenty minutes. I've got an idea for you, my boy.'

Ted had met Gerald Whitehead in the early sixties while cycling on top of a Swiss Alp; the two of them had celebrated by racing each other down the other side and been friends ever since. Gerald was, Ted explained in hushed tones, a highly influential member of Par-adise. Describing his friend, Ted used phrases like 'salt of the earth', 'owes me his life' and 'stand-up fella'. Over-looking the obvious question of why, if he was such a 'stand-up fella', he hadn't secured membership for Ted at Par-adise, I listened, feeling more and more light-headed by the nanosecond, as he outlined just what Gerald might be able to do to further my golfing career. If all went well, I learned, I could be a member at the Midlands' greatest golf club before the month was out.

'Don't get too excited, though,' warned Ted.

'Don't worry. I won't,' I lied.

The meeting was set for the following week. I arrived at Par-adise well briefed. 'Now don't go worrying about how well you play; it's going to be obvious to Gerry that you've got talent,' explained Ted. 'What matters is that you show him what a well-bred young man you are. The things that you learned from that little rules book: *they're* the important things. Gerry's a good fella, but he admires manners. Now – you just make sure you repair your pitchmarks and watch your "p"s and "q"s and I've got a good feeling that before long you could be the newest star player at one of Nottinghamshire's best clubs.'

'Thanks, Ted.'

'Oh, and Tom?'

'Yeah?'

'If you're getting a lift up to the club with your dad, you might want to suggest that he leaves the Sphincter at home.'

He needn't have worried. I wasn't leaving anything to chance. I arrived at Par-adise alone, having been dropped off by my parents in the car park of a lumber-yard half a mile up the road. My incessant argument that the occasion demanded a brand-new set of Mizuno irons might have fallen on deaf ears, but thanks to a tin of Brasso, a bucket of hot soapy water and the bathroom nail brush, it wouldn't take too much imagination to mistake my random, orphaned clubs for the Real Thing. My torso was complimented by a handsome Lyle and Scott tank top, complete with 'bilious diamonds' motif. My breath had been primed with an infallible cocktail of Colgate, Listerine and Fox's Glacier Mints. I was as ready as I would ever be. Emerging from the pines, I paused at the brow of the hill, and admired my new kingdom.

Gerald matched neither my preconceived image of a Par-adise dignitary nor my preconceived image of Ted Anchor's best friend. A tight-lipped, frugal man, he immediately made it clear that there were a thousand and one things he'd rather be doing than playing golf with a precocious little brat like me. His conversation was strictly limited to a muttered 'I think it's your turn to play' here and an 'I'm taking a free drop' there. I think at one point he might have asked me how I'd done in my GCSEs, but it could have been the wind thrashing through the pines. Unlike his Cripsley equivalents, Gerald seemed neither impressed nor depressed by my golf. It simply didn't penetrate his universe.

I guessed, though, that this was all part of the test. Well, bring it on, I thought. I was in what professionals call 'the zone' – the exact place I couldn't seem to find in all those county tournaments – and nothing could touch me. If Gerald wanted to wait for me to make the mistakes, he could wait as long as he liked.

I handled the whole thing, I thought, with model decorum. Ted had advised me not to worry about the way I played, and I hadn't, unduly. Par-adise had brought neither me nor the bowed shaft of my five-iron to my knees, yet I'd shown it the respect it demanded. My round was pragmatic, reliable, unspectacular, and that was clearly what the occasion called for. I had repaired my pitchmarks. I had replaced my divots. I had beaten Gerald by eleven shots.

'Good game,' he muttered, as – careful to apply just the right, respectful level of firmness – I shook his hand on the eighteenth green.

Clearly, something was playing on his mind. It could have been the crushing defeat, but I sensed otherwise: he had, after all, spent most of the round regarding my performance with all the excitement of a man with a ringside seat at the quarter-finals of the World Needlework Championships. As he invited me into the clubhouse for muffins (Par-adise was obviously too posh for teacakes), he had the look of an FBI inter-rogator who knows his suspect is guilty but hasn't quite located his weakness. I nipped into the locker room and checked myself out in the mirror, discovering to my immense relief that my shirt was tucked in, my flies were zipped up, and no one had covertly scrawled 'Marxist Deviant Sex Offender Hippy' across my forehead.

The events of the following hour might have been a series of coincidences and bad breaks. That's certainly what they felt like at the time. Now that I lay them out in my head, however, it all begins to look somewhat predestined. I wonder, for example, if it was mere chance that led us to the particular one of Par-adise's several imperious-looking bars which played host to the icy, grey-haired man in the dark suit. I muse over whether Gerald's prolonged visit to the toilet, leaving me in the company of this man and his remorseless manner, was just an acute attack of irritable bowel syndrome or something more contrived. I puzzle over whether the questions that the man put to me were his way of making conversation, or something worked out in a committee room the day before.

'Do your parents play golf, Tom?' said the icy man, by way of greeting. He was looking at something forty-five degrees to my right. I followed his gaze to see if it led to another Tom, but saw only a wall filled with framed photos of Par-adise's past captains. He was talking to me.

'No. They never have.'

'What or who made you take it up, then? An uncle?'

'No. Just thought I'd give it a go, really.'

'And what line of work are your parents in?'

'My dad's a supply teacher. My mum teaches English as a second language at an inner-city primary school.'

A perceptible drop in temperature. 'Hmmmph. Do you . . . Do you *know* anyone at our club, Tom?'

'Only Gerald.'

'And what makes you want to become a member?'

'Well, I've always loved the course. And I'm looking for a challenge, to help me become a better player. I aim to be down to a scratch handicap by the time I'm eighteen.'

'And how do you feel about the social side of golf? Do you enjoy it?'

'I . . . erm. It's . . . I . . . It's fine.'

At which point the interrogation drew to a close, and Gerald — who'd probably been watching the whole thing through a double-sided mirror with the remainder of the club's greens committee — returned, bearing a tension-relieving plate of muffins.

Ordinary teenagers principally have the misfortune of hanging around with only two types of old people — their schoolteachers and their relatives. They make up for the indignity of hanging around with the former by inventing cruel nicknames for them and leaving stray drawing-pins on their chairs, and generally do their best to spend as little time with the latter as possible. Golf teenagers aren't so fortunate. They are abandoned in an almost exclusively adult world where everyone under eighteen is written off as a 'junior', yet somehow expected to communicate on a civil level with people far less energetic and happening than them. The one factor that makes this bearable is the game itself. Colin Burroughs, for example, whom I played with in Cripsley's Rover Cup, might, for all I knew, have been a closet fascist with an Enoch Powell apron and an extensive collection of Barbara Cartland novels, but he, like me, could relate to the difference between an eight-iron and a mashie niblick and the tingling sensation associated with a creamy one-iron from a tight lie. These things brought us closer. Without them, I was his worst nightmare.

Which is perhaps why I never hit it off with Gerald and the Human Coolbox. I *tried* to talk about Ian Woosnam's winning putting streak and the new range of TaylorMade woods, but they didn't seem interested. They didn't seem interested in much, least of all my own golfing achievements. I might as well have been a face on the wall, and they probably would have paid more attention to me if I was. Every so often they would talk just out of my earshot, and I would pick up odd words like 'committee', 'disciplinary', 'union' and 'function'. Most of the time, they munched on their muffins and stared longingly at their beloved past captains.

'I'm due to play in the Midland Youths Championships next month,' I casually mentioned to Gerald, in an attempt to pep the conversation up slightly.

'Mmm?'

'Yes. It's at Stoke Rochford. I think I'm in with a good chance this year.'

'Hmmm. Well, good luck.'

Was that it? 'Well, good luck'? I might not have been Boy Wonder, but I was used to more deference than this. I was the youngest ever club champion of Cripsley, but I was marginally less important than a muffin at Par-adise. Reluctantly, I balled my fists, controlled my breathing, and swallowed my pride. After all, I was here to improve my golf, to get away from the evil temptations of Granny on Wheels and Ching!, and Nick Bellamy and the pro shop. I was here because it was a place where I wouldn't be distracted from the serious business of golf by the fun business of aiming punched one-irons at a tractor driven by someone called Stig or Reg or Rog. I wasn't here for the diverse culture, pithy conversation and lively nightlife. I was here strictly to do business. If the ice twins were going to play it cool, I could deal with that. Providing, of course, that they offered me membership.

I left that day not quite sure whether they had or not.

Stony Thrapston, the micro-suburb I lived in when I was sixteen, was, despite its rustic name, a classic eighties Meccano village: a vaguely aspiring middle-class community, surrounded on all sides by vaguely apathetic working-class ones. If you ignored the smoke billowing from the burning Gazmobiles on the council estate a hundred yards or so to the rear of our house, you might even mistake Mornington Road for quite a peaceful street, where burglaries didn't happen once every fortnight. The Human Coolbox was understandably unfamiliar with the place but – uncharacteristically, I thought – insisted on driving me home anyway, since it appeared to be roughly on his way. Conversation didn't exactly flow on the journey

('So, what exactly does teaching English as a second language entail?' 'I don't really know.'), but for the first time I began to review my day's work and feel positive. I'd withstood the onslaught of etiquette and stoicism. OK, I hadn't done *much*, but I hadn't done anything *wrong*. At least – I was pretty sure I hadn't.

Then I remembered the Sphincter.

By the time I thought of it, we'd already turned into Mornington Road, and it was probably too late. I toyed briefly with the idea of asking to be dropped off next door, at the house belonging to Mr and Mrs Singh, and trying to pass them off as my parents, but, foreseeing the problems that might be involved in explaining my Sikh adoption to the Par-adise committee, thought better of it. My one remaining hope was that my dad had, on a whim, decided to lock his precious jalopy in the garage for the evening. It was, admittedly, a slim hope, given that – with the exception of environmental health – there was no logical reason to lock the Sphincter away for the night since the only exterior parts of it that hadn't rusted already were the tyres, the windows and the headlights, and even they were beginning to look a bit on the orange side.

Who was I kidding? I was asking for a miracle. I closed my eyes and asked hard. When I opened them, I saw an empty drive.

It belonged to the Jacksons, the couple who lived opposite us.

In my own drive, as ever, squatted the Sphincter – looking less roadworthy than ever, it had to be said. I noted with interest that somewhere on the way home from the lumberyard earlier in the day my dad had managed to lose the car's one remaining hubcap. Through the rear window, it was possible to see the bin liners full of decomposing garden refuse intended for the local tip. If you peered hard enough at a small area of part-preserved paintwork beneath the rear bumper, it was just possible to make out the car's original beige hue. In the left-hand window – the side facing us – was the 'Ban the Bomb' sticker that my parents had bought at a 1982 CND funfair.

Had Coolbox – I still hadn't discovered his real name or what desperately important, clandestine function he performed in the Par-adise machine – spotted this (only just) living insult to the automobile industry? It was hard to tell. But if he hadn't, he was certainly just about to. And if he wasn't, he was going to catch a whiff of the burning vest smell that the Sphincter always gave off if it had been driven more than two miles at some point during the previous twenty-four hours.

'Well, thanks for the lift,' I said, squeezing out of the passenger door, trying to inflate my body in order to block out the view behind me.

'Yes. Well . . .' He seemed distracted.

'I guess Gerald will be in touch?'

211

'What?' Putting the car in gear. 'Oh, yes, you'll hear from Gerald. At some point.'

I watched and waved with a sinking heart as he sped off back up the road, still with my doubts as to whether he'd fully evaluated the putrid heap of scrap behind me, but instinctively coming to terms with the knowledge that I wouldn't be seeing him again.

The following month unfolded with inevitable, desperate silence, which soon devolved into normality. 'How did it go?' Ted had asked. 'I'm not sure. Well, I think,' I'd told him, not yet wanting to concede that all hope was gone. After another four weeks of silence from Gerald and apologies from Ted, the news came, the lateness, vagueness and spuriousness of the verdict – 'Unfortunately Par-adise has decided it doesn't have room for any more junior members at this stage' – an insult to my ambition and Ted's friendship. By then, though, I'd long since given up.

A couple of months later, at a tournament near Kidderminster, I found myself paired, uncommonly, with one of Par-adise's low-handicap adult members, a man I hadn't met before nor heard of – strangely, considering the close-knit nature of the Nottinghamshire scene. While waiting for the green ahead of us to clear, I found myself striking up a conversation with him about the state of Nottinghamshire junior golf. He seemed a genial enough fella, and I asked him, just out of interest, how his club's junior section were fairing that season.

'Ooh, not bad. The odd good round,' he replied. Then he paused, as if considering something right under his nose for the first time. 'Of course, there's always the problem of numbers.'

'Really?' I said. 'How many under-eighteen players have you got at the moment?'

'Ooh . . . let me think,' he replied. 'Eight, I reckon. Yes, that's right. Eight. Seven or eight.'

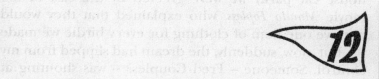

12

'No! *No!* What on earth are you talking about? No! Of course I'm not drunk. It's eight in the fuckin' morning . . . Will you just get off my case, for *once in my life*? . . . What are you talking about? *What?* Why do you have to be the most boring person in the world? Can you not just be, you know, cool, just for five seconds of my stupid *life?* Tell me. *Can* you? Mmm? Look. You're embarrassing me. I'm here with my friends and you're embarrassing me . . . No – of course I don't have to tell you. In fact, I don't have to tell you *anything*. I'm almost *fifteen!*'

The dream had started serenely enough: the American professional Fred Couples had called round at my place, *as usual*, wondering if I fancied a swift nine holes at the luxury Pebble Beach complex in California. There'd been a bit of trouble getting permission from my mum and, frankly, I thought the seat belts on Fred's Lear jet could have been better designed, but Fred said he had a surprise in store, so I went along with it and as we stepped onto the tarmac (Fred had his own reserved landing spot in the clubhouse car park) we were greeted by the cast of the movie *Mondo Topless*, who explained that they would remove one item of clothing for every birdie we made . . . But, now, suddenly, the dream had slipped from my control. Someone – Fred Couples? – was shouting at me, and I couldn't understand why.

I bolted awake as the phone slammed into its cradle. 'Parents, huh?' grumbled a voice. It seemed a bit feminine to belong to Fred Couples, but it was definitely the same one that had been yelling at me, even though its tone was surprisingly pleasant now. Removing a piece of sock fluff from the corner of my mouth, I traced my way through the rubble of beer cans, underwear and golf balls at eye level in an attempt to locate the voice's owner. Every time my gaze stretched beyond the three feet of carpet directly in front of me my head rattled like a quarter-full piggy bank, but I wasn't going to be discouraged. With a gargantuan mental shove, I looked up, and saw a girl – not a member of the cast of *Mondo Topless*, but not un-attractive – clad in ripped jeans and a T-shirt with the slogan 'Cool As Fuck' emblazoned across the front.

'Morning,' she said droopily.

Reaching deep inside the piggy bank, I found that I

could dredge up three salient facts about her: that her name was Letitia, that she was famous for being un-usually nasty to her mum in public, and that, of all Mandy Routledge's friends, she was the one I felt most comfortable about the concept of getting off with. That must have been her mum on the phone. Whether or not I had got off with Letitia was as yet unclear, since the events of the previous night were being pushed through the slit in the piggy bank at an excruciatingly slow speed.

Was it really only three hours since I had passed out on the living-room floor? At least, I assumed I had passed out on the living-room floor, since that was where I'd woken up. Data was arriving at the piggy bank not only slowly but also at random. I remembered Robin gently inserting a golf glove into Bushy's snoring mouth. Elsewhere was a foggy recollection of Jamie sabotaging some pampas grass in the garden of whosever house this was, while Mousey dementedly recited the jingle to a soft drink ad – 'drink it in the sun' – intermittently substituting the word 'mum' for 'sun'. Abruptly, it struck me just how funny these things were. Not just snigger-snigger funny, but belly-laugh hilarious. We really were genuinely amusing people. I shook my head at our genius, then dimly remembered that the girl sitting across from me – Letitia, that was it – had made a comment aimed in my general direction.

Surmising that, since I'd forgotten what it was she'd

said, it couldn't have been important, I brushed myself down and made the wobbly ascent to a vertical position, removing the small furry elephant that was, for some unfathomable (but, I could rest assured, very funny) reason, stuffed down the back of my shirt. I grinned enigmatically at Letitia – because, if you thought about it, she was pretty funny as well – and stopped at the bottom of the stairs, hearing giggling from one of the upstairs rooms. Then, stealthily, cheekily – this, too, was a stunningly humorous thing to do – I let myself out the back door of whosever house it was and set off in the direction of Cripsley, thinking, If I hurry, I might just make my 8.36 tee time in the Saturday Medal tournament.

I'd spent most of the previous three years doing my best to ignore Mandy Routledge. We all had – including, it frequently seemed, Mandy herself. With a voice that made Mousey sound like James Earl Jones and a habit of blending in to any social function to the point of invisibility, she didn't do herself any favours. She always acted, I thought, particularly shy around me. If she hadn't been Cripsley's only significant girl player, it's quite possible we might have been forced to overlook her existence entirely, mistaking it for a shadow or a particularly light breeze. It wasn't that Mandy wasn't pretty or graceful or sweet; she was all these things. But the bottom line was: she played golf. This in itself made her an asexual being in our eyes. It wasn't that we didn't want to hang around with girls who played golf; we just didn't want to hang around with the kind of girls you found at golf clubs (*British* golf clubs, anyway; Portuguese ones were an exception). Mandy, from the little we knew about her, seemed precisely that kind of girl.

'Look at Mandy. She *wants* you,' we would taunt one another, rolling our eyes mock-seductively, upon registering Mandy's nervous presence on an adjacent fairway. The concept of Mandy wanting anything beyond a My Little Pony and a skipping rope seemed quite frankly obscene. 'See those eyes. She's *gagging* for it.'

Most of the time we were hard pushed to see anything beyond the odd arm or leg. Where Mandy went, her mum went first, considerably more boldly. Mandy's diametric opposite, Georgina Routledge was a corpulent, battleworn woman with the kind of complexion custom-made for midwinter gang fights in northern market towns. She was also one of the few Cripsley members who wasn't afraid to tell the club president just where he could shove his men-only bar. If we were perfectly honest with ourselves, belittling Mandy was our own way of pretending Georgina didn't scare the living trousers out of us.

News of the first party arrived from Georgina, punctuated with infinitesimal squeaks of enthusiasm from Mandy, who was standing behind her at the time. 'We're not taking any excuses,' Georgina warned, cornering three of us in the clubhouse car park. 'You don't want to let my Mandy down, do you? We're expecting you all to be there. And that means *you* too, Tom.'

'So,' I asked Robin, Bushy and Ashley later. 'You gonna go?'

'Neh. Can't be arsed.'

'Fuck that. *Top Gun*'s on TV.'

'Do I look like a cradle snatcher?'

The following Saturday, five virgins in Joe Bloggs jeans and too much Old Spice arrived at the front door of a sixties semi off Cripsley High Road, jostling and jesting with one another with the special kind of bravado that only the truly sexually apprehensive can flaunt. The decision to relent and give Mandy's party a try had been made for me – and, I would guess, for my friends – by a reluctant process of elimination. That is to say, I had gradually eliminated every attractive female I thought I had a chance of snogging, until I could provide no rational argument for not turning up at Mandy's. With Tina Williams promising to go out with me 'just as soon as you get a Harley' and Wendy Morrisall still mooning over Mr Hope, the student English teacher, my best bet for a date had been Joanne Hardy, a chunky blonde who'd paraded the shortest skirts in 5G, but my relationship with her had been getting more and more baffling for weeks. The previous Sunday, to my immense excitement, I'd found myself invited up to her bedroom to evaluate the new Erasure album. 'You're my bosom buddy. I hope you know that, Tom,' she had informed me, before complaining of the heat, and suggesting that it might be a good idea if she removed her top. 'You've got to promise not to look, though,' she added. I'd pondered the situation for a moment, before falling back on the advice offered to me by Ian Flack, an experienced sixth-former of the world: 'When dealing with a woman, Tom, honesty is always the best policy.' 'Joanne,' I explained, opening my heart, 'I can't promise not to look at your chest.' The top stayed on and by Wednesday I'd heard from a close friend of Joanne's that I'd been dumped for a more 'mature' man. His name? '"Flackie", I think they call him.'

All of which left me with two options: going to Mandy's, or watching Tom Cruise performing unrealistically hygienic big-screen sex with Kelly McGillis.

'Might as well see how it goes,' Robin had agreed.

'We can always bugger off to the pub if it's shit,' concurred Bushy, who by that point had been getting served for three years.

'She might have some fit friends,' reasoned Mousey.

Though we always reassured ourselves that we were stooping to make a semi-ironic, semi-benevolent gesture by attending Mandy's parties, we were actually extremely fortunate. Mandy was educated privately at one of the Midlands' most elite all-girl schools, which meant her typical social acquaintance tended to be a uniquely sympathetic kind of fifteen-year-old girl who, though perhaps not a golfer herself, wouldn't feel sullied by the prospect of being chatted up by one. The key participants were Marcy, a secretly naughty redhead who gave the outward appearance of being even more squeaky and shy than Mandy; Camilla, who, though initially agreed to be the most 'up for it' of the group, turned out to be permanently insecure about the intentions of everyone around her; Cecilia, who picked relentlessly at her lip and, in a gesture preemptive of the teenagers of the late nineties, had a habit of turning ordinary statements into questions?; Mandy herself; and Letitia, the mum-basher. Nothing palpable seemed to bind these girls in close friendship beyond their collective ability to titter once every twenty-four seconds.

Somewhat less giggly were Georgina – who, armed with a row of non-alcoholic lagers, set up camp on the leather chair outside the living-room door – and Tracy, Mandy's nineteen-year-old cousin, a fearsome automaton of a girl known to us as the Transformer (Robots in Disguise) who seemed to be in attendance in the interests of security. At least, so we hoped. The unthinkable prospect that Tracy might view us in a carnal way was enough to prompt the kind of nightmare visions that would have David Cronenberg quivering behind his autoerotic gearstick.

The parties invariably unfurled in four stages. As the overconfidence of our arrival mysteriously dissipated, the initial sixty minutes would be a mixture of nervous laughter and nervous golfspeak, with both sets of friends clumsily attempting to justify their presence. The bridge to the carefree second stage was provided by an alliance of the drinks cabinet and Robin's limbs, and could never arrive quickly enough.

It would begin with an awkward silence, and a smattering of giggles, as we all anxiously wondered – boys on one side of the room, girls on the other – what to do or say next. Then, promptly, Robin would be at our rescue, squatting in the middle of the living-room rug, wrapping his neck around his little toe.

His repertoire of positions was awesome, light years beyond everyday double-jointedness. There was the Pylon, a convoluted manoeuvre which required Robin to bend his legs and arms backwards, yet somehow seamlessly meld them until they became one, while simultaneously keeping them perpendicular to his spine and putting his entire body weight on his genitals in order to stay upright. Also known as the Evil Weeble, this position was just a warm-up. Authentic crowd-pleasers like the Octoprong and Spatula Joy would, for any other supple human being, have required a team of highly qualified plastic surgeons, a DC

Comics editorial meeting and several tons of Plasticine.

From here on, the alcohol began to kick in, and the two sexes converged around Robin in the centre of the room. The third stage would last from now – nine-ish – until about two in the morning, and involve anything from dry humping to re-enactments of the 1990 Dunhill Cup via the medium of spoons, and encompass vomit fights and kitchen utensil theft along the way. Traditionally, around midnight, Jamie and I would wrestle, as – stirred up by seven cans of Red Stripe – our bottled rivalry fought for expression, spilling over into the street outside. Then, after Jamie finally outran me, I would pass out in the middle of the cul-de-sac, returning to consciousness intermittently to hum the BBC golf theme tune and ask anyone who happened to be in the vicinity if they had 'seen my caddy'. Georgina appeared to be utterly thrilled that all this mayhem was in some vague sense revolving around 'her Mandy', and watched proudly from her seat. Tracy's was the sole slightly grumpy presence, but she was essentially tolerant, as long as we didn't vomit on her body parts (I guessed she was worried about them rusting).

Then, when it was all over, we would all get into bed with one another.

It's important that I clarify a few details here. By 'get into bed', I do *only* mean 'get into bed'. By 'bed' specifically, I mean the king-size one belonging to Georgina. And by everyone, I mean everyone except

Georgina and Tracy. Stripped down to its intrinsic elements, the whole ritual made pre-teen games of mummies and daddies look licentious. The most surprising thing is that, in a whole year of parties, it never really progressed to anything. Clothes remained stringently a part of proceedings, and at the first sign of any furtive unzipping, unbuttoning or unstrapping, the offender would be put into a headlock by a couple of Robin's elastic limbs (Robin's pliability dictated that he could also apply this rule to himself if the need arose), then locked in Georgina's wardrobe for anywhere up to two hours. There was tickling, and the odd intrepid hand, but never much else.

That said, I couldn't say for sure, since my time under the covers was usually short-lived. After ten minutes of suspect odours and knee–mouth interfaces, it became clear that even Georgina's Emperor of all Beds couldn't comfortably house the writhing hormones of ten hyperactive teenagers, and Camilla and I were customarily the first to seek refuge in the spare room: Camilla, because by this point she would be convinced that the whole house was involved in some grand conspiracy to alienate her, and me, because I couldn't stand the smell of Ashley's feet.

'Mandy hates me,' Camilla would confide, as the two of us attempted to get settled, a slim partition wall away from all the fun. 'They all do! Do *you* think I'm fat? I'm not as fat as Marcy, and they don't hate her! And why's

Robin so bothered about Letitia and so horrible to me? She can be a real cow, you know. You wouldn't think it, but it's true. She gets forty quid a week allowance. Can you *believe* that? Even more than Mandy and she——'

'Nobody hates you, Camilla,' I would cut in. 'You're not fat. And I like you a lot.'

But I wasn't going to get off quite so lightly.

Over the following two hours, Camilla would talk, while I dredged up everything in my Sensitive Potential Boyfriend repertoire, right from 'Mmmm' to 'No – I really don't think Kylie Minogue's figure should be seen as a benchmark for the young female of today'. Every so often, a lewd enquiry would be thrown in our direction from the other bedroom, along the lines of, 'You getting any in there, TC?' This would start me wondering if they were getting any in *there*, and if I was a fool to miss out on it. Around daybreak the house would at long last fall silent and I would drift off for two hours with Camilla's head on my shoulder, before unaccountably waking up on the living-room floor with a mouth lined with an obscure stringy substance and Robin attempting to stuff a stale leather golf glove down my shirt.

Those, at least, are the things I *like* to remember about Mandy's parties.

The darker side usually stays well suppressed, beneath the clutter of selective memory, but it's there too, and I can't deny it. Sometimes I'll wake up with a jolt in the witching hour, too terrified to peek under the covers on the off chance that my wife is wearing plus fours. Other times, the Fear will manifest itself in a series of images. A boy running through a suburb, lost, glancing desperately over his shoulder. Laura Davies, the celebrated WPGA professional, in suspenders. A mouse. The pink fluorescent shaft of a ladies' eight-wood.

I knew Mandy fancied me. Even as the kind of person who needs to be felt up in public – twice, if at all possible – before he knows someone fancies him, I knew she fancied me. Her mum made it obvious. What I mean is this: after three years of Georgina buying him drinks, winking in his general direction, making up cuddly nicknames for him and gently coaxing him into the seat next to her daughter, a crash test dummy might have got the hint that he was being lined up for something.

Dissociating Mandy from Georgina seemed to me like removing some exotic seafood from its shell: fiddly, messy and probably not worth the unpredictability of the end result. Where some girls had big noses or food allergies or bad dress sense, Mandy had Georgina. I was pretty sure that I didn't fancy Mandy, but it was hard to get past the mum imagery and properly work it out. It wasn't so much that something was missing, more that something *wasn't* missing.

nice jumper

Right from Georgina's 'and that means *you* too, Tom' speech, I'd begun to get the creepy feeling that these parties were an elaborate ruse to get Mandy alone in the same room as me. I didn't dare voice these concerns to my friends, and told myself I was being paranoid, but even in my most misty drunken states I kept my foglights on and was always precisely aware of Mandy's whereabouts. While I'd like to think I comforted Camilla out of an innate warmth and generosity, or even because she had a nice bottom, the truth was she provided a perfect excuse for me not to end up in the same bed as Mandy.

I lasted out until the fifth party.

I don't remember where I'd been immediately before it happened – destroying some pampas grass or hiding a sieve behind the cistern in the downstairs toilet, probably – but I remember suddenly being trapped between the front door, Georgina, Tracy and the living room, where Mandy was sitting, alone and expectant.

'We've been looking for you, Tom,' said Georgina.

'Well, here I am,' I slurred.

'Tom?' asked Tracy. 'Why don't you like Mandy?'

'I do like Mandy,' I said, fumblingly.

'Well,' said Georgina, 'in that case, why don't you kiss her?'

'I just . . . don't.'

I was struck with the sense that the rest of the party

228

had deserted me. Upstairs – from where I could hear Letitia yelping and Camilla, Jamie and Marcy laughing – seemed like an adjoining country.

'Are you saying there's something wrong with my daughter?' asked Georgina.

'Of course not,' I replied.

'Is it that you think Camilla's prettier?'

'No.'

'Well then . . .'

'She's waiting for you,' said Tracy, who seemed to be gaining a more formidable, metallic quality by the second.

'Go on,' urged Georgina. 'You just go in there and give her a great big kiss on the lips.'

I looked into the front room, towards the settee, where Mandy was perched. 'Heee-hee-heee,' she said.

'Be a man about this, Tom,' said Tracy, taking hold of my elbow. 'You know it makes sense.'

I was cornered, and in a few seconds, I would be more than that – I'd be alcoved. I told myself I had three options: push Tracy away, fling open the door, and make a run for it; sit down and talk this through calmly with the three of them; or enter the living room and face the music.

What was I talking about, three options?

I turned, fumbled for the door knob (unlocked: phew) and scrambled into the night, wibbling for my life.

* * *

I've asked but no one can tell me what I did for the next six hours. My memory offers up flash sessions of the sixteen-year-old me running along Cripsley High Road, perspiring; sitting in the hut to the rear of seventh green; kneeling in the central reservation of the A43; being thrown out of a pub which I hadn't had the chance to enter by a bulbous-faced bouncer; but these images make no sense, come in no particular order and, besides, could quite possibly be borrowed from another drunken golf night. What I know for certain is that, at 7 a.m., I woke up in Ashley's living room with a confused-looking Ashley standing above me, and my clothes – *all* my clothes – in a neat pile beside me. A pile far too neat to have been arranged by someone who had consumed eleven cans of Red Stripe the night before.

'How did I get here?' I asked Ashley, whose mum and dad always left their back door unlocked.

'I was just wondering the same thing,' he replied.

'Who took my clothes off?' I asked.

'I was wondering that, too,' he said, handing me my boxer shorts.

I never did broach that night with Ashley's parents (who, Ashley assured me, were both at home for the entire duration of my bender) but, walking past piles of fresh ironing in his utility room at various points over the following couple of years, would often get obscure pangs of déjà vu and come down with an un-accountable attack of goose pimples.

It was some time before I spoke to Mandy and Georgina again, and, when I did, the subject of that night remained off-limits, beyond Georgina's comment to Bob Boffinger that I made a 'surprisingly expressive drunk'. I still sometimes made illogical detours via the clubhouse car park in order to avoid the Routledges, but on the whole I felt less threatened, and gathered that they'd passed into a less spooky era of mother–daughter relations. Sometimes we would even see Mandy on her own, making people properly aware of her presence by forming fully intelligible phrases like 'good shot', 'fine, thank you', and 'Have you seen my pink sun visor anywhere?' A couple more parties were arranged. I found excuses not to attend – *Rain Man* was on TV – and learned to live with overexcited reports from Mousey of Letitia's mum turning up at three o'clock in the morning only to be chased out into the street by her daughter, and Robin 'unhooking Marcy's bra strap'.

Mandy and I had known one another half a decade – our entire teenage life, more or less – by the time we engaged in what the average person would recognize as a conversation. It happened in a nightclub in Nottingham town centre, at a birthday gathering for Ben's older brother, Alistair. By this point the Cripsley junior gang had become a less cohesive unit, and I wasn't helping matters with my unfathomable habit of quoting from art-house films and listening to scuzzy rock music conceived in outside lavatories. My friends were baffled by what I was becoming, and I was starting to notice it. Having just lectured Jamie on the idiosyncratic brilliance of the dance scene in Hal Hartley's *Simple Men*, I found myself wandering pointlessly, feeling strangely out of place, and happened upon Mandy. Within two minutes of talking to her, I was immediately struck by how wrong I'd been to write her off, how confident she seemed compared to my acne-ridden, parochial mates, and – even more shocking – that she was the only person at the party who knew who Soundgarden were.

I still didn't fancy her, and she'd probably long since lost interest in me, but that was fine. We both agreed upon how ridiculous it was that it had taken us this long to get to know one another. I felt stupid, but she seemed to as well, which had the culminative effect of making us not feel stupid at all. We cackled contemptuously at our former selves – selves that, in truth, we'd only just left behind – laughed about her mum, and talked excitedly about the forthcoming Screaming Trees tour. I haven't seen her since, but the rumour is that she now has a well-paid job in military intelligence.

When I see my teenage golf-life, I see a bucking bronco, and I see it in two ways. In the first way, which is the way I see it now, golf is the horse, and I'm on the back of it, trying to maintain my grip. In the second way, which is the way I saw it as a teenager, I'm the horse, and it's golf that's struggling to rein me in. The one consistent factor is that the further I progressed towards adulthood, the more jerky, frantic and slippery everything became for both of us.

When I was denied membership of Par-adise, I could have tightened up my practice routine, donned the psychological armour and, like many more convincing rebels before me, shown the men in suits what I was made of. The idea certainly occurred to me, but I lacked the strength and austerity of mind to carry it through. Instead, I turned the crime in on myself. I simply hadn't been good enough, I concluded. The only deception here, I decided, was my own act of thinking that I was somehow 'above' my fellow Cripsley juniors, that I, alone, deserved a better course, simply because I had the lowest handicap at the club. My way of making this up to my friends was to spend the following few weeks squandering too much time in the back of the pro shop, wasting too many practice balls in games of Ching!, secreting the furry head-covers of the septuagenarian membership in deep shrubbery, and attempting to 'find myself' by playing golf while still drunk from the night before. This is what hard-living rock and movie misfits describe as a 'lost weekend'. They have loose women, cocaine and sports cars. Mousey, Jamie and I had tee pegs, Fanta and motorized buggies. If you ignore the discrepancy in resources, the levels of excess were almost identical.

Right in the middle of this period, the professionals' shop vanished. That is to say: the shell of the building remained more or less intact, but everything else about it was irrevocably altered. Where there had been ancient decomposing mashie niblicks, newfangled irons winked under fluorescent lighting. Where there had been dust and dark and porn, there were top-of-the-range waterproofs. Where a caramel-coated rat's skeleton had guarded the entrance to an arcane storage chamber, a hi-tech swing improvement unit stood proud and chaste. Roy Jackson and Mike Shalcross were gone for ever, without a goodbye, like eloping retailers in the night. The only remnant of the old regime was Nick, who would turn up every so often during the weeks following Roy's departure and sit in the new shop, eyeing the new staff incredulously, recounting a legendary blow-job he'd received on the lower practice ground or announcing that he was 'this close' to qualifying for the European Tour – a comment with little foundation since to our knowledge he hadn't played more than five holes of golf in the preceding twelve months.

If the powers-that-be were trying to smoke us out, we were determined that it wasn't going to work. If the new shop wasn't going to be so easy to hide in, then we would just have to be more vigilant in the way we arsed about. As for the new pro and his staff, they'd come around to our way of thinking – eventually. We'd make sure of it.

The first obstacle arrived in the form of Cripsley's new teaching professional, Steve Kimbolton. Steve's first unique quality was his habit of soundtracking his every movement with an unusual low humming sound, the noise a cat and a hive of bees might produce while in the process of becoming friends. His second unique quality was his walk, which gave the impression of a man so laid-back as to be involved in a permanent belly-dance. Clearly nobody had ever told him anything about the traditional duties of the club pro, since he seemed quite content to fill his hours passing on his technical skill, repairing clubs, selling equipment and offering psychological tips to members. Unfortunately for us, this meant he was nearly always in the shop, unless he was out on the practice fairway taking a lesson. Even when he returned prematurely with his charge to find half a dozen of us sprawled out with the contents of his new Mizuno display window scattered around us, he remained unfazed. At least with Roy Jackson a sense of volatility had lurked beneath the absent-minded surface. Steve just belly-danced right through us in slow motion. We wanted a sense of risk. Instead we got this noise: 'zmmmmunnznnnzmmm'. Finding ourselves infuriatingly not even *wanting* to upset him, our pranks tended to backfire. On one occasion we used the shop phone to book a high-class sheepdog trainer for his Jack Russell/whippet hybrid, but having shortly afterwards met the dog in question, which turned out to be almost as docile as its owner and utterly adorable, we lost sight of our original motivation and jogged to the nearest payphone to cancel the appointment. Another time, Mousey, in one of his more obnoxious moods, had pilfered one of a consignment of Nick Faldo-endorsed Pringle sweaters, only to feel bad about it and sneak it back onto the shelf the next day.

Thankfully we didn't have to expend so much energy on Nigel, Steve's assistant. Nigel arrived at Cripsley in 1991 as a conscientious nineteen-year-old, the

possessor of a warm smile, a rapidly improving handicap and hopes of getting his professional's card before
the end of the same year, with a view to competing
at the highest level in the not too distant future.
He left three years later as a jaded, sex-obsessed twenty-
two-year-old, with a considerably worsened handicap
and an imminent interview for a factory job sorting
women's pants. It's quite possible that Nigel's destiny
was always in lingerie and not golf, and that there was
nothing anyone could do to prevent him fulfilling it.
It's also equally possible that he was hounded
and goaded by Cripsley's junior section until he saw no
other way out.

'GOOD SCORE IN TODAY'S CONDITIONS!' Nigel
would shout, as I arrived back in the shop after my
round. Nigel would bellow, 'GOOD SCORE IN
TODAY'S CONDITIONS!' whether I had achieved a
mediocre score on a calm midsummer's afternoon,
a good score in a hurricane, or my worst score ever
on a course I'd specially set up in my own living room
with buckets substituted for holes. It was his catchphrase. His other catchphrase was, 'WELL, THAT'S
RIGHT!' He said this to adult members regardless of
whether they had just made a pithy observation,
uttered something Nigel couldn't understand at all, or
expressed the opinion that all gay and black people
should be gunned down in cold blood. Nigel would still
have said 'WELL, THAT'S RIGHT!' to them if they had

just confided that they were planning to put a bag of cat litter forward for role of vice-captain next year. It wasn't as if there was any choice for him in the matter. He was, after all, an assistant pro.

Our nickname for Nigel, who was sharp-featured, was 'Fez'. He looked more like a stoat than a ferret, but 'Stoaz' didn't have the same ring to it. We called Nigel 'Fez' behind his back until the end of his first fortnight at Cripsley, by which point Fez's Fezness had become so extreme that calling him anything else to his face required a level of mental effort we didn't have the stamina for.

'Hi, Fez!' blurted Mousey one day, as we piled into the shop.

'WHAT? WHY ARE YOU CALLING ME THAT?' said Fez.

''Cos Tom says you look like a ferret,' said Mousey.

'Bollocks, did I!' I said.

'THAT'S NICE. I FEEL SO MUCH BETTER ABOUT MYSELF NOW,' said Fez.

'We don't mean it in a horrible way,' I said, cushioning the blow.

'HOW CAN YOU CALL SOMEONE A FERRET AND NOT MEAN IT IN A HORRIBLE WAY?'

'Some ferrets can be nice. People have them as pets. We just like to give everyone nicknames. It's affectionate, really. We've got one for Steve, too.'

'WHAT'S THAT?'

'Squiz.'

'WHY?'

''Cos he looks like a squirrel.'

'DO YOU THINK SO?'

'Well, he's got ginger hair.'

Gradually but irresistibly Fez developed until the only thing Nigel had in common with Fez was the body they shared as a vessel. Nigel continued to go about his business of impersonating a human bouncy castle for the egos of Cripsley's adult membership, but the instant they left Fez would come out, slurping at his upper lip, sniffing the air malevolently and evaluating which members of Cripsley's bridge team he'd most like to 'DO IT' with. The Cripsley juniors might have frequently talked in mock lustful terms about Mandy and Cripsley's younger lady members, but for Fez no decrepitude, political inclination, age bracket or brightly coloured waterproofs could represent a barrier. One of his favourite hobbies was 'Grunking', an act which involved his desk, the open drawer of his till, and a series of violent pelvic thrusts. Grunking usually took place not long after a highly regarded member of the ladies' committee had left the shop. Fez was never anything less than ferocious while grunking, and excitement was displayed in quantity rather than brute force. Between twenty and thirty grunks usually meant that Molly Ripdale, a 73-year-old cataract-sufferer who captained the ladies' greensome team, was in the vicinity.

'I'D SHOW HER A THING OR TWO ABOUT MIXED DOUBLES!' Fez would snarl.

A moment later the door would open and Molly's husband, John, would arrive, bringing news of an unfortunate tangle with a conifer to the rear of the thirteenth tee, to which Nigel would make his immediate, mundane, ear-splitting return.

'DON'T WORRY, JOHN. GOOD SCORE, THAT – IN TODAY'S CONDITIONS!'

As far as Fez was concerned, it wasn't so much that we'd created a monster, more that we'd been perceptive and benevolent enough to put a name to an inner beast struggling for expression. At the exact same rate that Fez flourished, however, Nigel's luck ran out. As Steve settled into a work rate more becoming of a club professional, Nigel began to slave harder and longer for his forty-eight pounds a week. When he did get to play – usually for no more than half an hour, in the kind of light where it was quite possible to mistake anything from a hedgehog to the Starship Enterprise for a flagstick – his golf became a comedy of terrors, encompassing the whole spectrum of afflictions from 'the shank' (a shot notorious for flying off the club destructively to the right, at right angles to the target) to the 'Oh shit, I've just hit the clubhouse roof' (a shot notorious for instilling fear into the hearts of the bridge team). Additionally, he drove his dad's Vauxhall Astra into a lamppost, causing several thousand pounds' worth of damage, and his childhood sweetheart dumped him, complaining of the late hours and the smell that lingered on his clothes after a twelve-hour-day dripping petrol into rubber grips in the club repair room.

Naturally, we all found the whole thing heart-breaking, and did our best to help limit the damage Nigel could do to himself.

'I MAY AS WELL JUST CHUCK THIS THING IN THE BIN!' cried Nigel after yet another shank, casting aside his favourite club, a deleted, highly sought-after 1987 model sand iron forged half from copper, half from titanium.

'I'll give you a fiver for it,' I said, making a swift detour from the opposite side of the fairway.

'YOU MAY AS WELL. IT'S NO GOOD TO ME.'

'OK. Let's call it two pounds fifty.'

Yet there was only so much we could do. With Nigel programmed to self-destruct, it would have been impossible to resist the temptation to take advantage of the gaps in his concentration every so often. And besides, Fez, when around, would actively encourage it. There was no escaping the truth: Fez was a more fun person to be, and be with. While Nigel would have never opened up a tab for the junior section behind the cash register, Fez told us to go ahead and help ourselves. With Nigel on patrol, the shop's one remaining inner sanctum, the club repair room, remained strictly off-limits for juniors. With Fez at the helm, it became the number-one party venue.

The dangers would arise when a lightning character change became necessary. As the bell on the shop door tinkled, Fez would race away, employing the back staircase in the same way that Superman employs phone booths, and leaving us alone with an array of solvents, solutions, concoctions and obscure implements worthy of Heath Robinson's tool shed. By the time Fez reached the top of the stairs, he would have settled into the persona of Nigel again. His inherent patience and the insatiable whims of his customers meant we could find ourselves alone in the repair room for anywhere up to an hour. It wasn't long before we began to experiment. What would we get if we poured this sticky stuff into this acidic stuff and garnished it with this dusty stuff? we wondered. The answer was always the same: A big load of sticky, acidic, dusty stuff. But that didn't discourage us from producing several gallons of it.

It was Ashley who happened upon the blowtorch. We didn't even realize that it *was* a blowtorch at first, I don't think; it just looked like something good for pointing at people. The fact that fire emerged from it was a bonus in every way, initially just as a prop for deranged cackling noises, and then for full-blown impressions of Arthur Brown. It wasn't until our third session with it that anyone actually caught fire.

Nigel had been upstairs at the time, listening to Magda Norris complain about her new six-wood and the trouble she was having potty-training her grandson. I had been standing with Ashley and Mousey, observing as Jamie used the blowtorch as a device to enhance the telling of a ghost story. The story was one we'd all heard before, but with a slightly different theme. Jamie had just got to the bit where the driver finds the hitch-hiker's jacket on the gravestone, when I noticed the golden flicker in his hair. What's funny about watching someone's head catch fire is how long it takes them to notice, hence the first instinct isn't always to shout, 'Watch out! Quick! Your hair's on fire!' so much as to think wryly, Isn't that weird? His hair's on fire, yet he's still telling that ghost story, as if nothing's wrong.

'Jamie. There are orange things coming out of your hair. I think they're flames,' I observed, finally.

As Ashley and Mousey began to beat Jamie's head with a tea towel, I decided it was my job as junior captain to take the situation into my own hands, which is exactly what I did. I did it by going into an unbridled panic and shouting 'Quick!' and 'No!' and 'Get some water!' Then I remembered: at the top of the stairs, I'd seen a fire extinguisher. I'd always wondered what it was for. Now I knew.

As I hurtled to the rescue, hydrant at the ready, I congratulated myself on my quick thinking and pragmatic approach in a crisis. Jamie would thank me for this later, and the outcome could be a more symbiotic edge to our golfing rivalry. There was just one slight problem: I'd never operated a fire extinguisher in my life. Still, it couldn't be that difficult, I surmised. After all – wasn't the thing designed for situations when a few vital seconds could make the difference between a full head of hair and first prize in a Duncan Goodhew lookalike contest?

I looked down and assessed my options.

The extinguisher had been constructed with physics professors in mind. It appeared to be a matter of releasing the nozzle on the left, and pushing the button on the right, but what did the nozzle in the middle do? And what was that twiddly thing for? I vaguely remembered someone on TV saying something about not pulling something when using a fire extinguisher or something else would explode in your face. I wished I'd been listening harder when they said it. I took a wild guess, and pushed the button on the right.

A drip of water eased out of a hole and plipped onto the floor in front of me in slow motion.

I looked up. My friends were staring at me quizzically. As far as I could tell, Jamie's hair had been fire-free for several moments.

* * *

These were the slipshod days that other teenagers spend on street corners. Though we spent as much time at Cripsley as we ever had, we played golf infrequently, and disdainfully, unappreciatively. Whole weeks were frittered away in the shop, filled with countless Cokes and Mars Bars on the tab, impressions of Mousey (some days we were so bored even Mousey did impressions of Mousey), Eight-iron Tennis, and the kind of teenage playfighting that starts in hotheaded frustration and ends in twice as much hotheaded frustration. Golf had never been something we were openly proud of, but until now neither had it been something we actively scorned. What brought about the change in attitude? Was it that we were now on holiday from school, and some of us had been relieved of its trials for ever, and access to the course was unlimited, so golf had lost its mystique? Or had my post-Par-adise disenchantment been infectious?

Whatever the case, I knew I was letting myself down. Suddenly, even my parents seemed more enamoured with the game than me.

'How did you play today? Any good?' my dad would ask, as he picked me up in the Sphincter in the fading light.

'All right, I s'ppose,' I would answer sheepishly, thinking about all those five-irons I could have been hitting while I was making prank calls to the international operator.

I felt like a fraud. Essentially, my desire to be the best golfer ever wasn't any weaker than it had always been, so why couldn't I summon the discipline? Had I forgotten about that first British Open victory? No. So why couldn't I leave my friends in the shop overdosing on sugar and lethargy and spend the afternoon on the practice fairway? It wasn't even as if the atmosphere in the shop was stimulating, or exciting (at best, it was sluggish and anarchic). Would my friends respect me any less if I gave it a miss? Probably not, in the long run. So, why?

In the autumn, I was due to start taking my A levels. I didn't particularly want to take my A levels. I'd agreed to do so only to placate my parents, in the aftermath of GCSE results that probably wouldn't have been noticeably worse if I'd recruited a selection of plant life to sit the exams in my place. Getting down to some further education would keep the folks off my back, and give me chance to retake my failed Maths GCSE, which I needed to pass in order to become a run-of-the-mill club professional, if I ever had to fall back on that (I hoped not). My college had been selected with two criteria in mind: proximity to Cripsley's first tee, and proximity to Cripsley's bottom practice fairway. On my day of enrolment, I timed the walk from the college gates to the pro shop. It took me nine minutes, going at a good clip, which I figured I could live with.

As the beginning of term loomed, golf miraculously regained its importance. Out of the blue I was once more playing like my life depended on it, notching up three home victories in the final weeks of August and a couple of top fives in Midlands junior events. Within the space of a few rounds, I remembered that I was an extremely good player, in the grand scheme of things, whether I was worthy of Par-adise and Worksop or not. I was sixteen. I had a handicap of three. One digit lower, and I'd be eligible for the regional qualifying rounds for the British Open. Two weeks before my college education started, I'd be defending my club champion's title, as favourite, with at least four of my friends snapping at my heels.

What happened next couldn't have been less convenient if it had been orchestrated by a committee set up precisely to bring about our downfall.

You might say we deserved it, of course. Setting fire to one another's hair and corrupting an innocent club professional's employee is no way to go about your business as upstanding members of a private golf club, and I concede that in some ways we needed to be taught a lesson, if only to remind us to get our minds back on the game. But, to our knowledge, nobody on the club committee knew what was going on in the pro shop, beyond the fact that we spent an unhealthy amount of time in it. And anyway, if they did, that wasn't what they decided to punish us for.

No. They decided to punish us for playing *too much* golf.

The jibes started coming thick and fast in the weeks leading up to the club championship. 'Don't you lads ever go to school?' carped Steve Berry, a locksmith, from the sixteenth green, at 1 p.m. on a Tuesday afternoon. 'It's not surprising you won the tournament, when you're up here all hours of the day,' griped Clark Allydyce, from the green of his twenty-eighth hole of the morning. 'One day you'll realize what it's like to go to work. Then it will hit you that these were the best days of your life, and you'll be sorry,' lectured Ernie Files, sipping a midday gin and tonic on the clubhouse veranda. 'Don't you have homes to go to?' huffed Jack 'Net Man' Mullen, as he reluctantly gave up the spot in the practice net that he'd occupied for the preceding two hours. As the prospect of another junior victory in the club's most important event drew closer, the undercurrent of bitterness in these comments turned into an overcurrent, until it was obvious to all of us: at least half of the adult membership would be happier people if we didn't win.

Terry Clampett was one of them. He'd been made captain at the beginning of that year, and conformed effortlessly to the stereotype of the traditional James Bond film baddie: impeccably courteous on the outside, with a vindictive core. His operations took a more insidious, subtle form than those of previous Cripsley tyrants, but their precision attained new toxic heights. Compared to Clampett, Hell's Trucker may as well have been auditioning as a *Play School* presenter during his captaincy. You would see Clampett on the course on a sunny day, smiling and waving, and mistakenly think he was glad to see you, when all the while he'd be checking to see that the socks you were wearing with your shorts conformed with the regulatory length stated in the club rules. By the time he'd wished you well on your round, he would have not only concocted your punishment, but decided which one of his goons would deliver it.

When Ashley hit his perfect shot on the sixteenth hole and I saw it heading towards Clampett's sister, Janice, I could see immediately we were in trouble. It was three days before the club championship, and Ashley, Jamie, Robin and I had been surprising ourselves by indulging in a serious practice round with a complete lack of dead legs, arm locks and Eight-iron Tennis. We were back doing what we did best: playing golf well, urging one another to greater heights of excellence. We could see that up ahead Janice, the lady captain, Eileen Stokes and Reg Forman, the new head of the greens committee, were indulging in a four-some, so we made a point of keeping our distance. (The fact that they were playing golf made us keep well back, too.)

'Playing into' the players in front of us was a perennial problem for Cripsley's juniors, as our forearms beefed up and our swings flourished. Our power increased in the same way that our voices broke – in vast leaps and tiny false starts, completely beyond our estimation. Often we'd be lucky, and our shots would sail over the group of players ahead of us, leaving four somewhat deaf senior citizens blissfully ignorant of exactly how close they had come to visiting the great golf course in the sky. On other occasions we'd get away with a near miss, a profuse apology and a quick ticking off. But Ashley's shot shouldn't, by rights, have fallen into either category. From the top of the ridge, I obtained the perfect view of its voyage. There was no doubt it was a strike in a hundred, but even with all Ashley's strength at the back of it, there was no way it was going to trouble Janice and her friends, three hundred yards up ahead on the green. We knew that – which is why we had considered it safe for Ashley to play it.

I watched as the ball soared, hung, dipped and rolled, finally coming softly to rest against the wheel of Reg Forman's trolley, situated to the front left of the green. There was nothing remotely destructive about its descent – anyone could see that. If a centipede had been in the ball's path during its final couple of revolutions, it might have been a little dazed but it would have got up, dusted itself down, assured its fellow insects that it was unscathed, and gone about its daily routine as if nothing had happened.

'Shot!'

'Is it near the green?'

'Close, but don't worry – it didn't hit them.'

We continued to play. But as we drew closer to the green, a funny thing happened: Reg, Janice, Eileen and the lady captain failed to vacate the green. They also appeared to be glaring straight at us.

'What's their problem?'

'Dunno. Do you think they're pissed off?'

'Dunno why. I was nowhere near them.'

Ashley and I approached Reg.

'We're really sorry about that. Did it hit your trolley? We had no idea we could hit that far,' we said, propriety itself.

'You want to watch out. You could have put one of us in hospital,' replied Reg.

'You juniors come up every day, and think you own the course,' added Eileen. 'You ought to learn some consideration for your fellow players.'

'But we said we were sorry. It was a genuine mistake,' said Ashley.

'That's all very well,' said the lady captain, 'but it's not the first time that it's happened, is it?'

'What do you mean? We've never rolled a ball gently against your trolley before,' I protested.

'You know very well what she means,' said Janice. 'Don't think I won't be having a word with the captain about this.' Even though he was her brother, she still called him 'the captain'.

'You should be ashamed of yourself,' said Reg. 'I mean, anyway, don't you have homes to go to?'

And that was how Cripsley's four best players got suspended and missed the club championship.

There were no disciplinary hearings this time. The news came quickly and unequivocally from Bob Boffinger: we were not to visit the club for the following month, for social or playing purposes. As ever, he broke it to us wearily, as a friend, and we knew that he'd fought doggedly on our behalf in the committee room, using the phrase 'abbbsolutely imperative' anywhere between eight and thirteen times.

By the time we returned the club championship had been won and the season was practically over. Clampett continued to greet us with a wave and a beatific smile, like a Mafia overlord who'd just taken our great-aunts as collateral. Fez, who only really performed for an audience of two or more juniors, went into hibernation, and I increasingly found myself alone at Cripsley and free of distractions. Through October and November I hit an average of five hundred golf balls a day. I still have some of the calluses to prove it, and the turf on Cripsley's bottom practice fairway is only now recovering from my relentless path of destruction. The result was the closest I'd come yet to permanently attaining that elusive back-garden swing. But it was too late. With no more tournaments until the following March, I'd have to wait to test-drive it.

I lasted just under a couple of months at Broxwell College. I don't remember much about the time, the place or the people, but I have retained a vivid mental picture of the back gate. A few years later, I came to be friends with a girl whom I had shared a couple of classes with, and she had no recollection of my existence at Broxwell, despite the fact that, from what we could work out, I'd spent the best part of six weeks sitting next to her. I'm sure she's not the only one. Holograms have cast more conspicuous shadows.

My parents accepted my decision to drop out with a level of stoicism not often associated with ex-hippies.

'Over my dead body will you leave that place!' said my mum.

'You're going to ruin your life!' said my dad.

'We've spawned a monster!' they both said.

I knew I had to stand firm, believe in myself, and sit out the couple of months until they started speaking to me again. In the ensuing communal sulk, a couple of reluctant bargains were struck: in exchange for a temporary life of leisure, I would stick around at Broxwell until late November to retake my Maths GCSE, and then find some way of rustling up twenty pounds per week board.

I still don't know how I passed my Maths exam. I turned up at the exam hall with the sole aim of mollifying my parents, safe in the knowledge that there was a much easier numerical test devised by the PGA which I could take if I ever stooped to earn my living as a club professional. So when I realized I'd forgotten my protractor, I wasn't unduly concerned. It was only a few seconds later, when I realized I didn't have my pencil, calculator, compasses, pen or ruler either, that in fact the only vaguely geometrical instrument on my person was a stray tee peg, that I started to concede I'd come slightly underprepared.

I looked across the hall, scanning for a kindly invigilator, and zoomed in on a well-groomed man in a green blazer. He looked familiar. Before I'd had chance to raise my hand, he began walking towards me. Now, where had I seen him before? From some angles, you could even say he looked a little like Colin Allerton, one of Terry Clampett's evil henchmen.

'Hello, Tom.'

Exactly like him.

With a wink, Allerton opened his big golfer's hands, revealing all the apparatus I would need to see me through the following two hours, and a bit in reserve just in case. It was quite possible there were a couple of teacakes for later in there as well – I couldn't tell for sure. I hadn't even been required to speak. Allerton might have been the most lethal of foes at Cripsley, but here in the outside world we golfers would always be fighting for the same cause. With that wink, it seemed that he instinctively knew everything: what I was there for, what I needed, what I was feeling. I couldn't help marvelling at the way he didn't seem surprised to see me at all, how there was no logic to his presence (I'd been told he worked full-time as a solicitor) and, most weirdly of all, how invisible he'd seemed to the rest of the exam hall, and it was perhaps then, for the first time, that I began to truly get the inkling that golf was a supernatural force – something that I would never be in total control of, no matter how many balls I hammered up the practice fairway.

I've always had one major problem with winter golf: I'm too good at it.

If he's seeking perfection, the shrewd amateur golfing prodigy looks to peak around May, just in time for the British Open qualifying rounds and to impress the county selectors. I, on the other hand, have always shifted smoothly up to top gear somewhere around the beginning of January, when birdies tend to get swallowed up in the great big frosty silence, and the people I most want to impress are doing something warm and sensible, like watching pornography or eating teacakes. Ice-hockey players who find the key to their inner genius while on safari will know what I'm talking about.

Amid the temporary greens, restrictive clothing and ankle sludge, a lot of very good things can be said for winter golf. One is the relatively small number of golfers you find indulging in it. Another is that you sometimes get the chance to make friends with parrots.

I first met Ken as I teed up on the final hole of a winter league match, just before Christmas, 1991. I use the word 'met' in the loosest possible sense. We didn't exchange phone numbers. I didn't train him to sit on my shoulder. Come to think of it, he probably wasn't even called Ken. Yet over the following couple of months, we struck up a mutual understanding of a depth rarely attained in man–parrot relations. As I hit my shots up the eighteenth, Ken the Parrot would watch thoughtfully, then communicate his approval (via a quick squawk) or disapproval (via a barely perceptible flutter of his crest). In exchange for his expertise, I would refrain from asking him patronizing questions, such as, 'Where exactly did you escape from?' and 'You're a parrot. What the fuck are you doing hanging out next to the eighteenth tee of a golf course in the middle of an ice storm?'

Ken rarely moved from his perch that winter, and probably didn't see much of interest, but what he did see almost exclusively involved me. He let out a sardonic chirp, as, upon reaching the eighth green, Bob Boffinger and I discovered a human turd secreted in the hole and found new meaning in the age-old 'Who should putt first?' debate. He watched stoically, as if muttering 'I told you so', as Mousey fell through the ice on the pond alongside the first green and I jumped in to rescue him (a much easier process than I'd been led to believe by the child safety ads, thanks to the shallowness of the pond). He frowned sympathetically on Christmas Day as I crunched through the frost to the practice ground to try out my new titanium-shafted driver in the fading light. He looked away in disgust as I missed a three-foot putt which would have sent me into the winter league final. He was a clever parrot. And my strict practice regimen of five hundred balls per day was sending me just a little bit bonkers.

Still – what else was there to do? I'd left school and college, lost touch with all but a couple of non-golfing friends. I'd turned my back on education for ever. My mum and dad were on the verge of disowning me. I was out in the real world now, and had to make it as a pro, or else – as my parents were fond of pointing out – I'd be spending the rest of my life cleaning out public toilets. Besides, compared to what I was doing in the evenings, obsessing about the tempo of my downswing and craving the endorsement of an errant parrot seemed like sanity itself.

That October, in order to cover my board at home and fees on the amateur circuit the following year, I'd taken a job as a waiter in the carvery of one of Nottingham's most commercial hotels, the Cresthouse. I'd never worked as a waiter (or at all for that matter) before, but the premise seemed simple enough: turn up, stick on a bow tie, switch your body to autopilot and your mind to the thirteenth green at the Augusta National, then wake up a few hours later several pounds richer. Millions of students and dropouts do the same thing every year. The only differences are that when they turn their mind off, they dream about sex or what's on telly that night, not the thirteenth at the Augusta National, and their boss isn't Big John Stegley.

'What I'm talking about, pacifically, Tom, is shit,' Big John Stegley explained to me the first time I met him. 'When shit falls, it goes down. And you're right at the bottom of the ladder, so it will probably fall on you. If you can learn that, you'll go far in this business. Look at me! I learned the hard way, but here I am, now, the restaurant manager at one of Nottingham's best hotels. You could be me, in twenty-five years. But only if you remember that: shit falls.'

Stegley met me and immediately saw a younger version of himself. Personally, I couldn't quite see it. Not only did my new employer have a Ford Cortina driver's moustache, pudding-bowl hair, at least six stone of excess blubber and an annoying habit of singing Christmas carols into your face in their entirety, he was also the special breed of cretin who doesn't just say 'pacifically' when he means 'specifically' but bristles with pride about it. In short, I'd have rather been adopted by Jim Davidson.

'Listen, Tom. I've been sixteen. I know how it is. To be pacific, I'm saying you're young, you're horny, your mind isn't quite on the job. You don't want to be cleaning cutlery. You want to be out on the town, sniffin' around. But one day you'll be the one telling some other lackey to clean the cutlery. And how will you feel then? You'll feel like me. And that feels good, let me tell you. Stick with me, fella. We're going to make you a star. You could be head waiter by the time you're thirty.'

Prior to my first day at the Cresthouse, I'd envisaged myself sashaying into a room full of inferior beings, boggling their minds with my tales of golfing excellence, then moving on, safe in the knowledge that I'd made a necessary pit stop on the road to fame and expended precious little unwarranted energy in the process. What I hadn't envisaged was being turned into someone's *project*. What did the guy see in me? I was sullen, monosyllabic, and smashed an average of three plates per shift. Yet here I was, my hours getting ever longer, leaving less time for parrot bonding and golf. This couldn't go on. But I'd promised my parents I'd be working until at least the end of February, so resigning was out of the question.

'You enjoying working here, Tom?' enquired Stegley, as I slouched inefficiently against the kitchen hotplate, tugging at my bow tie.

'Well, I—'

'I knew you were! That's a lad. Keep up the good work!'

There was only one thing for it: I was going to have to get myself fired.

This wasn't as easy as it sounds. In Stegley's eyes, a smashed plate coming from me wasn't so much a costly error as a vital stumble on the rocky road to catering utopia. Try as I might, I couldn't do a thing wrong. If a sous chef told me, 'Cheer up! It might never happen!', and I replied insolently, 'It already has: my hamster was run over by a JCB this morning,' Stegley would choose that exact moment to hotfoot it in the direction of a burning sausage on the opposite side of the kitchen. If I hid the head chef's favourite ladle in the fork drawer, I'd return three minutes later to find it returned to its rightful place in the kitchen. If I offended customers, or used condiments to daub modern art expressions on their tuxedos, I was let off like an overzealous child at a family barbecue.

Gathering that my actions were invisible to the people around me, I opted for the indelible mark of ink, graffiti-ing Stegley's beloved Carvery Diary with entries as diverse as: '3 p.m. Watch *Lovejoy* with Norwich City Reserve Squad' and '4.20 p.m. Make Sheffield Town Hall burst into tears'. Nobody seemed to notice.

Then, just as I was at my most worn down, I saw my chance.

I knew I recognized the curly-haired, Jewish-looking man with the John Lennon glasses from the moment he walked in, but it wasn't until I spoke to him that I realized he was David Baddiel. This was back around the time of the first series of *The Mary Whitehouse Experience*, long before Baddiel became a reluctant lad icon, but I knew him all right. I'd seen his show – I think I was waiting for a video of the 1988 USPGA Championship to rewind at the time – and even laughed at it. But I wasn't going to let that stand in the way of my masterplan.

'Can I take your order? Our starters today are the soup and the prawn cocktail,' I said to Baddiel and his dining partner.

'I'll have the soup please,' said Baddiel.

Obediently, I transported Baddiel's order into the kitchen, opened one of the huge tureens on the worktop and slopped a couple of ladlefuls of steaming vegetabley slush into a bowl. I then opened one of the small fridges used primarily for cream and slotted the bowl on the top shelf. After that, I went behind the glass cleaner and began working on my backswing.

My problem recently had been a tendency to let my hands slip slightly behind the ball at the address position. So, keeping an eye out for chefs, I went to work on that. I felt I had the trouble truly licked after ten minutes or so, and returned to the soup.

I dipped a finger (scrupulously clean: don't worry, David) into the brown murk. It was edging beyond lukewarm, verging on deathly: perfect, in other words. I gave it a stir anyway, for good luck. Making double-sure that Stegley was at his favoured front-desk post, only three or four yards to the right of Baddiel's table, I prepared a starter for Baddiel's friend, returned to the restaurant floor, set the trap, and snuck away to wait for the inevitable.

It took about thirty seconds.

'Er . . . Waiter?' said Baddiel.

Ever alert, I scuttled back over to his table. 'Yes? How can I help?' I said, ensuring this was loud enough for Stegley to hear.

'Er, this soup you've brought me is cold.'

'Really,' I said. 'Are you sure? This really is extremely good soup!'

'It really is very, very cold. It doesn't taste like it's been heated up at all!' exclaimed Baddiel, getting slightly upset now.

'Actually, you're right. I know! I'm really sorry! Let me get you some more!'

Seconds after I'd crashed through the heavy kitchen doors, Stegley was on me – just as I'd planned.

'What was all that about?' he asked.

'Cold soup,' I replied.

'Yes, I realize that. Why is it cold? The soup in the tureen isn't cold, is it?'

'No.'

'So why is it cold?'

'Because I left it for a few minutes while I was practising my backswing.'

'Practising your what?'

'My backswing. For golf.'

'What the hell were you doing that for when you should have been working?'

'I was bored.'

'You haven't got time to be bored. Do you know who that guy is you've just given cold soup to?'

'Yeah, he's David Baddiel. Off the telly.'

'And do you know what happens when we serve cold food to people off the telly? They tell other people off the telly how rubbish our restaurant is, and then nobody off the telly ever comes here.' He crouched and put an arm around me, lowering his voice. 'Now – I don't want that to happen again. But, having said that, I'd also like to congratulate you. That show of his is crap. Load of bloody student rubbish!'

As he turned to walk away, still chuckling, he remembered something. 'Oh, and Tom? I've put you down for an extra eight-hour shift next week. Hope that's OK.'

The following day, I admitted defeat, and handed in my notice.

The important thing now was keeping my parents under the impression that I was still in gainful employment for as long as was humanly possible. It wasn't really that I needed somewhere warm to eat and sleep, more that I needed a taxi driver for competitions, at least until I gained my driving licence later (hopefully) in the year. The subterfuge was elaborate, but I slipped into a routine easily enough. Five days a week, my dad would drop me at the trade entrance of the Cresthouse. And, five days a week, I would wave good-bye, count to twenty, then nip around the corner to catch the number thirty-five. My 'shifts' lasted exactly as long as I fancied staying at Cripsley, plus an hour for the bus journeys. Clubs weren't a problem; I kept them up at Cripsley, in my locker.

For the moment, money was tight, but I knew I could survive. I had roughly seven hundred pounds saved. Allowing for board, entrance fees and petrol money, I reckoned that would enable me to remain a man of leisure until around early May, at which point I'd look for another waiter's position, hopefully without career prospects. The season would start in earnest in just over two months. The chart on my bedroom wall, where I'd neatly (I normally have the handwriting of a five-year-old, but for some reason not when it comes to golf planning) mapped out next year's fixtures, beckoned. Soon we would see if all this practice was worth it. I still had Cripsley virtually to myself. Ken was still on his perch (on the first fine day of spring he would mysteriously fly away for ever). The other juniors seemed to be permanently indoors, giving me a head start. The quiet was deafening. I wore big trousers and felt invisible and picked up my practice balls with a plastic tube that went 'klop'. The spikes on my shoes made a satisfying clack as I walked across the car park asphalt. I could hit my six-iron like Davis Love III. I was a liar, a charlatan and a quitter.

Golf would never feel so special again.

15

I was the first to spot the Mercedes behind us, as we descended the hill to Mapperley Golf Club, the venue for the 1992 Nottinghamshire Junior County Trials. The way it swerved from one grass verge to the other could have passed for ballet in some far-off, apocalyptic era. Later, my dad would lower his voice in a cod-mystical way and say that as soon as he saw the car in his rear-view mirror, he had sensed that something terrible would happen. Not a premonition, just a recognition of bad driving, I realize now. At the time, however, I didn't care. I had my own premonition: I was going to be in that car before the end of the day, even if it meant deceiving my parents even more than I had done already.

Long before the driver's face began to crystallize, I knew there was only one man who could be behind the wheel. Since the demise of the old pro shop, Nick

Bellamy had been an enigmatic figure in my life, slouching into view in all the least likely places to boast of implausible golfing and sexual accomplishments, then vanishing for weeks, even months, on end. Was he still a member of Cripsley? What precisely did he do for a living? The answers to questions like these were no less elusive than the meaning of life itself.

He certainly wasn't here to play in the junior county trials: he was too old and, besides, he'd always lampooned the county golf scene. So what *was* he doing here? I sneaked another look out of the back window. The Merc's front bumper was now a matter of inches away from the Sphincter's rear one. Arms flailing, Nick was moulding his features into a familiar expression – familiar, because it was the one that Nutty Graham, the man in the dirty overcoat who stood outside my school gates soliciting pupils for spare milk, used to adopt just before shouting, 'Full cream! No semi-skimmed today!!' at passers-by. I knew he was trouble (Nick, that is; Nutty Graham was harmless by comparison). If I was going to consolidate my winter's practice in this, the first important tournament of the season, I'd do well to keep him at fairway's length. Today, after all, was what I had been working so antisocially for, what I had been waiting virtually for ever for. The Official Dawn of New Tom. The exact thing that I'd made my fingers bleed and served David Baddiel cold soup for. From here to my thirteenth and final British Open victory, in the summer of 2022, this was a job, not a hobby, and I needed pointless distractions like I needed a future waiting on tables for a living.

'Hi, Nick!' I said, bounding across the car park. 'Nice wheels. Wanna caddy for me?'

Over the winter, as a supplement to my practice routine, I'd pored over the printed works of history's greatest thinkers: Jack Nicklaus, Nick Faldo, Seve Ballesteros, Tom Watson. Mindful of the very determined way in which these men had sacrificed their adolescence in order to realize sporting perfection, I had begun to see myself as the archetypal loner: the kind of kid who would quite happily turn down a ride in a flashy car or an invite to a happening party for the chance to practise his mid-length bunker shots in a hailstorm. What I hadn't realized was how easy it was to see myself this way when nobody *was* offering me a ride in a flashy car or an invite to a happening party (or a ride in a happening party or an invite to a flashy car, for that matter). Now that someone *might* have been about to, I had a choice: knuckle down like a total square, or piss about like any normal sixteen-year-old? Having always believed in going with your gut feeling, I took marginally under three seconds to opt for pissing about.

I played the first nine holes as if I'd spent the winter working preternaturally hard on my badminton, then things really started to come apart. While Nick regaled me with details of Trevor the DJ's latest public urination and mimicked my playing partners, I made an abortive attempt to compile some sort of half-respectable score, then began to rationalize my ineptitude: the course was badly maintained, with the architectural intricacy of a sheep farm. The county trials was a pointless event. Regardless of who did what on the day, everyone knew that the top places in the squad would go to Worksop players. I'd probably make the team regardless, as an also-ran, but if I was truly self-disciplined in my role as loner, I shouldn't care either way. 'Making it' to me didn't mean craving the approval of the sycophantic Notts Union of Golf Clubs in-crowd; it meant achieving a handicap of zero – the elusive scratch – by the end of the year.

Tossing my card dispassionately onto the county selector's desk, I could think of several reasons not to hotfoot it out of Mapperley, none of which were as persuasive as the feeling in the pit of my stomach that if I stayed in the place a moment longer or was forced to reveal my score to one more Worksop parent I might have to start breaking furniture. If you're behaving like a proper sportsman in golf, etiquette suggests that, even if you've played like a moron, you should stick around and don your blazer for the prize-giving – support others, in the way you hoped they would support you, in other words. I decided, just this once, etiquette could swivel. In the car park, I ran into Mousey, who, having notched up a score of ninety-three and fallen out with both his playing partners (they said he talked like a girl; he hid some sheep shit in their bags), expressed similar sentiments.

'Bloody Mickey Mouse course, isn't it?' I said. Whenever we messed up on a particularly hilly or difficult course, we said, 'Bloody Mickey Mouse course.'

'I would have scored better halfway up Ben Nevis,' said Mousey.

'You boys fancy a lift?' said Nick, who'd popped up out of nowhere. He was back at the wheel of the Merc, and it was the offer I'd been waiting for. I looked longingly at the flawless curves, the gunmetal finish, the proud grille and headlights. It belonged to Nick's dad, of course, but that didn't make it any less impressive. Why couldn't my dad have a car like that, which he'd let me drive to tournaments in which I had no interest, for no apparent reason?

The plan had been for me to get a lift back with Bob Boffinger, who would be leaving in another hour or two. I thought about the final part of my conversation with my dad as he dropped me off that morning. (Dad: Now, you'll get a lift back with Bob, won't you? Me: Of course. Dad: You promise you won't go with Nick? Me: Don't be silly. You know me better than that. He's a maniac.) Then I picked it up and put it into a cupboard at the back of my mind marked 'Give A Shit?', which I'd been using a lot lately.

I turned to Nick, unable not to smile. 'What the hell do *you* think?' I said.

Watching from afar as Nick manoeuvred an Austin Allegro into a wheelie bin on a peaceful private cul-de-sac was one thing; sitting directly behind him as he hurtled down a heaving, narrow suburban street in a 2.5-litre death machine was something else entirely. If you discounted a couple of visits to Silverstone and Castle Donington, I had until this point only had one first-hand experience of genuinely fast driving: the time when I was four and my appendix burst, and my dad, foot stapled to the floor, had bravely risked the Sphincter's life in order to save mine. But next to this, that was an underwater slug race. As we careered towards them, the red lights seemed to change shape and show deference to the Merc, like normally hard-hearted bouncers spotting an esteemed punter in the queue. In our wake, pensioners didn't so much jump out of the way as freeze in the manner of mortal souls dealing with a paranormal force. As we clasped corners and shaved bends, gravity seemed to suck extra-hard in empathy.

After twenty minutes of illegal right turns, screeching brakes and obscure T-junctions, we rounded a corner and finally found ourselves back in front of a familiar-looking gate. On top of the gate was a sign. It said: 'Mapperley Golf Club'.

Out of it came a red Ford Fiesta XR3i, containing three members of the junior team from Sherwood Forest Golf Club.

'Are you thinking what I'm thinking?' asked Nick.

I knew what was coming next. This was no longer sheer hedonism; this was pride. Sherwood Forest juniors had beaten us in the league every year since 1982, and, if you ignored Worksop, probably represented Cripsley junior section's archest enemies. So what if we didn't even know the names of the kids in the car? This wasn't about specifics; it was about revenge. Through four red lights, we stayed glued to the Fiesta's tail. Lorries, bollards, no-waiting zones, pedestrians – these things were just scenery. At the junction with Carlton Hill, we nosed in front. But these boys clearly had local knowledge on their side. As we passed the Public Hair barbers' shop, we realized they'd dangled a right-only-lane carrot in front of our noses.

Now they were a couple of car lengths in front. At the pelican crossing before Gedling village, Nick decided it was time to get mean, swerving neatly around a Chihuahua and edging back level with the XR3i. By the time we reached the turn into Richmond Avenue, there was a very real possibility of us going past on the bend, where the road opened up for the bus lane. As Nick floored the accelerator and whipped around a bollard, I saw that it was actually happening: Cripsley were finally beating Sherwood at something! As we scorched past, hollering out of the open window, the Fiesta seemed to slow and admit defeat. From the back seat, I turned to give our enemies one final two-fingered salute.

And saw that they had stopped for fish and chips.

His adrenalin undiminished, Nick pressed on. I surreptitiously checked the speedometer: seventy now, in a forty-mile-an-hour zone. It was obvious he could handle it, but my big worry was the hairpin bend, coming up in about half a mile, where Mapperley turned into St Annes and the downhill slope to the city centre kicked in. Having been to primary school nearby, I'd seen the aftermath of smash-ups there: spacious family estate cars transformed into fun-size runabouts with one flippant tap of the accelerator. I thought about pointing this out to Nick, but concluded it would make me look squarer than a paving slab. Still, I decided now might be as useful a time as any to put my seat belt on.

'What's the matter, Tom?' asked Nick, clocking me in the mirror. 'You getting scared? Don't worry. I've driven on a professional rally track, y'know.'

He hardly had time to finish the sentence when we went in to the spin.

I remember it all in a series of freeze-frames now –

the wheels seemingly slipping out from underneath us, the Volvo looming, the surprisingly soft and yielding impact, the big stone wall a couple of inches from my nose. The collision wasn't remarkably scary, or life-altering, or dissonant, just remarkably slow even though, since Nick was driving at seventy-five miles per hour at the time, it cannot have taken more than a second or two. It was only when I stumbled out onto the pavement and went over the facts that I realized how lucky we'd been.

1. We had been in a high-speed, head-on collision with a Volvo.

2. We were all unharmed, if you ignored Nick's whiplash and Mousey's temporary loss of the power of speech.

3. I'd buckled my seat belt approximately point two of a second before impact.

4. The Volvo's exterior suggested that it had crashed at speed, but into a paper aeroplane.

5. The Merc looked as if a giant had picked it up, folded it in three, used it as chewing gum for twenty minutes, then spat it out.

6. If you drove past the scene, you'd look solemnly at the Merc in the knowledge that anyone who had been in it was going to spend the rest of his life in un-bearable agony, but only if he was very lucky.

7. Nick might be doing precisely that, when his dad found out about this.

For a moment, we were bona-fide local news: cars slowed, passengers stared, police and ambulancemen comforted, pedestrians lingered. It was tempting to make the most of the attention and complain about a partially fractured throat, but that would have been dishonest. I was no more shaken than I might have been if I'd fallen out of a dodgem. In fact, after the commotion dissipated, the entire experience swiftly became about as mundane as any other occasion when you have to spend an hour sitting on a mashed-in stone wall staring at the launderette across the road. I occupied myself by planning a way to keep all this from my parents, and wondering how I'd get home. After that, all I could do was wait for the inevitable: Bob Boffinger rounding the corner on his way back to Cripsley, double-taking at the view out of his side window like a man discovering he has woken up in the arms of a horse, and very nearly causing yet more heartache for Nottingham's overworked emergency services.

Then, one by one, we were all at it. First Ashley in the wheezing seventy-quid Fiesta his dad bought him for Christmas, then Robin in an obscure Japanese monstrosity known only as the Tank, then myself in the inherited Sphincter, then finally – quite a lot later – Jamie in (typical!) the brand new Vauxhall Corsa his parents presented him with on his seventeenth birthday. If Nick's crash passed quickly into Cripsley folklore, we learned approximately nothing from it. No matter how painstakingly our parents or driving instructors had grilled us on the rules of the road during our time as provisional licence holders, from the moment we passed our tests our frame of motoring reference stretched only as far as the space between the Dukes of Hazzard and Starsky and Hutch. Anything else was for grandads. We drove like rave musicians, not golfers. We all crashed and burned (almost literally in Ashley's case: he narrowly escaped when his Fiesta caught fire on the way back from a tournament in Staffordshire). We all wanted to. We all screamed things like 'Sheep', 'Gigolo Whippet' and 'Skirting Board' out of the window at passers-by while we did it.

Then, when we had done that, we started driving really, really slowly. Not safe slowly, but stupid slowly. The kind of slowly where you pack eight teenagers into the car, drive at eleven miles per hour in a forty-mile-per-hour zone for no sensible reason, wait while a queue of thirty or so cars builds up behind you, wait again until one of them tries to pass you, then, as they do, suddenly start driving *very very quickly* and pulling faces at them.

When we tired of the simple pleasures of holding up traffic, props were introduced. These were usually random plastic body parts, brought along by Ben, whose dad taught Biology at one of Cripsley's comprehensive schools. A fully reclined seat and a carefully placed endoskeleton could cause havoc in a traffic jam, but timing and placement could make the all-important difference between a convincing ghostly driver and a clavicle in the face. Far simpler yet equally satisfying was Wave Hello, Say Goodbye, the game where the driver turns the steering wheel from below with his real arms, while simultaneously waving to the car next to him with his fake ones. Failing that, there was always Spleen Throwing. This was the most adapt-able game, in that all it involved was a good throwing arm, a car (parked or moving – it didn't matter) with an open window or sunroof, and one of the apparently limitless number of plastic spleens that Ben's dad brought home from work. We didn't always hit our target, but even the best basketball players miss the hoop sometimes. And, besides, they have an advantage: they're throwing balls, not spleens.

When I look back and try to pinpoint the moment in my life when I first felt more man than boy, I don't think of stubble or voting slips or fumbling teenage sex; I think of driving at thirty miles over the speed limit, fifteen minutes after passing my driving test. One of the indignities of being an obsessive junior golfer is being made to feel that you're a lot younger than you are. At eighteen, you can conceivably still be a lowly 'junior'; at twenty-one, an only marginally more impressive 'youth'. Long after your college lecturers have started to respect you as an adult and your school uniform has gone to the charity shop, your golfing superiors are admonishing you for wearing trainers and talking down to you in the kind of tone that warns of after-game detentions. In space, no one can hear you scream. In a golf club, no one can hear your voice break. The introduction of a screech of teenage brakes into this environment is louder than bombs. By driving up to the golf course by our own volition, we were saying many things to the old grouchbags at Cripsley that our golf had only hinted at: 'Fear me! I'm coming up behind you! I'm bigger than you now, and soon I'm going to be even bigger than that!' It wasn't a co-incidence that all but a couple of us passed our driving test before our eighteenth birthday. It was a downright prerequisite. Without a car, we were trapped in a mini-kingdom where we could be punished for anything from an overhit three-wood to a wayward denim shirt. With a car, we were free.

Adults always talked approvingly about cars that would get them 'from A to B'. We didn't see much fun in that. We wanted vehicles that would get us from D to M, via C, X and, if at all possible, G. Every journey, whether it was to McDonald's in Cripsley town centre or the Sandmoor Future Masters in Leeds, was an adventure. I had longed for a driving licence to liberate me from reliance on my dad for lifts and furnish me with the independence to stay at the golf course for as long as I pleased. Countless times I had spread out my competition entry forms on my bedroom floor and dreamed of the time when I could take off to any amateur golf tournament I fancied. I'd looked at the course names – Beau Desert, Coxmoor, Whittington Barracks – and pined for pines, gorged on gorse. What exactly was a desert doing in Staffordshire and where did a beau fit into it? What was a barracks doing on a golf course? I felt like the answers to questions like these could change my life. But I hadn't even guessed at the unadulterated thrill of cramming five of your best friends into a vehicle that you're not responsible for and driving to your local garden centre for no obvious purpose besides seeing how many handbrake turns you can do before you make your tyres bald. I'd also overlooked the way a fragile ego can feast on the superficial popularity that can come from being the Man with the Lifts. Most heinously of all, I'd neglected to allow for the caprices and flaws of adolescent will-power. Again.

However, perhaps I'm being a little harsh on myself. On all of us. Was driving more fun than golf? Sometimes. But, in the long run, probably not. We probably sensed, deep down, that before long we'd look upon it in the same way as our parents did, and get behind the wheel with the awe drained from our soul and replaced by a sense of grim inevitability. Golf, on the other hand, would be here for ever. If it wasn't, why would so many of the living dead play it?

I now know that I am highly likely to relive the sensation of hitting a crisp, high, drawing three-iron over a lake into the heart of an elevated green or sinking a forty-foot putt over a hog's back green – potentially several times. Whether I will again find six close friends willing to cramp themselves onto the back seat of my hatchback, shout 'Pylon Lover!' at mid-afternoon shoppers and wave plastic body parts out of the window is, however, very much in doubt (though don't think for a minute I don't live in hope). Unless you're Michael Schumacher or a sales rep, driving is a duty which dresses itself up as an adventure for a fleeting, elusive moment. But golf, if you genuinely love it, is with you for *life* as an adventure – the exciting bits, the stressful bits, the crap bits, the dangerous bits – whether you like it or not. You can't run from it, you can't hide from it, and you can't use the harsh realities of the outside world to devitalize it. Believe me on this one: I speak with the long-suffering air of someone who, as he navigated the final, jagged passage to adulthood, had a bloody good go at doing all three.

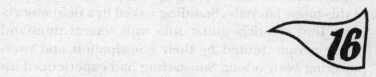

I had often heard about Sunstarling during my stint as
golf pariah. Within the social circle surrounding my
family, he was a shadowy legend, whose cautionary tale
could be viewed as the batik cushion propping up an
entire generation's morals. Although he was often
spoken of with affection by my parents and their
friends, I never met him, and whether he was fact or
fiction remained unclear – as did whether Sunstarling
was the name he used when he went to sign on for his
dole money – but I felt I knew his story almost as well
as I knew my own. In the late sixties, Sunstarling had
been Wales's star junior golfer, with a handicap of 0.4,
a set of hand-tailored clubs, a place in the England
youth squad, a swing like whipped cream,* and the

* My family and their friends didn't use phrases like 'a swing like whipped
cream', but, nevertheless, this was how I imagined it.

distinction of 'once being bought a drink by Tony Jacklin'. His future as the missing link between Tom Weiskopf and Jack Nicklaus had looked guaranteed until, at eighteen, he'd been invited to the Isle of Wight Rock Festival by a non-golfing friend, the angel of this hippy fairytale. Standing naked in a field absorbing a Jimi Hendrix guitar solo with several thousand young people united by their constipation and overpowering body odour, Sunstarling had experienced his epiphany: from that moment on, he would renounce uptight old golf and its venal mores, and devote his life to 'getting down with the land' (whatever that meant) and 'working on his music'.

I had three main problems with the story. One: it never seemed to end properly – we never found out just what Sunstarling *did* with 'his music'. Two: nobody ever mentioned who he gave his clubs to. And three: it all sounded a bit smelly.

At the same time, however, a part of me is jealous of Sunstarling. When *my* life-re-evaluating revelation came to *me*, it didn't come in the form of a Hendrix guitar solo. *I* didn't see God in the opening chords of The Who's 'Won't Get Fooled Again'. I didn't even get hip in time to bliss out to the Stone Roses at Spike Island. No. When I saw my life change direction in front of my eyes, the future spoke to me through the medium of David Byrne.

David look-at-me-I'm-so-weird-with-my-strange-jerky-

head-movements-and-Third-World-rhythms-but-kind-
of-safe-with-it Byrne.

David Byrne used to be the lead singer of Talking
Heads, the New York group who came out of the New
Wave movement and, with 1979's *Remain In Light* and
1980's *Fear Of Music*, made two of my favourite albums
of all time. In July 1992, however, I was only dimly,
reluctantly, aware of this. By July 1992, Talking Heads
were long extinct and Byrne had reinvented himself as
the kind of curtain-haired, early nineties, sensitive solo
artist who exists purely to help ease baby-boomers into
musical middle-age and its inexorable co-conspirator,
world music. This, I'm slightly ashamed to confess, is
The Man Who Changed The Course Of My Life. My
First Ever Gig. Which I Saw With My Parents And Their
Friends. From A Sitting-Down Vantage Point.

Still, Byrne certainly had been a genius and icono-
clast at one point in his career, even if he wasn't any
more. He didn't interest me because of his kooky
syllables or pseudo-Brazilian tunes so much as because
he was *playing music, at a louder-than-average volume,*
much of which seemed to whisper to me that there was
more to life than breaking par in the Midland Youths
Championship. The new songs might have been
mediocre, but the old ones were like a revelatory
trigger to an amnesiac. Hold on: I know every word of
this, I thought for the third time, and suddenly I was
blinded by the light. Yes, I had actually *liked* music

before I took up golf, hadn't I! I *still* liked music, if only I could admit it to myself! It was *good* to be part of a huge group of people who weren't going to let the fact that they had shot eighty-one/handed their essay in late/had a lousy day at work that day stop them having a good time together! That girl sitting directly in front of me *was* pretty sexy!

Let's just say David Byrne caught me at a weak moment.

By July 1992, I'd been competing on the amateur golf circuit for four solid months and working in my second stretch as a waiter for three. During this period I'd travelled from one end of the country to the other, signed up for every tournament I could, bled my bank account dry, twanged the patience of the people closest to me, finished in the top ten of two tournaments, snapped the shaft of four clubs over my knee, and won one set of 'deluxe' tee pegs. I'd also been forced to endure more easy-listening ambience tapes than I would inflict on my worst enemy, and my weight had dropped from comfortably over ten stone to just under nine (not ideal, since I'm roughly six foot tall). It would be a massive understatement to say that things weren't progressing fully as well as planned. It would be a massive understatement to say things weren't progressing a *quarter* as well as planned.

My typical working day would progress as follows:

3.00 a.m. Wake up with jolt from recurring nightmare

involving last place finish in that day's tournament.

4.00 a.m. Return to fitful sleep, having finally convinced myself nightmare wasn't real.

6.30 a.m. Get up and rush to window in order to check trees and bushes for wind strength.

6.31 a.m. Suffer anxiety attack, having deduced that wind is blowing in excess of five miles per hour.

6.45 a.m. Clean clubs covertly with bathroom nailbrush and mum's face flannel.

7.00 a.m. Watch Fred Couples video and practise positive visualization.

9.00 a.m. Get lost in nondescript Black Country village while searching for tournament venue.

9.25 a.m. Arrive at venue in panic. Suffer second anxiety attack as sky darkens.

9.26 a.m. Scramble over to pro shop to stock up on balls and tee pegs, while simultaneously trying to put on waterproof bottoms.

9.27 a.m. Fall over errant waterproof bottom-leg hole and land face first on putting green to horror of club president.

9.28 a.m. Arrive panting on first tee and meet allotted playing partners for the day, Barry and Roy, both of whom try to conceal distaste at my outmoded equipment.

9.29 a.m. Hit tee shot in what appears to be the perfect direction, only to be told by Roy that I have dunked ball into local sewer.

1.00 p.m. Arrive in clubhouse, having shot fifth worst score in entire field.

1.30 p.m. Stride to first tee for second round, revitalized by complimentary teacakes. Snarl encouragement to myself under breath, only to be given funny look by passing greenkeeper.

3.00 p.m. Decide it's time to get mean and stop being the course's 'bitch'.

3.01 p.m. Hook ball into neighbouring farmland, scaring cows.

5.00 p.m. Begin journey home.

5.02 p.m. Start to philosophize and rationalize mistakes. Use words like 'concentration', 'smooth', 'cocooned', 'Worksop' and 'buttclunk'.

6.45 p.m. Begin waiting shift at local theme pub. Get called 'lazy student fucker' by restaurant supervisor.

8.00 p.m. Get into argument over pronunciation of 'chicken escalopes' with fat chef.

9.00 p.m. Begin to wonder why there are only two waiting staff catering for forty-two tables. Perceive shedding of final supply of adipose tissue.

9.30 p.m. Accidentally on purpose spill horseradish sauce over strange beardy regular who attempts to befriend me by calling me 'Tommy'.

10.00 p.m. Begin to go slowly insane to the sound of Kate Bush and Peter Gabriel's hit duet, 'Don't Give Up'.

10.11 p.m. Serve girl from my old school who I used

to fancy. Ask her what she is doing now. She says A levels. She asks me same question. I say golf, and, well, this, what I'm doing right now. Conversation dies.

10.41 p.m. 'Don't Give Up' rolls around again. Kate and Peter actually feel like they're doing forward rolls in my brain now, sending me a message. Message seems to be 'don't give up'. Submessage seems to be nothing.

11.40 p.m. Stagger home across building site still in bow tie, jeered at by smoking juvenile delinquents, but comforted by fact that I have hidden fat chef's free supper beneath bar.

12.10 a.m. Lie in bed replaying day's golf in head: yardages, swings, concentration levels. Everything goes better. I win. Pete and Kate continue to sing. Why?

Had I thrown my eggs so forcefully into one basket that they'd smashed?

One thing was for certain: I was playing out the stereotype of the sporting hero who scrimps and saves and sacrifices and slaves then reaps the rewards on the playing field, with one missing element – the vital, final one. Granted, I still waved artificial limbs out of car windows and made prank phone calls to pizza-delivery companies, but I worked hard on my golf too, particularly in my head. Everything I'd read about the history of the game told me that my story would have a happy ending, but I was starting to get impatient. My handicap hung in limbo: two one week, three the next.

Terrific by most standards, but somewhat lacklustre by the constricted, fanatical ones I'd set for myself. With no school or college to bolster me and the bemused gaze of my parents turning more sceptical with every tournament I botched, golf defined me to an extent that it never had before – which would have been fine, had I been playing it well or feeling comfortable within its pedantic, conservative social infrastructure. Unfortunately, I was doing neither, and it was starting to scare me. The question 'What the hell am I doing here?' was only just below the surface, tempting me to abandon my childish vanity and look it straight in the face.

I arrived in July at the Beau Desert Stag tournament in Staffordshire knowing that it was one of my favourite competitions of the year, at one of the most testing courses in the Midlands, and that even if I played brilliantly in it, I'd still be thinking about all the opportunities, money and energy I'd wasted earlier in the year. In that frame of mind, something had to snap, but for once it wasn't the shaft of my five-iron. I forget my score now, perhaps because it was the first one that year that I didn't record on my wallchart, but I'm almost certain that on any other day I could have beaten it blindfolded, with a golf bag full of garden hoes and one hand tied behind my back.

By the eleventh hole of the afternoon round, I'd reached the single lowest point of my golfing existence.

My tee shot had been ostensibly a thing of utmost splendour, sailing over a ridge into what I'd presumed would be a scrumptious lie in the middle of the fairway, but I'd skipped down the hill only to find it nestling in the tracks of some abstruse burrowing animal – an elephant, by the looks of things. When this sort of thing happens on TV, a long delay ensues as the professional in question calls in a referee from the opposite side of the course, who leafs through his local rules book until he happens upon Rule 593.2, 'Ball buried in woolly mammoth shit', at which point he allows the pro to remove his missile and drop it without penalty onto some more verdant terrain a couple of yards away. For an amateur like me, however, there was no such relief.

I peered ahead, beyond a channel of heather, over a cavernous bunker, to the flagstick, which, from what I could work out from my yardage chart, was located somewhere in North Kenya. The most depressing aspect wasn't the impending task's gruelling nature, but its devastating lack of significance. Even if I pulled it off, my playing partners, Barry and Roy, would still think I was just another ploddingly decent low handi- cap golfer who couldn't handle the pressure of tournament play. I'd still go to bed that night with a reef knot in my stomach and a slow-motion replay of my round on repeat play in my head. My dad, who was walking round the course watching me, would still look at me in that way that simultaneously said, 'Hard luck,' and 'How much longer?'

Then it hit me. This didn't need to be a dead end. There was *one* way of changing this. If I just picked my ball up, shook hands with my playing partners, walked peacefully back to the car and stopped worrying about tomorrow, everything would be OK. Sure, it would be an irresponsible act, contravening every rule of decorum and conduct that had been drilled into us by our superiors, but what if I gave it a go? *Could it make me feel any worse?*

'Barry, Roy,' I said, picking my ball up. 'I'm going in.'

'You're going in where?' said Barry and Roy.

'In from the course. Away from here.'

'Oh,' said Barry and Roy.

And that was all it took.

As I walked back to the car, I kept checking behind me, but nothing exploded. Odder still, no one struck me down into a blazing pit to roast for Satan's delectation. *It was all so easy.* Moreover, it felt *good*.

Journeys back from tournaments with my dad invariably involved an extensive post-mortem – me berating my fortune and self-discipline, my dad trying to help in whatever psychological way he could, while simultaneously dropping subtle hints about a return to college. This one was an anomaly. Why break the peace inside my head with inane chatter? For once, it felt glorious to shut the sodding hell up, and it was only as we passed back over the Nottinghamshire border that one of us finally punctured the silence.

'I've got a spare ticket to a concert tonight, if you fancy it,' said my dad.

He could have said it was for David Byrne. He could have said it was for Val Doonican. He could have said it was for an inanimate carbon rod. By then, it didn't matter. I was his.

Once unlocked, the floodgates slid open with ease. David Byrne begat Neil Young, who begat Sonic Youth, who begat (much to their own chagrin, I'm sure) Smashing Pumpkins. Within a month, I'd quit my job at the theme pub, enrolled for a Media Studies course at South Nottinghamshire College, and raided every vaguely bohemian, rebellious record collection I could lay my sweaty, deprived mitts on. I'd shut music out of my life for the entire period that most people spend discovering it, and now I had some serious catching up to do. Having spent the previous few months ricocheting between the personalities of a seventeen-year-old (in the pro shop), a thirteen-year-old (in the clubhouse) and a thirty-five-year-old (on the course), it came as a comfort to find out that, with music by my side, I could be seventeen all the time.

A jumped-up little git, in other words.

For so long, I had wondered if I was the one who was

wrong for feeling uneasy about the prospect of wearing baggy slacks and ridiculously tight polyester sweaters. I had seen the half-mocking, half-bewildered looks on my friends' faces and fretted about the doomy, out-of-kilter songs my dad made them endure as he drove us to tournaments. I had puzzled over whether it was just me who put his sun visor on, looked at his reflection in the mirror, and thought, You look a bit of a tosser, don't you? I had asked myself if it was me alone who heard echoes of the Third Reich in the ritual of sucking up to an estate agent from Southwell and calling him 'Mr Captain'. Rock music helped clear up these issues for me, reassured me that I might have been right after all, and left me a more self-assured individual. But it did more than that, too. It made me a missionary for its cause.

Recently, I've gone back to some of the songs that soundtracked the transitionary period of my life that followed my seventeenth birthday. The vast majority sound bloody awful – the equivalent of several heavy pieces of furniture falling down some stairs while a pissed-off teenager shouts about the eternal injustice of being made to tidy his bedroom. The odd few still sound terrific, but even those are somewhat different to how I remember them. Sonic Youth's 'Teenage Riot' now sounds like a song about a teenage riot, where I could have sworn it used to be about a teenage riot at a golf club. And someone seems to have doctored my vinyl copy of Soundgarden's 'Rusty Cage' and edited out the bit where the golf officials get strung up by their legs from the iron bars.

Back then, it all sounded like the Truth or, better still, My Truth. Music had shown me the way, and I knew it could show others too. It was just a simple matter of conversion.

'What do you reckon?' I asked Ben and Jamie, as my copy of Smashing Pumpkins's 'Gish' kicked into gear in the antiquated tape player that Fez kept in the basement of the pro shop.

'Sounds like a couple of warlocks fighting to the death over a flank of dead cow,' said Ben.

'I know. Brilliant, isn't it?'

'No. It's shit.'

I knew I'd get them hooked in the end, if I persevered. The problem was that they obviously didn't think I was serious. I could see their point: for the last few years, they'd known me as Tom, their golf buddy. A slightly obsessive golf buddy, with curiously uncompetitive parents, perhaps, but, all the same, not one given to launching into anti-corporate diatribes inspired by the lyrics of New Radiant Storm King. Acknowledging this, I decided I needed to go to extremes and show my commitment to the cause in every facet of my appearance. I let my hair grow, and bought the most profane band T-shirts I could find, wearing them on the car ride to the golf club and showing them off in the general vicinity of the place for as long as my courage would allow, before hurriedly changing into my golf clothes in the locker room.

'WHAT'S THE MATTER WITH YOUR HAIR?' asked Fez as I scuffled into the shop one day. 'YOU LOOK LIKE DOUGAL FROM *THE MAGIC ROUNDABOUT*.'

'I'm growing it,' I explained. 'It's much cooler to have long hair. Haven't you *seen* Evan Dando?'

'EVIL DILDO? WHO'S HE?'

'*E-van Dan-do*. He's the lead singer of the Lemonheads. I'll do you a tape of their album if you want.'

'NEVER HEARD OF THEM. WHY ARE THEY CALLED THE LEMONHEADS?'

'They just are. It's far-out.'

'SOUNDS PRETTY FUCKING STUPID TO ME.'

'Do you like my T-shirt?'

'"TOO DRUNK TO FUCK". WHY ARE YOU WEARING THAT?'

'It's a Dead Kennedys T-shirt. They were an eighties anti-fascist punk band from San Francisco. You should hear them. I think they'd change your life.'

'WELL, I'M NOT SURE I'D WANT TO GO ROUND WEARING A T-SHIRT SAYING THAT. IT'S LIKE GOING ROUND WEARING A T-SHIRT SAYING "MY NOB HAS SHRIVELLED UP".'

By now I had started college again and bought the full student lifestyle package, with its accompanying set of slightly arty mates: a group of people I was quick to portray to my golf friends as at least six times more fascinating than it really was. This included Matt, Richard and Karina, all of whom – though known to get mildly annoyed from time to time – might be surprised to find themselves classed as 'raging, anarchic punk subversives'. With them, I would attend gigs at Nottingham's Rock City, a venue most notorious for the adhesive quality of its floor and the sadism of its bouncers. 'Gigs' here would normally consist of an in-distinguishable sonic mudstorm played by men in plaid shirts, topped off with a face full of sweat courtesy of the crusty with the arse-length dreadlocks who had been standing directly in front of us. This, the four of us agreed, was Living.

I was, in brief, an indie elitist tosser of the highest order. I had seen a couple of rancid, whinging scuzz-rock bands, and bought the badly made, off-the-shoulder bootleg T-shirt, and as a result I thought I was Johnny Rotten, acerbically spitting my rage at everything bourgeois and bloated. What did these pathetic little golf people think they were doing? I scoffed to myself from the front seat of the Sphincter, surveying the scene as I hared across the clubhouse car park to the strains of Mudhoney's 'Touch Me I'm Sick'. What were they gaining with their big cars and afternoons off, and motorized buggies, and healthy lifestyles? Didn't they know there was *more* to life waiting out there?

Confusion was my weapon, and I wielded it in the general direction of the golf course like a giant, out-of-control combine harvester, stopping only to replace my divots and ensure that my polo shirt was tucked in. As my hair crept below ear-level, I could see the strange looks intensify. Passing my driving test helped immeasurably, too. What is this . . . *thing*, with its screeching brakes, complaining music and elongated speeches cribbed from arthouse movies, and why is it corrupting our green Utopia?, I could see them thinking. Well, either that, or, Who's that self-righteous little tosser?

'Didn't get in 'til three a.m. last night,' I told Nick Crawley, a nine-handicap landscape gardener, by way of greeting, as we teed up together for the St John's Bowl. 'Went out to see Pavement last night. They were, y'know, really *angular*.'

'Oh,' said Nick Crawley.

My sole ally seemed to be Robin, who, complete with flowing locks, now looked more like the lead singer of Soul Asylum than Chesney Hawkes. He probably didn't know who Soul Asylum *were*, of course, but I could live with that, since I sensed an anti-establishment thunder within him that I could feed off.

Together we would delight in arriving at Cripsley via the back entrance, adjacent to the thirteenth tee, in our 'disguises': Robin in ripped jeans, backward baseball cap and oversized trainers, me in Dinosaur Jr T-shirt, cut-off Rupert the Bear trousers and Doc

Martens. There we'd wait, outside the iron gate, feeling like Leisure Rebel and Alterno-Man, until a group of members arrived on the tee. No matter how many times we acted it out, the scene that ensued was always the same, and just as much fun.

The voice would pipe up as we clanked through the iron gate.

'Er, boys?' it would say.

'Yes?' we would reply, continuing towards the clubhouse.

'I suggest you stop right there. This is a private golf club, don't you know?' it would say.

'We're fully aware of that, sir,' I would say.

'Well, I suggest you leave as quickly as possible,' it would continue, and, if it was feeling particularly haughty, 'and trundle on back to whatever scumhole you crawled out from.'

'Well, sir, we would do exactly that,' Robin would say, putting on his poshest accent, 'were it not for the fact that we've paid our membership fees and very much planned to have a game of golf here today. If you'd like to verify this fact, I suggest you look on the list of past winners of the club championship. On it, you'll find the name of my friend here, Tom Cox. It's mounted above the men's bar door, if you're in any doubt.'

This would provoke a stutter at best, a stunned silence at worst, and we'd move on, past the bushes, through to the eighteenth tee. Once there, we'd quietly erupt, high-five one another, and throw a couple of balls from the spud bag back over the bushes onto the thirteenth fairway, just to confuse the old buggers even more. Then we'd tear along the path that ran adjacent to the first hole, scramble up the locker-room stairs to get our clubs, clang our metal locker-doors shut with a force that would wake the dead (or at least some of Cripsley's more senior members), run-walk over to the first tee, and play some of the best golf of our life. Sneering, punk-rock golf, punctuated with elaborately constructed fantasies about thrashing Lee Westwood and his hi-tech weaponry in front of the national junior selectors while armed with only a hickory-shafted forties seven-iron, then turning down the chance to play for England as 'a statement'. Golf that, by rights, should have been out fighting a revolution, directing a student theatre group, or raising funds for sick animals.

Jesus, we were pretentious.

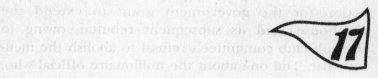

When I was seventeen years old, there was a chillingly real possibility that I knew Cripsley Edge better than I knew myself. Whether I was in or out of love with it at the particular moment you asked me, what I couldn't tell you about the place could have been written on the bottom of a tee peg. After four years as part of the scenery, I'd hit my ball into every dyke, nest, swale, trap and furrow that nature could fling at me. I knew every short cut, slope and hiding place. I could have told you which particular dignitary's wife was jealous of his curvy young mixed-doubles partner, pointed out the precise gorse bush the senior vice-captain favoured when stopping for his mid-round piss, and briefed you on the exact time on a Friday that the head green-keeper and his wife usually chose to stage their weekly quarrel. If a scrap of gossip was skittering through the undergrowth, the chances were I'd be on a fairway, under a tree or upside down in a holly bush somewhere within earshot. I knew all the rumours. The one about the Reg Varney lookalike who offered the clubhouse barmaid eight hundred pounds to come back to his place to look at his 'etchings'. The one about the application for the government grant to extend the clubhouse, and its subsequent rebuttal, owing to the golf club committee's refusal to abolish the men-only bar. The one about the millionaire official who, charged with the responsibility of getting a bell to alert players that the eighth fairway was clear, chose not to put his hand in his pocket, but to ring round local schools for cast-offs instead. I could have told you it all.

What I couldn't have told you, though, was how to make a dignified path from the tool shed at the back of the eighteenth green to the car park, via the main clubhouse door, while not wearing any trousers.

Until now, the tool shed had represented rare unpioneered territory for me, and probably would have remained that way had I not spotted, as I snuck out of the locker room, a couple of members of the ladies' bridge team crossing the car park, and been forced to make a dive for safety. Not having the patience for gardening or breaking down communication barriers with the greenkeepers, I'd never seen much point in hanging out in a dank, stone building full of secateurs. But now, as the icy January wind whipped through the slit in my boxer shorts (I *knew* I should have got my mum to sew that button back on), I couldn't help regretting my complacency. I'd forgotten Golden Rule Number One of the Hunted in the Land of the Hunter: Know Your Surroundings Like You Know Your Own Heart. If I could just have been here before – even once, briefly, with the express purpose of tying Rick Sweeney's leg to a lawnmower – I might at least have an idea of a useful escape route.

As it was, I appeared to be stranded. Every time one gaggle of adult members ceased their after-match chortling in the car park and I thought I saw my chance, another gaggle promptly replaced them. Hence I found myself performing a piece of mutant physical theatre based on a man with a stutter: start to run . . . hide again . . . start to run . . . hide again. Not only that; it was getting dark and cold and the unctuous, wriggling shapes in the murk in the corner of the room beside me suggested that, within a few minutes, my nether regions could be subject to the attentions of anything from a baby squirrel to a fully grown local radio DJ.

I was beginning to rue my bravado. If only I'd chosen to gamble a less vital article of clothing – my golf glove, perhaps, or a sock – I'd probably be at home by now, tucked up in front of my *Seve: The Legend Continues* video, or at least in a semi-warm car, listening to the new Wing-Tipped Sloat album.

Still, today's game had been a skins match, and

everyone knew the two unspoken rules of a skins match at Cripsley: 1. Risk Everything, and 2. Boast Like Crazy. Skins represents golf's most popular form of gambling: competitors put down a nominal amount of money for each hole, along with bonuses for eagles and birdies. If a hole fails to produce an outright winner, the money accumulates and moves on to the next hole. The bigger number of players, the bigger the prizes, the more loaded the atmosphere.

Junior skins matches at Cripsley had been ushered gently into existence around six months previously, typically with games involving no more than four players – all of whom were required to contribute twenty pence per hole and ten pence for birdies, but could generally get away with not paying up if they sneaked out of the locker rooms surreptitiously enough afterwards. However, by January 1992 skins had evolved into a twenty-legged monster with the potential to vacuum up an entire monthly allowance.

This had been the biggest game yet. By the sixth hole, I'd already gambled and lost the wages from the Saturday supermarket job I held down, but I wasn't worried about that because now, as we reached the eighteenth hole, the money from the previous nine holes had rolled up. If I won, I probably wouldn't *need* a Saturday job ever again. We were talking serious jackpot here: twenty pounds, or perhaps more.

'Who's it going to be, then?' asked Robin. 'Who's

got the bollocks? Big money, boys, remember.'

'Me,' I replied, feeling the adrenalin surge through my fingertips. 'It's obvious.'

'You gonna put your money where your mouth is?' asked Jamie.

'I'll do more than that,' I said. 'I'll put my trousers there.'

I don't know where it came from, either.

'What?'

'My trousers. It's a skins match, isn't it? Well, if I don't make a three up this final hole, I'll give these to the winner.'

I looked down at my grey slacks, formerly an integral part of my school uniform: they'd seen me through a lot, but I couldn't picture myself missing them. Much rather them, for instance, than the rest of my utility golfwear. Put it this way: I certainly wasn't going to give away the stripy, quasi-ethnic grandad shirt I'd bought from Nottingham's 'alternative' boutique, Ice Nine, the previous week.

Obviously I'd prefer to drive home with trousers on, given the choice, but I didn't see any problem sneaking into the house. My mum would probably be out at a garden centre and the chances were that my dad wouldn't even hear me come in over the cacophony of his new Bhundu Boys album. That just left the seventy-yard journey to the car to consider, and, while my golf friends could be malicious, I knew they'd at least let me get behind the steering wheel before I stripped. At least, I was pretty sure I knew.

But what was I worried about? I was going to win anyway.

I teed my ball up, using an old technique I'd learned from a Jack Nicklaus video. This required me to focus on the flag, in the distance, then on a spot of grass just ahead of me, directly in line with the hole, then on the flag again. The one flaw in this technique was that every time you looked back at the flag, you would forget which patch of grass it was you had originally focused on. That was the problem with grass: it all looked the same after a while. Still, I felt pretty sure I was taking dead aim at the target. The hole was 321 yards long, a gentle par four, with the wind helping. That meant if I struck my driver well, I could hit the green in one, setting up a possible eagle.

I wound up my shoulders for a big one, picturing my swing as liquid silk and driving my wrists down into a clean, springy hit. I watched as the ball probed the sky, upsetting some pigeons, then eventually dipped as if attached by a drawstring to the green, took one abnormally huge bounce, skipped up the bank at the back of the putting surface, across a concrete path, through a door, and into Steve Kimbolton's swing-improvement room. I stood stone still and gaped. The ball, I deduced, could only have landed on one of two objects: the plastic sprinkler head at the side of the green, or a passing armadillo. One thing was certain: there was no way back from here, unless, unbeknown to me, the club had recently introduced Local Rule 37.5, 'Free relief for ball hammered into teaching equipment'.

'OK, Faldo,' said Ashley. 'We wanna see you strip.'

Now, three quarters of an hour on, with ice-cold air where my empty pockets should have been, I peeked through a crack in the tool-shed door. Already I was forgetting what it felt like to have legs. And was the car park ever going to clear? I wondered what conversational topic could be so interesting that Jenny Abrahams and the rest of her fourball had to hammer it out out here in the cold, as opposed to in the snug clubhouse lounge over freshly toasted teacakes. I'll level with you: I was descending into panic. It was all very well flouncing across the clubhouse car park in an indie band T-shirt with the words 'Suck Me: I'm A Moose' emblazoned across it, but faced with the prospect of making the same journey in a pair of big flapping pants, the punk subversive inside me seemed to be taking a fag break. I pictured the scene the following morning as the club steward dragged my frozen, squirrel-mutilated body from among the shovels and rakes, and the subsequent wild celebration, hosted by Hell's Trucker and Terry Clampett.

'Well, Terry, I won't say I told you so, but we knew this one would come to a sticky end.'

'That's right, Truckster. I saw it coming that day in August 1989, when I first saw him fail to repair a pitchmark.'

It was no good. I was going to have to run for it.

Seeing that Abrahams and friends had turned their backs, I crept out across the mushy leaves, ducked briefly behind a magnolia tree, then tiptoed across the asphalt – some idiot seemed to have turned its volume switch up – as nimbly as I possibly could to the door of the Sphincter, hyper-alert, key at the ready. Safely inside, visible to the outside world only from the shoulders up, I exhaled deeply, turned the key in the ignition, and paused for a moment, waiting for the car heater to rasp into action. Then, sensing something at the periphery of my vision, I turned my gaze ninety degrees to my left, into the car next to me, and looked directly into the limestone eyes of the lady vice-captain.

Decked out in a pink sweater and cloth cap, she sat as still as stone. From her Medusa stare, it was impossible to tell whether she'd watched my entire journey, just the last bit of it, or none of it at all. In fact, I wasn't completely sure she was alive. Still, she must have seen *something*. For a full ten seconds, we assessed one another unblinkingly. I knew that something had passed between us, but being pretty confident it wasn't love, I decided there wasn't much point sticking around, clunked the gearstick into first and headed for home, driving with a new-found prudence of the kind exhibited only by the old and the semi-naked.

And, again, like the old times, the weeks that followed yielded nothing in the way of repercussion. Once more, the powers-that-be at Cripsley confounded me. The irony was infuriating. They could quite happily overlook us running around in front of their wives in our underwear, yet when it came to rolling a ball gently into one of their trolley wheels or failing to replace our divots on the practice ground, the competition room would suddenly be made over to resemble a scene in a John Grisham novel.

Take my hair, for example. By this point, it had been carefully cultivated to reproduce the length and texture of a month-old Magic Mop. Yet somehow it remained invisible to the close-cropped Cripsley committee. If they disapproved, they chose to show it indirectly. To wit: the 1992 Cromwell Cup, where I shot a round of seventy-two, which gave me the prize for the best scratch score of the day. Upon strutting into the competition room after my round, I was met by the 1992 captain, Roy Skilling, and the competition manager, Clark Allydyce.

'Hi, Clark! Hi, Roy!' I said, buoyantly flicking a curly lock out of my mouth.

'That's a very fine score you've done today, Tom,' said Clark. 'But there's a pressing matter which we'd like to have a word with you about.'

'Oh, really?'

'Yes. It's about your attire.'

I quickly surveyed my reflection in the window opposite: shorts, shoes, stripy ethnic top. Nothing too controversial there.

'It's the socks, Tom,' the captain cut in.

'They're the wrong colour,' continued Clark. 'It states clearly in the local rules that only white socks should be worn with shorts.'

'I didn't know that,' I said.

'Well, you should. Now – I suggest you show some respect and apologize to the captain.'

'Er, sorry, Roy,' I said, with as much feeling as I could muster.

'"Mr Captain", you mean,' corrected Clark. 'Now, it's high time you juniors started showing some respect. It's all very well shooting seventy-two, but I suggest you please wear socks that are white, and not grey, in future, or you could be looking at another suspension.'

'But white socks are for Darrens.'

'What do you mean, "for Darrens"?' asked Roy.

'Y'know: "Darrens". Townies. People with no dress sense.'

'I don't care about dress sense. I care about the rules of this club. This is *the captain* you're talking to here, don't you realize? And do you know who's in the room next to us? The president, that's who.'

'What? George Bush?'

'No, *Mr Peters!*'

I'd spoken to Mr Peters, who owned the club, only a few times during my membership. I could never understand why the other adult members spoke of him in such hushed, fearful terms. To me, he seemed like a repressed old man who mumbled a lot. Only the previous week I'd walked straight past him in my Never Mind The Bollocks T-shirt and he hadn't batted a cataract.

'Now,' continued Roy. 'Come back when you're decent.'

But I would never be 'decent' – not any more. All pretence that I could sculpt my personality to fit this strange, protocol-fixated environment was starting to crumble. At last, after years of being told by my parents that a graceful backswing might not be the only recipe for existential fulfilment, but stubbornly refusing to believe it, I was relenting. For the first time, I was acting unreservedly like a normal, messed-up teenager. Naturally, my dream of making it onto the USPGA tour and winning the US Masters hadn't completely died, but I was beginning to feel the true weight of all the history standing in my way: the sheer boringness of the preparation required to get to the top in my favourite sport; my own pathological lack of self-control; the fact that nobody had ever sunk a winning putt on the eighteenth green at Augusta while wearing para boots bought from their local army surplus store. Besides, if I did play on the European Tour, most tournaments climaxed at the weekend. How would I make it back to Rock City, to headbang my way through Alternative Night with Jez and Dogan, the two ageing punks I'd befriended, if I was three off the lead with one round to play in the European Masters in Cranssur-Sierre? Had I ever thought of that?

Something had died – not just for me, but for all of the Cripsley juniors, and perhaps Bob Boffinger too. You could sense it in the way that we teed up without assigning professional alter egos to one another ('I'll be Fred Couples. No. Sod it. I'll just be Tom.') . . . in the way we only got fired up about golf when we were playing it for money or trousers . . . in the stoic, resigned look on Bob Boffinger's face as we complained of our hard luck in some godforsaken sandy hellpit.

For the first time, it was possible to arrive at the pro shop on a Sunday afternoon without the pre-ordained knowledge that there would be at least two of your mates sitting on Steve Kimbolton's big leather chairs and throwing novelty pitchmark repairers at one another's heads. One by one, we began to drift. Robin became a chef. Ben started a garden furniture business, and, having had his own epiphany in the form of a telepathic conversation with a dead Portuguese garden-centre owner, spoke excitedly of selling 'energy waves' to the masses. Bushy took up male modelling.

Ashley started college, dropped out, started college, dropped out. Jamie – still young, and perhaps Cripsley's one remaining hope for professional tour glory – took his GCSEs and began to spend more time with the Worksop team than he did with his own. Fez left for the world of lingerie. Mandy turned into a woman apparently overnight, began dating a thirty-year-old computer programmer and was never seen again. Nick Bellamy, meanwhile, vanished off the face of the golfing sphere, taking a large chunk of Cripsley's magnetism with him for ever.

I was probably the biggest surprise of all, with my ill-fitting clothes, mystifying slogans and insanitary music. Yet, for all my rebellious posturing, I often felt like the only one trying to hold the whole thing together. There was Mousey, too, of course, but he was a permanent fixture in the pro shop by now – a living, breathing, part of the furniture, more than any golfing being you could actually rely on. I was alone, constantly on the phone – convincing, persuading. Just because my golf friends preferred the *Top Forty* to the John Peel radio show, it didn't mean I was going to relinquish my role as the junior section's binding permanent element. Even as I was baffling them with obtuse tales of indie revolution and heaving moshpits, I was organizing seventy-two-hole scratch events, desperately striving to persuade my friends to cancel their new lives and keep our gang together.

I'd fallen off the bucking bronco hard this time, but still I tried to scramble back up.

At the end of my final year in the junior section, my fragmenting team finally won the county team championship. After Mousey and I slam-dunked pressure putts on the final green to beat Rushcliffe's juniors, the five team members drove the trophy back to Cripsley, where we were greeted by Bob Boffinger, Pete Boffinger, Ted Anchor and Scampi, the clubhouse cat. If anyone else noticed or was pleased or proud, they forgot to say so.

We had always seen ourselves as the stars of Cripsley's wretched sitcom. If we weren't, we contended, then why on earth would all those adults devote so much energy into the lost cause that was moulding us into gallant young men? Even when we had been burned by golf at its most preposterously pedantic, we had always assumed there would be some profound point there, *somewhere.* Now it was dawning on us that perhaps there wasn't. For all our bluster and pranks, we were hurt and shocked that our arch enemies didn't care.

I'd read enough golf books and seen more than enough golf videos to be only too aware of the way it worked. If you were eighteen, and your handicap was no better than it had been when you were sixteen, the odds were that you were never going to be Greg Norman. I'd tried, simultaneously setting my standards too low and too high in all the wrong areas in the process, and obviously failed. I was even prepared to admit that it might not have been my destiny to succeed, and that I was out of my element. *But was this really all there was?*

If the seventeen-year-old failed golfing prodigy feels like a tiger squeezed into the cage of a kitten, his eighteen-year-old equivalent feels like that same tiger left for dead on the hard shoulder of the motorway. Perhaps that's too severe a metaphor – we're talking golfers here, not starving Iranian orphans – but you get my point. As soon as we were old enough to vote, we were old enough not to matter, but, infuriatingly, not quite old enough to command respect. No one told us that there were other jobs to be gained in golf, besides those of world number one or assistant professional slave. Everyone told us that we were wearing the wrong-coloured socks.

We still knew how to mess about, but the knowledge that we would never prove the fogies wrong by winning that first British Open title took the edge off the anarchy somewhat. When we stole a soda water bottle from behind the men-only bar and soaked one another under the disapproving gaze of the Past Captains wall, or hid random items from lost property in the pro shop, we did so with the lacklustre aura of those who know there's more to life, but aren't quite ready to admit it.

A new generation of juniors had arrived – nearly all,

Bob Boffinger reliably informed us, considerably better behaved and less motivated than us. If we didn't get to know them or teach them in the ways of mischief, it was because we hardly ever saw them. One of the few rebels among them was turfed out of the club after having the misfortune to drive his ball into the same committee member's trolley two weeks running. When we heard this, we didn't shout in indignation, or plan our retaliation; we merely nodded and frowned vaguely – a reaction which, a year before, would have been unthinkable.

When we claimed the county team championship, we gave Bob Boffinger his long-deserved recompense for his love, time and patience, but something was missing. It wasn't that it wasn't a classic victory. Nor was it that I didn't contribute to it. You could even say for once that I fulfilled my expectations. And there was certainly nothing wrong with the barbecue at Bob Boffinger's place later the same night. Yet buried deep at the core of the triumph was the implication that that's all it was: a triumph. At club level. With your mates. Not a step or a bridge or a kickstart. Not the road to anywhere particular. Not a crusade. Not even a David Byrne concert.

Don't believe everything you hear about revelations. They don't always arrive in one big flash at moments of transcendental artistic brilliance or great natural beauty. Mine came in two parts: the first during a passable version of a song I'd loved as a kid, the second a year later over a spare rib. As I masticated wistfully, and surveyed my friends – people who were closer than any schoolmates could ever have been, people I loved, people I could feel moving away from me, some of them perhaps for ever, even right now as they said and did familiar things – then and only then did it finally hit me that I never wanted to play golf again.

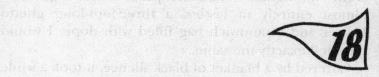

No matter how deep a part of him his territory has become, a fanatical golfer can never quite prepare himself for the first time he sees his home course at midnight. Beyond the overwhelming darkness and the ensuing transformation of conical ceramic tee markers into genuine health hazards, a more subtle sense of transformation overpowered me as I tramped up Cripsley's sixth fairway for what I was sure would be the last time: something pristine that the daylight, or the proliferation of ten-tone knitwear that came with it, or maybe just my escalating cynicism, had served to blot out. *This place was beautiful.* OK, so perhaps local ruffians occasionally hopped over the chainlink fence and took a shit in one of the holes, but overlooking that, this was the nearest thing to heaven you could find within the boundaries of the A37 ring road. Being somewhere so familiar yet feeling so illicit – it was like buying a ticket to a private view of the inside of my own head.

The weirdest thing was: I was sure that even if I hadn't been accompanied by two notorious lyricists from Nottingham's hardcore punk scene, a girl clad almost entirely in tassles, a three-foot-long ghetto blaster and a sandwich bag filled with dope, I would have felt exactly the same.

Covered by a blanket of black silence, it took a while for us to find the precise spot, but my orienteering skills surprised me in this oddly, wrongly exotic place. Unnervingly, my feet seemed to be performing Braille, my subconscious navigating them over and around the hazards – the gorse on the eighth, the stream on the twelfth, that funny little crater on the ninth. A few paces behind me, my friends – Dogan, Ellen and Smelly Jez – did their best to keep up, occasionally tripping over the lip of a bunker, frequently shouting 'Fore!' or 'Birdie!' or 'I've got a big shaft!' or one of the other things non-golfers used to shout whilst taking the piss out of my favourite pastime . . . things that would have annoyed me, not so long ago.

Did they notice how quiet I was? Perhaps – though I don't imagine they knew the reason we were here, beyond the superficial one that, after five pints of Red Stripe, breaking into your local golf course to smoke a joint and listen to the new Archers of Loaf album seems like a brainwave of history-altering proportions.

I eyed them through the gloom and found myself struck by the enormity of the fact that not one of them knew what a greensome stableford was. Not one of them had ever felt the compressed rightness of a cleanly dispatched nine-iron. Not one of them had ever been told off by a fellow human being for not calling him 'Mr Immediate Past Greens Committee Chairman' or reprimanded by the same human being for wearing a sweater without a shirt collar underneath. I'd known them all for not much more than three months, having met them in the mosh pit at a Dinosaur Jr gig at Rock City. In that time, we'd learned a lot about which bands one another liked without learning much else, or feeling that it was important to. Until now, I'd shielded my golf life from them, referring to it – if at all – like you would refer to a particularly irksome skin complaint that you had left behind for good. They were here not because I wanted to show them my dark past – if I gave them even the remotest hint of the person I'd been a couple of years ago, surely they'd dump me for ever – but because I wanted to prove to them, and myself, that that's what it was: a past.

Yet, right now, they seemed sort of intrigued.

'What's an eagle?' asked Smelly Jez.

'It's a score of two under par for one hole.'

'And what's par?'

'It's what a good player would be expected to complete the hole in.'

'So being below par is actually a good thing in golf?'

'Yeah.'

'That's fucked up, man!'

'I know. So is golf.'

'Is golf sort of, like, really boring, Tom?' asked Ellen.

I gave this one some serious thought. 'Well, yeah and no.'

'So that's why when you see it on the telly, you hardly ever see anyone playing, but you always see the camera focusing on some horse in a field nearby or a fat bloke in the crowd?'

'Sort of. But . . . it *can* be really exciting. There are just quite a few pauses in the action.'

On we hiked, looking for the place. Thinking in the kind of black and white terms that only those who locate life-enhancing qualities in the lyrics of Jane's Addiction can think in, I'd pictured this moment as something momentous and final. But now I was losing sight of exactly what. Perhaps it was just the weed interfering with my sense of purpose. At least, I hoped so.

Maybe it didn't matter if we didn't find the exact spot. After all, there were plenty of landmarks on this course that had contributed equally to my metamorphosis from golfing squarepants to world-weary anarchist rebel. Wasn't it utterly arbitrary to pinpoint only one? Surely the point was in the act itself, the finality of the thing I was going to do when I got there?

Finally, we stopped. I couldn't remember exactly

where Ashley's ball had made contact with Reg Forman's trolley, all that time ago, but where we stood, a few yards shy of the sixteenth green, seemed near enough – and, even if it wasn't, it didn't make any difference. It was Cripsley I was saying goodbye to – as a whole, not a hole. Dogan handed me the practice ball bag, I turned it upside down, and an avalanche of balata raced itself to the ground. Ellen clicked 'play' on the ghetto blaster, and for probably the first and only time, insomniac residents of the villas overlooking Cripsley's most gruelling par five were privy to the high-octane opening chords of The Archers of Loaf's 'Web In Front'.

I couldn't see the reservoir, but I knew it was there, beyond the line of ghostly willows ahead of me. We had the rest of the night, and we were probably going to need it. There were around three hundred balls in total. The ones that didn't make it to the water would probably wind up on the playing field of Alfred Crown, the local secondary school, where they might be put to use by a budding player, or – more likely – pelted at the class spanner. But I couldn't afford to worry about that now. The whole point of this exercise was that the concept of destination – destiny itself, even – had to be a thing of the past: my past. I didn't believe in it any more.

I steered the first ball into an inviting lie with the sole of my driver, and took aim. My friends watched, almost as awestruck as they were perplexed. The strike was business-like. The shiny white dot climbed and probed impressively – more impressively, somehow, than it ever could have in daylight – before being sucked up into the Marmitey darkness for ever. It felt good, not seeing it land.

'Fuckin' 'ell!' said Jez. 'Why would anyone want to give that up?'

Epilogue

It could end there, if you wanted it to.

It could end with me smashing the last of my practice balls into the great unknown and trudging back home with my flinty mouth and overburdened eyelids to leave big bad golf behind for ever and begin my groovy new life – the one I should have been living all along. I could start editing a fanzine on American lo-fi rock, snag a job writing for the music press, meet endless fascinating people, none of whom will use the phrase, 'Got your putting boots on today, son!' or be materialistic or narrow-minded or unaware of art-house cinema. I could keep golf in a seedy little drawer somewhere, stashed away for an ironic day.

You could stop reading here.

You could do that. Or I could give you the more complex version of events: the one that reflects the frailty of character (well, mine, anyway), the non-linear nature of life, and the realities of adulthood.

I did intend to leave golf behind for ever, that unearthly hour in the summer of 1993, when I walked home from Cripsley with my new friends, to a dawn chorus of chinking milk bottles. I was snotty enough to think that was not only The End, but A New Beginning. I did start a fanzine, I did get a job as a journalist. I did meet people who couldn't believe I played golf. I did do all the things I said, kind of.

But, at the same time, I kept going back – tentatively and mockingly at first, then, as I learned more about the outside world, increasingly confidently and accept-ingly. There was the first time, in 1997, when I regained my handicap, played every week for six months, got my hair cut, wore a complete lack of offensive T-shirts, won a couple of competitions, and *still* got told off for wearing the wrong-coloured socks in a manner that most people would reserve for scolding mis-chievous toddlers for pulling the legs off insects. There was the time the following year when I visited the club for a reunion party, got drunk with my old friends, and as I talked to them in a brand new way – i.e. without the lingering subtext of who'd played the best golf recently and managed to look least bothered about it – felt a dysfunctional part of my fifteen-year-old self rise up out of my body and leave me for ever. There was the time just after that, when I went to clear out my old locker wearing a Led Zeppelin T-shirt, and got seriously 'checked out' by the security guard the club had installed in the car park (I swear I even saw him pick up his radio at one point and mouth that he had a 'one-eight-six' or something in progress).

Meanwhile, layer by layer, my post-golf idealism was being stripped away. In the outside world, the coarse little realities slinked up on me. Perhaps loving music *wasn't* synonymous with being a wholesome person. Perhaps being left wing and working in the media and wearing sandals *didn't* go hand in hand with an inherent lack of duplicity. Perhaps I *did* prefer the Carpenters to the Jon Spencer Blues Explosion. Perhaps I *did* need to get some fresh air.

My subconscious kept drawing me back to golf. Maybe it *was* a great game after all? Maybe it *was* a more enjoyable way to spend your free time than standing in a pool of vomit swigging watered-down lager while three bearded Americans attack their guitars with violin bows?

I started to get the tee peg dream again – naggingly, relentlessly. The following day, I would find myself en route to my local driving range, without having made any quantifiable decision to go there. Having arrived, I would line up in my enormous flares, comedy sideburns and unruly hair, and ease ball after ball into another time zone with yesteryear's equipment, while men with baseball caps and space-age drivers looked on, perplexed. I felt addiction kicking in. Out of the corner of my eye I saw people in tank-tops whispering about me. I arrived home with flaps of raw skin hanging off the palms of my hands. I started to break things in the house with my clubs again and concoct preposterous excuses in front of my wife. ('I don't know how it happened. I just walked into the room and for no reason a picture frame dropped on to the lamp, which fell off and smashed the mirror. No: of course it was nothing to do with my putter!') Doubtfully, I told myself it was all 'research'.

There was one thing I still needed to do, and then I'd know.

I arrived at Cripsley in July 2001 with a few things I'd never arrived there with before – a hairstyle I was comfortable with, a semi-modern, smooth-running automobile, a sense that there was more to life than golf but not much more – anticipating that the place would counter my personal development with its own. Since I'd last been a serious golfer, Tiger Woods had revolutionized the game, breaking ancient barriers of race, class and age, but Cripsley seemed somehow oblivious to all of this. The painted white line still warned of the hideous retribution available to those unscrupulous females who dared cross over into the men-only bar. Around the corner, a couple of silver-haired oldsters sat, each with one eye on me and one eye on the TV, which showed the tee shot of an incredibly dull-looking, badly dressed young British professional with the kind of haircut that should, by rights, be torn off the head and thrown high into the air and shot at as a statement. His name, the graphic below informed the viewer, was Justin.

I'd arranged to meet my playing partner for the day, Pete Boffinger, at 1 p.m., which gave me ten minutes to kill. Pete would be older and thinner on top than when I'd last played with him, just as my sideburns would be bushier and wider than when he'd last played with me, but until then, time seemed to be standing still. In the car park, the same security guard looked up from his *Daily Mail* and eyed me with the same ill-disguised suspicion that he had done a few years before. In the practice net, Jack 'Net Man' Mullen bashed away, still searching for that elusive backswing trigger. I watched him, becoming momentarily distracted by what sounded like a bee attacking me from behind, and turning to see Steve Kimbolton bellydancing a plate of teacakes over to the pro shop.

'Hi, Tom,' said Steve, as if he'd seen me at some point in the previous four years.

'Er . . . Hi, Steve.'

Was someone screwing with my mind here?

Outside, the world had changed immeasurably. The internet had arrived, and quickly mutated into the world's biggest shopping mall. Global leaders had risen, fallen and committed inappropriate acts with cigars. Pop music had coughed out its dying breath, keeled over, then got up and eaten its own corpse for the hell of it. I'd gone from punk to soft rock, from elitist anger to cheerful uncoolness. But golf hadn't moved. It had merely been waiting for me to stop revolving.

I glanced down at my clothes, noting that, after years of sartorial felonies, I'd inadvertently found my natural look in the fashions of the 1976 British Open. I looked at Pete, who'd joined me on the tee – not some alien golfing being from my past, but a downright ace fella, with whom I could discuss the recorded output of Crosby, Stills and Nash. I looked at the immaculate fairway. I looked at the brilliant white ball, sitting squarely – securely – on the tee peg, inviting me. In this sleepy corner of my past, I felt every event nudging me further towards myself, and let it.

EDUCATING PETER

By Tom Cox

Available in August
as a Bantam Press Hardcover

Here's a taster . . .

Mama Told Me Not to Strum

The way I remember it is something like this.

He drags himself into the room, eyes to the floor, hands buried in the arms of his long-sleeve t-shirt. Jenny says, 'Pete, meet Tom'; he mumbles hello. He roots around in the cupboard for a packet of crisps. I ask him what CDs he's bought recently; he mumbles something about the second AC/DC album. He shuffles away, back to his bedroom.

I say, 'So. I'll pick him up a week on Tuesday, then?'

Jenny says, 'If you could, that would be wonderful. He's got fencing class from ten till eleven, then he's all yours.'

I say, 'Right. Er, cool. I guess I'll be off.'

Jenny says, 'Mind out for those roadworks on the North Circular.'

And that's how it all started.

Did I miss a bit out? Possibly. There's a chance he picked up one of his bass guitars and plucked disconsolately at it for thirty seconds before he rooted around for the crisps. Perhaps we even shook hands. What's pretty certain, however, is that our first meeting couldn't have been described as 'unforgettable'. Nothing screeched, sparked or went 'Kapow!'. Nobody called the police or drove a 1969 Aston Martin.

Like many men who'd grown up playing with too many model cars and watching too many films starring Warren Oates, I'd often fantasised about this moment: the beginning of my Great Road Trip. I'd pictured Jeff Bridges haring out of nowhere in a Dodge Charger to save Clint Eastwood from a shower of bullets during the opening scene of *Thunderbolt And Lightfoot*. I'd pictured a big sky, a fast car, a hopelessly romantic meeting of inseparable outlaws, perhaps with the added bonus of a couple of loose women looking for a ride to nowhere in particular. But now this was it: I was here, finally embarking on my adventure, and all I could see was a North

London kitchen, the first flowering of acne, some rather fetching Ikea units and a Slipknot t-shirt.

Outside the window, a wicked wind took a running jump down Alexander Palace hill, whipping along Crouch End Broadway, making a couple of local underfed aesthetes unsteady on their feet. Double-parked, my slightly-lower-than-middle-of-the-range Ford Fiesta waited for some action beyond the hot wax it had been lavished with earlier that day. Upstairs, in his room, the Thunderbolt to my Lightfoot attempted to master the riff to Metallica's 'Enter Sandman'. North London slept. Nothing continued to not happen. I decided, on balance, I'd settle for it.

Then again, by this point I would have settled for just about anything.

My whole life, I'd been playing some kind of four-wheeled journey into the unknown, but as the years piled up – that is, the years when it is still dignified to drive around for the hell of it while dressed in a loud shirt, listening to even louder music – my Great Rock And Roll Road Trip had become in danger of turning into My Great Bag Of Hot Air. The original idea had been something fairly vague that I'd dreamt up on receiving my first plastic pedal car as a seven-year-old: I would drive, anywhere, mindlessly, just for the thrill of driving. In my late teens, this was modified to the cliché of all Great Road Trip clichés: I would fly to New York, buy an ineffably cool second-hand car, and drive cross-country to San Francisco, picking up hobos, buskers and itinerant jazz musicians on the way. However, in 1997 as I was travelling back from an Italian holiday, the plane had been struck by lightning, plummeting 1,000 terrifying feet before righting itself. As a result, I'd vowed not to take to the air for the foreseeable future, thus making America a less viable option. Additionally, I'd finally got around to reading Jack Kerouac's *On the Road*, rather than just talking about it, and discovered it was a vacuous pile of antelope droppings.

More recently, my thoughts had turned towards the winding B-roads and endless Little Chefs of my homeland. Everyone talked about the American Dream, but what about the British equivalent? Did it exist and, if so, what did it look like? How come you never saw rootless outlaw types cruising through the Lake District just for the existential hell of it? Was drifting banned in Britain, and had someone forgotten to tell me?

I wanted to discover the real Britain. Whatever this was, I felt certain it was out there: a rock and roll place every bit as weird as the backwoods America that writers like Hunter S. Thompson and Tom Wolfe had discovered. But more than anything I wanted an excuse to drive around aimlessly, getting lost in places with names like Snafbury and Little Piddling. All I needed was someone willing to ride shotgun: a relentlessly-up-for-it soulmate – the kind of partner who'd be willing to help me out of a gambling debt, come to my aid in a tussle with Hell's Angels, or, more importantly, navigate me out of a council estate on the outskirts of Hull. But circumstances had changed since I'd begun to lay down the plans for my Great Rock And Roll Road Trip. Many of the friends who'd shared with me in the nihilist's vision of films like *Vanishing Point* and *Two-Lane Blacktop* as twenty-year-olds now held down steady jobs in insurance and the civil service. Most of them simply couldn't afford to up sticks and abandon their jobs and girlfriends for six months. The ones that could, meanwhile, just couldn't see the same romance in driving up the M4 listening to Fairport Convention as they'd once seen in cruising along Route 66 listening to The Byrds. There were still the isolated loose cannons who I knew I could count on, of course: Colin and Surreal Ed, a couple of relentlessly cheerful womanisers with a penchant for jumping out of cars at red traffic lights and running into nearby woodland for no apparent reason.

These, though, were the kind of insatiable single and free party animals for whom 'a good book and an early night' meant the latest issue of *Mayfair* and only two nightclubs instead of the normal four. In other words, great company in moderation but a veritable health hazard if you were talking about six months on the road, and not one I could afford as a married man with a mortgage and five pet cats to support.

In short, I was beginning to lose hope.

The call from Jenny couldn't have come at a more desperate moment. Jenny, I could be fairly certain, wasn't the type of woman who would jump out of your car at a red light and hide in adjacent shrubbery. She was fifty-three, for a start – the same age as my parents – and in full-time employment as a college lecturer. I'd known her since my third birthday party, when, seated in her lap, I'd smeared an ice cream sundae in her hair for reasons I can only remember as 'to see what it felt like'. Since then, I'd enjoyed the kind of respectfully distant relationship with her that one enjoys with surprisingly cool friends of one's family whom one has disgraced one's self in front of. I tended to see her, when it came right down to it, at fiftieth birthday parties and weddings. Jenny liked a lot of good blues music and, unlike many of my parents' other friends, still occasionally found time to go out to the cinema, but it had never occurred to me to call her up to arrange a friendly drink. You just didn't do that kind of thing with your parents' mates. Besides, she and her ex-husband, Ian, had their hands full with Peter, a teenage son whom I'd never met but whom relatives assured me was just making the transition into the 'melancholy' stage of adolescence. For a couple of weeks now, my parents had been hinting that she might get in touch with me with a mysterious proposal, but I couldn't guess what it could possibly be.

'It's about that road trip you've been planning,' Jenny explained to me, after we'd caught up on some random family gossip.

'Oh. You heard about that? Bit of a non-starter, really.'

'Yes, well, I had a bit of an idea that I'd like to put to you that might make it a starter again.'

Abruptly, my mind filled with incongruous images of me and a flame-haired ex-hippie cruising along a sun-splashed highway, radio on, sunroof open, discussing the meaning of life. Part of me kind of liked the idea. Part of me didn't. The remainder was alive with questions. What would my wife think? Where could this journey possibly go? How many times would we have to stop at Ikea?

'It's to do with Pete,' continued Jenny.

I let out a silent lungful of relief. 'Oh yes? How old is he now?' I asked.

'Well, let me tell you all about him,' said Jenny.

And, for the next half an hour, she did.

Peter, Jenny explained, had recently turned fourteen, and, virtually overnight, an unfathomable transformation had come over him. Just yesterday, it seemed, he'd been a cheery, fluffy-haired kid whose main priority in life had been where his next Pokemon toy was coming from; now he stalked the house in black clothes, guitar slung over his shoulder, a stormcloud in trousers looking for somewhere to rain. The funny thing was, Jenny couldn't remember ever buying him any black clothes. And what were those strange dangly chains that hung from his trousers? Try as she might, she couldn't work out what had detonated the change in her son. It could have been a friend. It could have been a video or record he had heard. It could merely have been a new set of hormones. Peter certainly wasn't giving anything away. But he was certain about one thing: one day, in the not-too-distant future, he was going to be a rock star, and he wasn't going to let anything stand in his way.

Jenny didn't have anything against siring a rock musician, per se. She'd liked plenty of rock music when she was younger, and had even been on dates with a few of the hairy people who made it. But now, three or four months into her son's obsession, it was becoming obvious that it was having an adverse effect on his schoolwork. Peter's teachers were starting to use words like 'enigma' and 'unfulfilled'. And it got worse, said Jenny. Two weeks ago, Gaynor, the nanny who Jenny relied on to look after Peter when she was off to Europe on lecture tours, had handed in her notice, having decided to go and work on a kibbutz in Israel. Meanwhile Ian, who worked as an actor, was due to spend most of the summer as part of a travelling theatre on the American West coast. It was going to be a busy summer for Jenny, too – lecture tours in Norway, Greece, France and Spain – and she was beginning to panic: about the effect her son's new interest would have on his future; about what he would do with his free time; about where she would find a nanny as reliable and inspirational as Gaynor. But, during a conversation with my parents at a friend's fiftieth birthday party, a strange idea had popped into her head – a long shot, which wouldn't solve all her problems, but which might just work.

It's always hard to work out what your parents tell their friends about your life, but you can normally guess that they make it sound considerably more interesting than it is and backdate it at least a couple of years. I couldn't tell exactly what mine had told Jenny at the party, but it had given her the idea that a) I wrote about music for a living, b) I hung out with rock stars all the time, c) I had a lot of free time this summer, d) I was desperate to take part in a road trip, and e) I was a responsible adult. What, Jenny had started to wonder, if Tom were to give Peter a kind of summer school in the realities of the rock musician's lifestyle? What if he were to take Peter around Britain, visiting landmarks and musicians, passing on his knowledge. Yes, Jenny would still have to find a new nanny, but it would take some of the pressure off her. It would also mean that Peter had someone to hang out with who was closer to his own age. Peter might be equally determined to pursue a career in music afterwards, but at least he'd have a more pragmatic, less impulsive view of his future, and plenty of ammunition to make decisions pertaining to it.

'So what do you think?' asked Jenny.

'Er . . . phwew!' I said.

'I know it's a strange proposal, and I'll totally understand if you want to say no. But er . . . don't. Please!'

The truth was, I didn't quite know *what* to say, or whether to find her belief in me flattering or misguided. In reality, I probably wasn't quite who Jenny thought I was – or at least not any more. I *had* made my living by writing about music for national newspapers for much of the previous five years, but I was in the final stages of a career change. Like many of my contemporaries who'd opted to move from music journalism to other forms of writing, I'd gradually had my soul sucked dry by the industry, until listening to new CDs and conducting thirty-minute interviews in hotel rooms were in danger of becoming what I'd never thought they would be: chores, like those you encounter in real jobs. But I wasn't kidding myself that The Man was to blame for my weariness with a career deconstructing Eminem lyrics and being horrible to The Stereophonics. The *real* blame could be assigned to three much more persuasive factors:

1. With a few rare exceptions, I only liked music made between 1957 and 1980.
2. Gigs made my ears hurt.
3. I would rather be playing golf.

These days, my music writing amounted to an article every couple of months, focusing almost exclusively on the work of someone dead with a beard who'd once been in possession of an alarmingly large collection of lutes. The last CD I had bought was Chicago's *Greatest Hits*. The only semi-famous band I had ever made friends with had stopped returning my calls after one of them was invited to appear on *Never Mind The Buzzcocks*. HMV bewildered me, MTV made me want to hide behind the sofa, excessive live music was known to give me ear infections, and the indie rock I'd bought as a teenager now sounded tuneless and I couldn't recall how or why it had ever sounded any different. I could hardly remember the last time I had stayed until the end of a gig, much less hung out backstage.

'The thing is, Jenny,' I told her, 'I love the idea in theory, but I might be a bit rubbish.'

'The thing is, Tom,' said Jenny, 'I don't mind. I'm not asking for much here. It's not that I want Peter to meet anyone really well-known or anything. Even if you were just to pass on some of your experiences, play him some records, take him to meet some of your mates – you know, even people who are involved in music in a minor way – that would be enough.

'I mean, surely you can rustle a *few* of your old contacts up? What about that bloke, the one in the photograph that your mum and dad have got? You know, the one where he's sticking his tongue in your ear.'

'Oh, Julian Cope?'

'Yeah, that's him. He'd have time to meet up with you, wouldn't he? I bet he could teach Peter a thing or two.'

I pondered this for a second. Cope, who licked his fans' ears almost as often as he modelled his hair after a root vegetable (i.e. at least three times per month), had once been the lead singer of the excellent new wave group The Teardrop Explodes, but now divided his time between writing books on Neolithic Britain, recording the occasional solo album, and turning up unannounced in small villages in Wiltshire to play gigs with his novelty band, Brain Donor, while dressed in preposterously large leather boots. I thought back to the last time I'd met him: the electricity in his handshake, the inspiring logic at the heart of his surreal, breathless ramblings. It *had* been like meeting a real rock star, hadn't it?

I couldn't be sure that Cope would agree to meet with me. He was kind of elusive, and at one point in the mid-Eighties had locked himself in his room for several weeks, surviving only on the water biscuits his wife pushed under the door. But perhaps there were more like him out there. In fact, I knew there were. I'd met a few of them over the last few years: eccentric, damaged icons, folk heroes and psychedelic loons who shunned the corporate trappings of the modern music industry, yet found their own niche within the essential musical fabric of the British Isles. I might not manage to locate many of them, and those that I did find might not fancy spending time in the company of a golf-loving Eagles fan and a bored teenager in oversized trousers, but a sliver of hope began to emerge. Maybe I wouldn't find that elusive 'real' Britain after all, but here at least was the chance to have a lot of fun failing to do so. I tried to think of the worst thing that could happen. All I came up with was getting lost in an industrial estate in Greater Swindon. I *wanted* to get lost in an industrial estate in Greater Swindon.

'Come on Tom,' said Jenny. 'It will be fun! Why not come and meet him, and we'll take it from there?'

Irresistible vanity washed over me: I was going to be in charge here. This would be *my* version of a musical education. I could do this in any way I chose.

'Which day's good for you two, then?' I said.

One factor I hadn't really stopped to consider was Peter himself. What were fourteen-year-olds like these days? Moreover, what were *teenagers* like? It had been only seven years since I'd been one, yet it struck me, somewhat frighteningly, that I seemed to have entirely forgotten what that was like. Now, when I thought of adolescents, I thought of the pavement

outside the London Astoria in the build-up to a nu-metal gig:
the pseudo-threatening band names . . . my inadvertent need
to cross to the opposite side of the road . . . the accou-
trements of a new kind of hollow-eyed corporate rebellion . . .
the cries of 'Nigel, where's Jasmine? She's got my System Of
A Down t-shirt!'

I'd found teenagers scary and slightly confusing when I
was one myself; now I just found them perplexing and
unsavoury. I did my best to live and shop in places where
they didn't, and generally avoided them in the street, half-
convinced that they were either going to ask me to give them
a counselling session or beat me up for looking at their 'bird'.
Earlier in the year, a national newspaper had commissioned
me to write a feature which involved manufacturing my own
boy band. My editor had instructed me to head out on to the
streets of the capital to recruit 'talent' between the ages of fifteen and eighteen, but I'd spent the afternoon browsing in
second-hand bookshops instead. In the end, my band,
Boyzcout, had been constructed out of a group of friends in
their mid-twenties, all of whom, after the influence of make-
up, had the common trait of looking twenty-four instead of
twenty-seven. We'd tried hard to pack plenty of *NSync har-
monies and hip, modern references to text-messaging and the
dot com world into our single, 'Zcouting For Boyz' – 'I'll zcout
for you babe while we're out zcouting for boys' – but record
company A&R men had rejected the demo for being too
mature. 'It's a bit like *Mojo* magazine in musical form,' said one.

I knew I was turning into an old fart, perhaps prematurely,
but I didn't care. There was no shame in my love of The
Eagles, Journey's 'Don't Stop Believing', fuzzy dressing
gowns, Sainsbury's Taste the Difference range, weak beer,
golf and the VH1 Classic Rock channel; just lots of self-
righteous enjoyment. I'd spent the previous seven years
becoming increasingly scornful of my former self. I'd sold his

records, taken the piss out of his hairstyle and mercilessly mocked his tactics with women. Occasionally I felt the odd bit of reluctant affection for him, of course, but ultimately I thought he was a wally – although I certainly believed his spiritual descendants to be a thousand times worse.

I was fully aware that it was a cliché to feel like your generation had made better things of their youth than the generation that followed, but that didn't stop me feeling the same thing with every fibre of my being. To put it bluntly, today's teens repelled me. I didn't like their grunting, complaining music, I didn't like their shapeless clothes, I didn't like the three prongs of plastered-down hair on their fringes, I didn't like their baseball caps, I didn't like the big speakers in their cars, I didn't like their piercings and I didn't like the way they hassled me for bus fare in the market square of my home town. And, from the little bits of evidence I could gather, they probably weren't gagging to add me to their speed dial either. When I had tried to convey my honest sentiments about youth trends such as nu-metal, skateboarding and gangsta rap in a newspaper article, I'd inevitably received an angry letter in response from a frustrated sixteen-year-old with a name like Toad or Jemima, lambasting me for a) my lack of understanding of the isolation the modern adolescent feels, and b) my lack of comprehension about why Slutbone or Composition Of A Horse had to insert the word 'plasma' into every second verse of their lyrics. This, naturally, had the effect of making me feel even more righteous.

Peter was an anomaly in that he didn't fit into either of the categories in which I'd come to define teens: he didn't remind me distastefully of the old version of me, but he didn't remind me distastefully of the people I used to have fights with at school either. From our initial, fleeting encounter, I'd worked out several things about him: that he was tall for his age, that he was considerably better educated than I had been at his age, that black was his favourite colour, that he was uncomfortable with his hair, and that he had watched the Oliver Stone biopic *The Doors* at some point in the previous twenty-four hours. He was the essence of sub-Jim Morrison hangdog adolescence, yet he was something alien to me, too – a kind of teenager that I'd never been in a position to have to understand. Jenny might have been friends with my parents from her student days, but while they still lived in a cosmopolitan enough area of North Nottinghamshire, she had long ago moved to a sub region of North London where it was possible to buy a jar of pimento-stuffed olives from any one of seven local outlets at three o'clock in the morning. She'd sent Peter to the local independent school, where, among the children of art gallery owners, daytime TV presenters and pop stars, he was groovily encouraged to learn in the direction that he wanted to learn. Having been to a comprehensive school whose twin areas of progressive excellence were football and beating the living crap out of the year below you, I didn't quite comprehend what this style of education involved, but I was almost certain that it meant Peter knew a lot of bigger words than I'd known at his age, and probably a few bigger ones than I knew now.

Would we get on? Did Peter have any enthusiasm for the project, or did he just see it as something his mum had pushed him into? It was far too early to tell. By the end of Peter's first encounter with me, his only gestures of communication had been 'Mmmmawwwrighttt' and 'Yeah, s'even better than *Back in Black*.' Jenny, ever helpful, had assured me that in normal English this translated, respectively, as 'Hello! You must be Tom, the music writer who is going to help me further my development and learn about multifarious aspects of our musical heritage!' and 'I'm so glad we both like the work of AC/DC! I think this provides an indication that we're going to get along just spiffingly!', but I wasn't so confident. It occurred to me that, as a premature fogie, I'd spent my whole adult life hanging around with people older than me, people who treated me as their equal but always with the unspoken agreement that I was their apprentice. It didn't matter how many Hall And Oates albums I bought; providing my mates were older than me, I would always feel slightly wet behind the ears. Now the situation was reversed. I was about to spend six months feeling old for the first time in my life, and I wasn't sure I liked the idea. My parents, who had both made a living as teachers while I was growing up, had warned me from an early age not to follow their career path, and I wondered if I was about to find out why. Sure, moulding Peter in my image would be a great way to get my own back on a generation that got on my nerves, but I could see, from five minutes in his company, that there would be minimal effort on his part. He wasn't going to make me feel like he was the least bit interested in me, my life or my friends. And I would have to learn a whole new way of speaking and acting: patient, cool, encouraging, effervescent, selfless, yet somehow disciplined and slyly exemplary.

In the week that preceded my first official journey with Peter, Jenny and I began to draw up an itinerary for the summer. Due to Peter's school commitments, this would be no ordinary road trip: it would take place in carefully planned stages, featuring minimal late nights and plenty of wholesome food. Long journeys might be a problem, particularly on school nights, as would the distance between my house, in Norfolk, and Jenny's, in Crouch End. I started to wonder just how much time I would be spending on the London Orbital and what I would do to relieve the boredom. So much, I thought, for my loose, free-livin' road trip, where every day was a magical mystery tour.

I began to make lists of people Peter could hook up with, but always in the sceptical knowledge that rock stars are an awkward bunch and getting them in the same place at the same time as a recalcitrant adolescent might be a task no less arduous than persuading your favourite fragmented musical casualties to reunite and perform at your birthday party. In my planning I leaned heavily towards mates of mates and the kind of real people who'd be generous with their wisdom, and tried to ignore the more famous, plastic ones who might, if we were lucky, grant us twenty-five minutes of platitudes in a hotel room with their press agent eavesdropping outside the door. I could guarantee that *someone* out there would want to talk to us. What I couldn't guarantee was structure, or that Peter would become a more rounded person as a result. Jenny explained again that she simply wanted Peter 'to get more ammunition to enable him to make the right decision about his future, and to fill his spare time with something that wasn't computer games'. Was it just British music she wanted me to teach him about? 'No. Not really. Anything.' Did she want me to persuade him that he *didn't* want a career as a musician? 'No. I just want him to be sure of what he's getting himself into.' The problem was, I wasn't sure that *I* knew what he would be getting himself into. I wasn't even sure whether the people I was taking him to meet would know what *they'd* got themselves into. That was the point of rock and roll, surely: it wasn't supposed to be a carefully planned career choice.

Gradually, reality was beginning to replace my Thunderbolt and Lightfoot fantasy. Originally, I'd thought only of the *concept* of me teaching a teenager the laws of rock and roll on the road, as if the whole thing was nothing more than a movie, a series of easy-to-swallow images spliced together by Steven Spielberg for popular consumption: Peter and me in the car, arguing over a late-Sixties folk album; Peter and me being taken to an archaeological site by Julian Cope; Peter and me getting lost in Runcorn.

Well, okay. Maybe not Steven Spielberg.

The point was, this was going to be nowhere near as easy

as I'd thought. Looking at the coming months with a clear head, the chances seemed slim that I would be picking up random hitch-hikers and playing surreal practical jokes at traffic lights. What had seemed like a great opportunity to be even less responsible than normal was suddenly looking like the most responsible thing I'd ever had to do. I wasn't going to be spending countless hours sitting next to a caricature of a teenager; I was going to be sitting next to the real thing, with all the messy eating habits, imbalanced taste and raging angst that that implied. I was devoting the best part of my summer to this, I realised, as I set off home from Jenny's place. I'd gone past the stage where it was going to be possible to back out. What was more, in all my pontificating I'd forgotten to circumnavigate the roadworks on the North Circular, and was bringing up the rear in the South East's most monotonous traffic jam.

Not every great road movie starts with a bang, does it? I thought back to the sleepy opening frames of seventies films like *Vanishing Point* and *Badlands*: nothing events in no-horse towns with negligible hints of the mayhem to follow. Besides, who said I was at the start? The real beginning could come at any moment I wanted it to, in virtually any setting. I was director, writer, producer and cinematographer here. There was scope for freedom, anarchy and adventure in this project, after all – it was simply a matter of loosening up, using my imagination and letting it happen. Liberated by this thought, I clicked *The Best Of The Steve Miller Band* satisfyingly into the tape machine, pushed the gear-stick back into neutral for the ninth time in as many minutes, and turned my attention to the evening's shopping list.

**Read the complete book –
coming in August from Bantam Press**